Jacques Lacan

Anika Lemaire

Jacques Lacan

Translated by David Macey

Routledge & Kegan Paul

London, Boston and Henley

Originally published in Belgium in 1970
by Charles Denart
This edition revised by the author and translated by David Macey
first published in 1977
by Routledge & Kegan Paul Ltd
39 Store Street,
London WC1E 7DD,
Broadway House,
Newtown Road,
Henley-on-Thames,
Oxon RG9 1EN and
9 Park Street,
Boston, Mass. 02108, USA
Reprinted and first published as
a paperback in 1979
Reprinted in 1980 and 1981
Set in Monotype Imprint 101 by
Kelly Typesetting, Bradford-on-Avon, Wiltshire
and printed in Great Britain by
Lowe & Brydone Printers Ltd
Thetford, Norfolk
© Charles Denart, Bruxelles 1970
English translation © Routledge & Kegan Paul Ltd 1977

British Library Cataloguing in Publication Data

Lemaire, A

Jacques Lacan.
1. Lacan, Jacques   2. Psychoanalysis
3. Languages—Psychology
I. Macey, David
150'.19'5   BF173.L15   77–30106

ISBN 0–7100–0350–1 (p)

Contents

Contents

Preface by Jacques Lacan

A good thirteen years ago, I used to say to two of those people we call nonentities, which for public opinion, or at least for student opinion, simply better entitles them to occupy the professor's place, 'Don't forget that one day you will give what I am now writing as the subject for a thesis.'[1]

As though from a wish that they might look into it: where I would check whether the zero really does have any idea of the place that gives it its importance.

It has happened, then. Nothing has happened to them, only to me: thanks to my *Écrits*, I am now the subject of a thesis.

That this should be due to the choice of a young person is nothing new. To my surprise, ten years after its publication my Rome lecture made the adventure of an intellectual emerging into an American university from a trapper's tunnel.

As we know, it needs a second swallow to make a summer. The second is therefore unique in this place, even if there are several of them. A smile multiplies when it is that of a young person.

Anthony, Anika . . . what a sign of a new wind is insisting in these initials?

May she forgive me then, if I take the opportunity to designate what she effaces by showing it.[2]

My *Écrits* are unsuitable for a thesis, particularly an academic thesis: they are antithetical by nature: one either takes what they formulate or one leaves them.

Each of them is apparently no more than a memorial to the refusal of my discourse by the audience it included: an audience restricted to psychoanalysts.

But, precisely by including them without retaining them, each article shows by a further twist that there is no knowledge without discourse. For what would such knowledge be: the unconscious one imagines is refuted by the unconscious as it is: a knowledge put in the place of truth; this can be conceived only within a structure of discourse.

An unthinkable discourse, because it could only be held if one was ejected from it. Perfectly teachable, however, by a half-speaking: a technique which realizes that truth can only be half-spoken. This presupposes that the psychoanalyst never shows himself except in an asymptomatic discourse, which is, in effect, the least one can expect of him.

In fact, this 'impossible' is the basis of his real; a real from within which the consistency of the discourses in which truth limps can be judged, precisely because it limps openly, as opposed to the inanity of the discourse of knowledge, which, asserting itself with its closure, makes the others lie.

That, indeed, is the operation of academic discourse when it makes a thesis out of the fiction it calls an author, out of the history of thought, or out of something that styles itself progress.

Illustrating an incompatibility such as that in question with an example is always fallacious.

Obviously, it concerns the pupil.

I could draw a contrast and say that, in 1960, my two L's beat together as two wings (*deux ailes*), because one of them was such that it had to be taken universally or not at all. By that I mean the lichen which unifies the forest for you when the forest has to hide the tree from you.

At that date, it was a question of nothing less than making my teaching understood, my teaching which for seven years had been stated once every eight days in the most eminent site of French psychiatry in an unpublished lesson for those to whom it was particularly addressed: psychiatrists and psychoanalysts, who still leave it to one side.

This singular phenomenon is the doing of segregations, there as elsewhere effects of discourse, but which, to make concrete inferences, here enact promulgations different in origin and date.

First, the segregation of psychiatry in the Faculty of Medicine, where the university structure displays its affinities with the managerial system. This segregation is supported by the fact that psychiatry itself performs the office of social segregation. The result is that psychiatry designates a spare room on the strength of the University's liberal funds, those who have a right to this lodging being repressed into the ghetto which was once, and with some reason, known as the asylum.

Such a site lends itself to the exploits of civilization, where the fact of the prince (my friend Henri Ey, as it happens) is established.

A liberal diktat may arise there, as it may wherever the arbitrary finds itself a crack between domains of necessity.

What happens to me in my field because of Bonneval, the fief of Henri Ey, proceeds, therefore, from no other favour, from no dialectical progress.

If one thinks about it, the field of the psychoanalyst, the habitat he found in psychiatry, is motivated by a political configuration rather than by any connexion of practice. He was ordered there by his antipathy to academic discourse, an antipathy which is no less effective for having received its rationale from my teaching alone, when, as a symptom, it is translated into institutions conveying secondary benefits.

As for the segregational articulation of the psychoanalytic institution, it suffices to recall that the privilege of entering it after the war was to be measured against the fact that, some years earlier, *all* the analysts in

Central Europe had fled to the Atlantic countries – and then the batch – who would perhaps have to be restricted by a *numerus clausus* – announced by the anticipated Russian invasion.

The result is a sequel maintained by the established domination of academic discourse in the USSR and its antipathy[3] to sectarian discourse, which, on the other hand, flourishes in the USA, since the country was founded by it.

This symptomatic play explains the prodigious fact that a certain Ipepée [IPP] could effectively forbid access to my seminar to all those in its obedience who were less than fifty years old, and see its decree confirmed by the student herd, even in the 'guard room' four hundred yards away from the Clinique Universitaire (cf. the spare room) where I used to speak at lunch-time.

The present fashion should not consider itself any less gregarious; it is only a metabolic form of the growing power of the University, which shelters me just as well in its courts. The discourse of the University is desegregative, even if it does convey the discourse of the master, since it relays it only by freeing it from its truth. Science, it thinks, guarantees the truth of this project. Insoluble.

However, let no one underestimate the autonomy of this discourse in the name of its budgetary dependence. That settles no one's account. What is torn there can be surprised only by another discourse from within which the stitching can be seen.

It is more accessible to demonstrate academic discourse's inability to return to the discourse out of which it is patched together, an equivalent process.

The two paths merge when something of the discourse it represses happens to make itself felt within it, all the more so in that nowhere is it secure. This, one day, was the experience of a Politzer, who had a sensitive soul as well as being a Marxist.

Reopening the paperback in which this *Critique des fondements de la psychologie* has been republished, against all likelihood of the author's consent, you've no idea of the formulae with which he asks if thoughts left to themselves are still acts of the 'I'. To which he at once replies: 'Impossible' (p. 143 of the paperback).

And on p. 151:

> Unconscious wishes . . . are perceived by consciousness, but at no moment does *an act with a human form* [author's emphasis] implying the 'I' intervene. But this wish is still subject to transformations which are no longer acts of the 'I'. . . . Systems which are too autonomous break the continuity of the 'I', and the automatism of the processes of transformation and working over exclude its activity.

This is what the would-be critique comes down to at the demand of postulates held to be extremely backward even where they persist –

namely in academic psychology – only because they remain basic to it, whether academic psychology likes it or not.

It is not by resorting to the author from whom academic discourse might well proceed that I will explain how, rightly promoting the 'story' as the very thing around which the analytic experience centres, he emerges as a ghost because he never looked at it.

It is in the nominalism essential to the modern university, the university with which capitalism befuddles itself, that I would have you read the scandalous failure of this critique. This is the discourse in which one can only become more and more caught up, even, and especially, if one curses it. (What a laughable operation if one thinks about it.)

My L's get out of it by casting this 'first person' out of the unconscious with a flick of the tail. They know very well how, to please them, I refer to this unconscious as speaking in more than one person (*je l'entu -ile*). [4] It would be better, they tell us, to bundle it up 'in person'.

They could, however, have remembered that I make truth say 'I speak', and that if I state that a discourse is sent out from somewhere only for its message to return there in an inverted form, this does not mean that the truth which an Other sends back in this way is on intimate terms with that Other.

I would have suggested to Politzer the image of the innumerable I, defined only by its relation to the unity of recurrence. Who knows? I might have put it in the transfinite.

But this jesting is not important. It should have been strikingly obvious to my two L's that I had dispensed, and with reason as we can see, with a reference they take up only because they want to make a bow to the only people it affects – those who have nothing to do with psychoanalysis.

CNRS Marxism [Centre National de Recherches Scientifiques = academic Marxism] or phenomenology of forms; the (species) hostility or the (conjunctural) friendship that these positions show towards the only discourse in question derive from it the efficiency for which they are summoned there: once neutralized, they become neutralizing.

The idea is beginning to dawn on those for whom a discourse, of which they have not heard because they have kept quiet about it for seven years, affects a very stiff and starchy attitude that all they have to reinstate is the philosophical umbrella, and much good may it do the others.

After all, if it can be exported, this is an opportunity to save up currency which is legal tender in the Alma Mater.

This becomes obvious when the report on the unconscious is put on the unofficial market, which, aptly enough, is overlooked by *Les Temps Modernes*.

The sensibility of the professional common market is becoming more refined.

What will become of the unconscious in all this?

For the sake of propedeutics, let us limit ourselves to what articulates it in the apparatus of the signifiers. One could say that I did nothing else in introducing Signorelli (as the entry of forgetfulness into discourse!) to the Société de Philosophie. But that was because of the context: the substantialist prejudice, which could not fail to have affected the unconscious there, derived from an intimidation to be produced by the crushing weight of its language-matter, if not from a disarray to be borne by leaving it in suspense.

Here, it is a question of people (at least if one insists upon speaking with valid interlocutors without composing a third party), of people, I say, whose myth is accredited by a practice. Here, as in any faith, the fabulous arms itself with the solid. It [*ça* = id] is dripping with strong ego, and swimming in aggression; to say nothing of the genital supreme, which really is well cooked up.

To limit oneself to what I have established as the algorithm appropriate for writing the relationship between the metaphor as significant structure and the return (once the fact of the signifier has been demonstrated) of the repressed becomes valid only as an extract from a construction whose design, at least, could be indicated.

The mental ground of today's reader, let us say the young reader, has been swept clean by the converging effects of the discourse to which I have contributed, not without the question of the distance required for maximal effect having left me speechless before I had thought about it. He can have no idea of the inaudibility, so few years ago, of these remarks of mine, which are now running about everywhere. In doctors who are not yet Balinted, he can perhaps still measure the extent to which it is possible to live whilst completely ignoring the unconscious, which to him means (immense for him, thanks to me, poor): to ignore the unconscious, i.e. the discourse.

I can well see the embarrassment of my two L's at approaching this masonic gathering. I do not think this is sufficient for them to take a free decision to do away with all recourse to the graph constructed for them in my seminar on the formations of the unconscious (1957–8).

That apparatus, in which figures ... (God knows it's a risk), in which the *apparole*[5] figures (let the ambiguity of this monster-word be welcome), the *apparole*, I say, made out of that spendthrift[6] the Other (known as the Great Other), so that the basket of desire can be hung up by its four corners and stiffened into a phantasy by the 'a', the ball-object. It is astonishing that bringing out this rigorous apparatus did not make the haggling over the double inscription a secondary issue or a resolved question, since it was resolved by Freud himself when he promoted, I shall say in my expected style, the *mystic pad*.[7]

The difficulties in work which count for a lot in the directions for psychoanalysis are certainly not revived for nothing in the passage that makes the analyst. For they are essentially concerned with the relationship with truth.

(This last word is not easy to handle, but this could be because its meaning vacillates, whilst its usage is correctly settled.)

I myself would not be caught up in analytic discourse if I here avoided the opportunity to show precisely what is carried away by academic discourse.

Let us begin with astonishment.

Let us admit that it is correct to use the formula for metaphor just as it stands, just as I give it in my text in Schreber, namely:

$$\frac{S}{S'} \cdot \frac{S'}{x} \rightarrow S\left(\frac{1}{s}\right) \tag{I}$$

As the subsequent passage shows, this scription is there to bring out the function of the signifier 'Phallus' as a sign for the 'signifier's passion'. This is what the x, habitually used to designate the variable, indicates.

The original formula (original in more than one sense) given in *The Agency of the Letter*, is:

$$f\left(\frac{S'}{S}\right)S \cong S(+)s$$

The entire text of this *Écrit* is a commentary on this formula, which does not lend itself – and this should hold back our L – to the transcription we are about to see.

I refer to the transcription made on the basis of . . . analogy with a scription of the arithmetical proposition which must be stripped down by being put into figures:

$$\frac{1}{4} \cdot \frac{4}{16},$$

which does in effect give $1\left(\dfrac{1}{16}\right)$ (and it's still an accident).

But that this $\dfrac{1}{16}$ can be written (no accident) as

$\dfrac{1}{16}$ is no reason for transcribing Formula I, with its

$$\frac{4}{4}$$

on the letters, as

$$\frac{\dfrac{S'}{s}}{\dfrac{S}{S}}$$

In a word, what has the line with which Saussure inscribes the impassable gap relating signifier to signified, and in which I am (falsely) charged with finding the barrier between the unconscious and the preconscious, to do with the line, whatever it may be, indicating Euclidean proportion?

A little of the buzzing of the dialogue I had with M. Perelman in June of the same year in order to refute his 'analogical' conception of metaphor (cf. *Écrits*, pp. 889–92) would have sufficed to stop anyone fascinated by it from taking that path.

It fascinates him, but how? What is the term whose three suspension points (preceding the term analogy) show that I do not know which saint to dedicate it to? What is the word to designate the similarity with an idiot's manipulation of an abacus?

There's nothing to hum and haw about. It's my discourse all right which the author permits himself to adopt after his own fashion – which is not the right fashion, for all that it is the fashion in which the academic listens to me, and even if it is instructive.

I have to admit it: when, at a difficult moment, I despaired of the psychoanalyst, I naïvely placed some hope, not in the discourse of the university, which I did not as yet have the means to pin down, but in a sort of true opinion which I imagined there to be in its body. (We know who would have said Henormous!)

I saw a few members of this body being attracted by my pasture. I expected their votes. But they turned it into a schoolboy essay.

And what became of my L, still a little chicken of an L (*aile de poussin*)? His wings are now strong enough for him to imagine this formula: the unconscious is the condition for language.

That comes from him: one of the faithful assured me that he then expressed himself in those phonemes.

Now, what I say is that language is the condition for the unconscious.

It's not the same thing; in fact it's the direct opposite. But one cannot therefore say that there is no relationship between the two

L would have been flustered if he had said that the unconscious was the logical implication of language: in effect, no unconscious without language. That could have been a step towards the root of the implication and of the logic itself.

He would have got back to the subject presupposed by my knowledge (*au sujet que suppose mon savoir*).[8]

Perhaps – who knows – L might thereby have outstripped me in that which I am reaching.

This is precisely where his lower $\frac{S}{S}$, which as such can only mean that one signifier is worth another, could have taken him from the moment that (and he was aware of it) he admits that a signifier is capable of signifying itself.

For, knowing the difference between the formal usage of the signifier, notation $\bar{S}$, and its natural function, notation S, he would have understood the very detour on which the so-called mathematical logic is founded.

But, as one cannot re-discover everything by oneself, his lack of information really must be put down to laziness, the unfathomable amongst the sins out of which the tower of the deadly sin arises.

To make up for it, let L ask himself the question posed at the point I have reached, namely: what satisfaction is there to be found in forcing S, the natural signifier, to experience what a still more advanced formalization of its practice reveals in it to be irreducible as language.

Could this be what ties the knot that stops knowledge detaching itself from *jouissance*, but still means that it is never anything but the *jouissance* of the Other?[9]

Ah! Why does he linger over what Freud has for ever designated as the narcissism of minor difference. 'Minor' – that is sufficient for it to differ from the interval separating truth from error.

What Freud does not seem to have known he could be grateful to is that narcissism, that narcissism to which he owes the fact of being Freud for ever, throughout his lifetime and after it for a whole circle of people, and that fact that he can never fail to be quoted as insurpassable in what he says.

The fact is, he has the good fortune not to have the unversity pack at his heels.

Only what he calls 'his gang'.

That allows my gang simply to verify his discourse.

But they behave oddly towards me. When, beginning with the structure of language, I formulate metaphor in such a way as to account for what he calls condensation in the unconscious, and I formulate metonymy in such a way as to provide the motive for displacement, they become indignant that I do not quote Jakobson (whose name would never have been suspected in my gang – if I had not pronounced it).

But when they finally read him and notice that the formula in which I articulate metonymy differs somewhat from Jakobson's formula in that he makes Freudian displacement depend upon metaphor, then they blame me, as if I had attributed my formula to him.

They are, in a word, playing about.

When, after years of sleep (the sleep of the others), I have to summarize what I said to the mob at Bonneval (the tree springs up again, and on my arms, all the birds, all the birds . . . how can one survive their eternal twittering?),[10] all I can do in an *écrit – Position de l'inconscient –* is to recall the object 'a' is the pivot around which every turn of phrase unfolds in its metonymy.

Where is this object 'a', the major incorporeal of the Stoics, to be situated? In the unconscious or elsewhere? Who can tell?

May this Preface be an omen to one who will go far.

The good use she has made of academic sources inevitably lacks what oral tradition will designate for the future: texts faithful in pillaging me, but never deigning to pay me back.

Their interest will be that they transmit what I have said literally; like the amber which holds the fly so as to know nothing of its flight.

Notes

1 This does not refer to S. Leclaire and J. Laplanche. We will come to them later. (*Anika Lemaire*)

2 Let me make myself understood: by showing it as it should be shown. (*Lacan*)

3 Naturally, the refusal of segregation is basic to the concentration camp. (*Lacan*)

4 The neologism defies translation. It is a condensation of *en* (in) *tu* (you, thou) and *il* (he, it). The formation of the neologism is aided by its phonetic association with *intituler*: to entitle. (*Translator*)

5 *Apparole* is a condensation of *appareil* and *à parole* (apparatus, speaking). (*Translator*)

6 *Panier percé* means both a spendthrift (metaphorically) and a basket with a hole in the bottom (literally). (*Translator*)

7 In English in the text. (*Translator*)

8 A reference to the seminar given on 10 June 1964: 'Du sujet supposé savoir, de la dyade première, et du bien', now included in J. Lacan, *Le Séminaire. Livre XI: Les Quatre Concepts fondamentaux de la psychanalyse*, Seuil, Paris, 1973. (*Anika Lemaire*)

9 There is no real English equivalent for *jouissance*, which covers the fields, 'pleasure', 'domination', 'possession', 'appropriation', etc. It should be noted that the verb *jouir* also has the slang meaning of 'to come'. (*Translator*)

10 A reference to the image used in 'The unconscious: a psychoanalytic study' by Laplanche and Leclaire (48). Cf. Part Four, Chapter 9 of the present text. (*Translator*)

Foreword by Antoine Vergote

The author wished to see here a statement on Lacan's work by someone with the authority of a longer familiarity with psychoanalysis and the human sciences. Within the limits of a foreword, there can be no question of recording, and still less of justifying, Lacan's theories, his critical reading of Freud and his epistemological elucidation of psychoanalysis. I should simply like to outline some of the master ideas which carry Lacan's teachings, to show the originality that distinguishes them from other conceptions of psychoanalysis, and to bring out their impact upon analytic practice. A rash project, since no original work – and Lacan's less so than many others – is capable of being delimited by an inventory. There is no need to worry. My brief note at the beginning of this work is a simple mapping out of some essential indications.

The major contribution of Lacan's work to psychoanalysis and to all the human sciences is to be found in the twofold movement of a return to Freud and a recourse to the sciences of language which allow the science of the unconscious to be articulated.

In Lacan, all the so-called human sciences combine to recapture the experience generating psychoanalysis, and to elucidate its principles and the architectonic of its theories. Lacan's readers and writers know the profit he has been able to derive from cultural anthropology, psychology and philosophy. A true interpreter of Freud, he knows that understanding a work does not mean repeating it literally or reducing it to some thought foreign to it. In rescuing psychoanalysis from a positivism which encloses it in compulsively repeated formulae, he has not, however, subjected it to psychological or philosophical theories which might mutilate it. He has been able to rethink it through a ceaseless coming and going between the basic texts, analytic listening and the immense contribution of all the human sciences. The fascination exercised by his teaching appears suspect in the eyes of a serious world which is not tolerant of provocation, but, regardless of a certain scandal and the spell of the language, many researchers and practitioners have felt that psychoanalysis has been freed from a social or a scientific imprisonment, from a sort of cultural domestication, and has acquired its scientific status.

Amongst the sciences he interpellates, Lacan accords a privileged place to the sciences of language and speech: A. Lemaire's study is therefore devoted essentially to an exposition of the Lacanian conceptions of language and their application in psychoanalysis. Is Lacan making a sacrifice to scientific actuality, or is this due to a spirit of philosophical subversion? Or is it not rather a return to the gravitational pole of psychoanalysis? For the site of its theory as well as its practice is speech. How does man become himself and liberate himself by the act of speech? This is the only true question posed for us by psychoanalysis.

It is surprising that established psychoanalysis should have forgotten to examine itself as to its experience and power. Worried about its peculiar condition, it has tried to borrow its theoretical principles from various sciences: phenomenology, the psychology of conditioning or motivation, the sociology of alienation and identification, even from orthopedagogy. . . . In the image of the individual or cultural neuroses psychoanalysis examines, it has forgotten the origins of its own traditions. And its origin, untranscendable and constitutive, scandalously permanent for anyone who dreams of scientific progress, is the constantly repeated observation that the neurotic is suffering from memories and from discourses which have been buried, and that speech alone has the power to regenerate him.

Some come back to Freud in order to criticize the hybrid concepts – inherited from the biology and physiology of his day – which encumber the theoretical formulations of psychoanalysis, even if they do preside very happily over its birth. Their concern for 'scientific' exegesis aims at the recovery of psychoanalysis from its audacious assertions in order to integrate Freudian thought into the anthology of received truths. Lacan goes right to the site kept to by Freud: paying attention to that part of the unconscious in the discourse (through free association), discourse which, not wishing to be at its own disposal, allows the advent of discourses which are none the less effective for having been suppressed from the ego. Hence the attention he pays to Freud's many notes on the language of the unconscious and its interference with conscious language. He resuscitates these nodal texts, obliterated by a hotch-potch of subsequent theories, and gives them back their bite. Whatever the occasionally touchy and exclusive tone of his linguistic centrism, his fidelity to the original matter and perspective of psychoanalysis must be acknowledged.

The same intellectual commotion shook doctors, psychologists and philosophers when they were confronted with the Freudian texts on language. Successive reformulations: behaviourist (Dalbeiz), neurophysiological (Ey), existentialist (Sartre), phenomenological (the early Merleau-Ponty), or culturalist (Kardiner and M. Mead) had permeated our reading of Freud. They want to free us from interpretations which are too 'sexual' for their liking or from ludicrous prejudices; they promise to rectify theories which seem to lack a scientific basis. It will be noted that not one of these forms of thought is foreign either to man or to the unconscious, but in trying to capture psychoanalysis in their concepts, they suppress that latency of the unconscious which defines it. Their attempts at reconciliation end up by covering up what has been unveiled.

It was forgotten that Freud had an explicit knowledge of his own principles. Witness his texts on mnemic traces or on the effect of displacement. The neurological or behaviourist references alone were retained, whereas Freud always upheld their structure as a language. Lacan has rethought these texts, which are inaugural for both theory and practice; he has made explicit and founded the connexion between consciousness and the unconscious, the line which holds them at a distance – a distance which can never be crossed – the spreading out of the complex in delirious discourse. . . .

As A. Lemaire shows, a whole 'philosophy of man' arises out of the analytic experience recognized in the irreducibility of its object. We now know that man's young, the *in-fans*, accedes to speech and hence to recognition of the other and of the self, and to the order of language by way of the perilous passage through the 'Oedipus complex'. But language is often reduced to being merely a means of communication within a constituted order. For Lacan, such discontinuity between existence and language signals the failure of anthropology, for language is inseparable from the meaning of existence. In its social and kinship relationships, the order of culture is equivalent to that of language. Not that existence, cultural figures and kinship structures can be converted into a linguistic design! Some percussive phrase or other may certainly have allowed a linguistic idealism to be apprehended. I think rather that Lacan intended to develop in all its consequences the central fact that, for man, the word symbolizes and renders symbolic the essence of things. Everything which has meaning for man is inscribed in him in the very archives of the unconscious by language, understood in the full extent of its semantic, rhetorical and formal structures.

For this very reason, any significant relationship follows the formal laws of language. This is without doubt Lacan's most important contribution, and the most difficult to grasp. This is why I am soliciting the reader's special attention, in order that he might try to understand the link between the order of language and the order of culture. For the circumincession of language and of kinship and of social structures allows psychoanalysis to be more rigorously conceptualized and clears up a lot of misunderstandings.

I shall point out only a few questions of doctrine. The consideration of the structuring effect language has because it is by nature structural allows us to go beyond a purely genetic conception; from the outset of the pre-Oedipal relationship, language imposes its order and at once introduces the symbolic rupture into the Imaginary. One can recognize in the Oedipus complex the humanizing efficacity of renunciation of the imaginary omnipotence of being and having; for, in it, the sexual relationship is ordered under the sign of the Phallus, to which no human is equal and which no one possesses. Dead in his phantasmatic opacity, the father imposes himself as the holder and the guarantor of the law, the order of the family and the cultural structures which are the basis of all possibility of human existence.

Freud had already seen that the form of language constitutes the law of culture. We need only refer to his observations on the genesis of language in the child, penetratingly annotated by Lacan, or to his remarks about the connexion between the father and language, an idea in which Lacan has grasped the principle for interpreting the Oedipus complex.

Superfluous metaphysical constructions? In any case, the theory of the conformity between the order of language and the order of culture, which is in agreement with much contemporary research in anthropology, allows the efficacy of re-effecting the process of becoming human to be assigned to the discourse of the cure. It extends Freud's Metapsychology and preserves analysis from the alienating misunderstandings into which it was toppling under the effects of a psychology and a philosophy centred upon imaginary representation.

The ego is in fact born to itself and to the intersubjective relationship through the necessary mediation of the perceived image; and in our anthropological theories, we always run the risk of reproducing the imaginary mode of thought. A sub-linguistic schema, the imagination, which is productive of 'Imagos', has left its archaic forms in numerous key terms in psychology. Thus, becoming human is conceived after the mode of identification with a represented model; the body is reduced to the image of the body projected on the plane of representation; and affective maturity is conceived as being adaptation to the socio-cultural model of the environment. 'What is the ego?' Pascal asked himself. Lacan tells us that in wishing to grasp it, we identify it with the ideal image, a reflection in our desire of the form designed for it by the gaze of the other who judges or seduces. Emerging to itself in a mirror relationship in which it risks being swallowed up, the ego is called upon by Lacan for the cathartic denuding of full listening and full speech. The somewhat abrupt critique of the Imaginary and of 'ego psychology' has the austere accents of a mystical theology of language. Completely removed from any mysticism of affectivity and of imaginary reciprocity, it recalls the negative theology that broke idolatrous images. An iconoclast of the mirrors of Narcissus, Lacan awakens an anthropology trapped in the snare of speculary reduplication.

The Lacanian study of the mirror stage can be read in this volume. Should the reader extend this analysis, should he discover in certain theories of inter-human relations the permanence of this mirror stage, which inaugurates our being for another and our being for ourselves, then he will understand Lacan's aims. The demystification of narcissism cannot be limited to a genetic consideration of the subject.

It takes its place in the very heart of all human relationships in order to denounce the imaginary slidings in them. Psychoanalysis is a structural analysis of the position of the subject, who always moves at the intersection of the imaginary representation and symbolic speech.

In psychoanalysis, theory of language is therefore much more than a study of the rhetorical forms proper to the dream or to symptoms. It is the site of the truth. For speech alone tears the veil from mirror enchantment, and speech alone allows the truth of the subject to come to light.

That Lacan should have translated Heidegger's study of the Logos proves the measure of his linguistic theory. Freud trusted in the discourse of patients, never doubting but that the discrete voice of reason could be heard there. In the Lacanian view, reason is carried, harboured and manifested by language.

Brought back to its site, the revelatory action of language, psychoanalysis finds once more its original ferment of regeneration. It restores subject and object to their origins. The archaic in man is not the immature, the chaotic, the seething or the shapeless: deposited in us by the laws of culture, whose spokesman is the father, language is primary. The full speech of the liberated man tends to rejoin it in its primal integrity.

The reader may be surprised by Lacan's refusal to subscribe to the ideology of continual progress. Like Freud and Heidegger, he sees in the successive cultural facts so many detours which take us away from the primal truth and which displace the true question of the human being. The texts on the line which irremediably separates signifier from signified invite reflection. Could one hold that the signifieds, the significations we give to the world, and to experience, obscure the fundamental signifiers more than they manifest them? The analytic experience proves to us in every way the power of occultation and deception which our rational elaborations and moral justifications may conceal. Is it not the same for the cultural forms in which man moves. There exists, no doubt, no other way to exist and, for man, every truth conquered is paid for by something being forgotten. Nothing obliges us, however, to denounce the pure lure of displacement in partial truths. To see only faded derivatives in the cultural figures of the mind would, I think, mean forcing Lacan's theory towards a new Manicheanism. Similarly, to reduce consciousness to a shake of the dice over the unconscious would imply disrespect for the Freudian architectonic. Besides, what power could be assigned to the cure if analytic theory condemned man to be irremediably captive to his illusions? The insistence upon the line which irrevocably separates signifier and signified reminds us, however, that the dream of integral lucidity is also a flight into the opacity of the Imaginary. We are summoned to the never-ending labour of a catharsis in the movement of the truths which speak in us and which spread to infinity the network of their significance.

As soon as psychoanalysis returns to its birthplace, where forget-fulness and reminiscence are exchanged, it is no longer the complacent ally of the blemishes that burden society. To lead analysis towards adaptation to the models of the surrounding world would be to render men strangers to their own origins. For if it is true that man speaks only when he has first been seized by spoken language, and that he accedes to his human status only through culture, society still cannot pretend to offer an unfailing truth. Wishing to take the objective model for his existence from society, man alienates himself in images which have taken on the appearance of law. A psychology directed towards adapta-tion chains up the subject and makes the forgetting of his own virtuali-ties of existence pass for the first pact between individual and culture. One can understand Lacan's denunciation of the terrorism of such psychology. His attempt, subversive to some eyes, aims at restoring to psychoanalysis its regenerating virtue. For, in the conduct of the cure, as in the analysis of cultural forms, it is incumbent upon psychoanalysis to go beyond the fiction of adaptation. The primacy and anteriority of the signifier over the signifieds opens up in man a primal *béance* [gap] which posits him as subject and as desire; and recognition of the law breaks the circle of an imaginary coincidence with oneself and with the desire of the other.

My preliminary words, which are perhaps enigmatic for those familiar with a philosophy of consciousness or for the devotees of a psychology of adaptation, will be illuminated by a reading of the present work. Let the reader abandon himself to a naïve astonishment, let him allow himself to be interpellated by considerations which provoke him; let him put received concepts into parentheses, and let a work which goes back to the origins of his existence work upon his conception of psychoanalysis and of man.

Some readers may be disappointed that Lacan does not give a complete exposé of the analytic science. Perhaps they will miss some point of doctrine which they value: the study of the body, of affectivity, or of intentional consciousness. What analyst could lay claim to a perfected doctrine when he defines man by the gap between signifier and signified, and by the asymptotic project of truth?

The reader will at least recognize that such an understanding of analysis presents the theoretical foundations which allow a conception of the body, of consciousness and of affectivity to be articulated. What-ever the modalities of the body and of affectivity may be, their expres-sion and resumption always passes through language because they are always inscribed in its semantic networks and its metaphorical or metonymic structures. This is why simply setting up human relation-ships does not liberate. It is the technical speech of the analyst which restores to these relationships their alienated truth. To show the linguistic structure of consciousness and of the unconscious is at the same time to justify the therapeutic mediation of speech. Analytic theory is therefore not foreign to its praxis. Yet how many therapists, analysts or not, dissociate Freud's theoretical writings from his practical writings. One may as well say that a few therapeutic rules are handled by being amalgamated with principles which deprive them of their power. To convince oneself that this is so, it suffices to observe the ravages exercised by 'analytic recipes' applied widely by analysts who have not taken the pains to assure themselves of their theoretical basis.

Lacan strives to demystify the false technical power of the psychotherapist; hence his paradoxical formulae: the analysand's resistance is the analyst's resistance, or again, the cure comes as an extra. After the long years of work upon himself which free him from the image of his power, the analyst will recognize that his real power resides simply in this: making possible the emergence of the subject's truth.

A. Lemaire's study does not venture far along the paths of analytic practice; and I appreciate the discretion of the non-analyst who does not allow herself to go deeply into Lacan's views on the exercise of analysis. Born of praxis as much as of the hermeneutics of Freud and the frequentation of the various human sciences, the *Écrits* do, however, take their strength from their practical consequences. Long theoretical detours sometimes frighten practitioners who are in a hurry. But beware. No cure can be effective if it remains captive to cultural images and to the psychological images which presided over the patient's alienation.

The importance of the *Écrits* for the direction of the cure is obvious if one considers the paths in which therapy has sought its efficacy. Analysis has been centred upon the immediate transference relationship; some have thought to remedy psychical illness by the gift of an intimate benevolence which may have been missing in the patient's early life; others have devoted their efforts to the remodelling and the reinforcing of the ego, sometimes positing the personality of the therapist as an educational model. . . . I do not deny that these practices may provide some benefit of relief or support. But such therapeutic practices are still, in various ways, full of traps. They may alienate the subject in an imaginary model in which his liberty is exhausted; they may burden him with a culpability imposed from the outside by the illusory models of a strong ego; or they could quite simply open up in him an insatiable demand for affection.

Must not man come into his own? Not by imitating images which are proposed, not through a competitive duel with the therapist, but by allowing the significations inscribed in his unconscious to speak, significations which previously manifested themselves only in a distorted and debased manner. The conformity between structures of language and structures of kinship and society and the structuration of the subject speaking in psychical sites (conscious and unconscious) oblige the therapist to be the hermeneut who listens to and interprets words overdetermined in their signification. Language, the condition of his existence as a man, is the site of possible liberty and truth. To have demystified certain false powers of the therapist and to have founded interpretative listening as a science justifies Lacan's undertaking.

The author of the present study invited me to place the aim of Lacanian researches in the general perspective of tendencies in analysis and of the sciences of man. Reading her well-informed and well-thought-out work will give the measure of Lacan's concepts, which these preliminary pages are intended to introduce.

Université de Louvain   A. Vergote

Acknowledgments

I am grateful to Tavistock Publications for permission to quote from Alan Sheridan-Smith's translation of the following articles by Lacan: 'The mirror-stage as formative of the function of the I as revealed in psychoanalytic experience'; 'Aggressivity in psychoanalysis'; 'Function and field of speech and language in psychoanalysis'; 'The Freudian thing or the meaning of the return to Freud in psychoanalysis'; 'The agency of the letter in the unconscious or reason since Freud'; 'On a question preliminary to any possible treatment of psychosis'; 'Subversion of the subject and the dialectic of desire in the Freudian unconscious'; 'The direction of the analysis and the principles of its power'.

D. Macey

Introduction

The present work was written in response to a wish that has frequently been expressed to me: the wish that access to Lacanism could be facilitated by a complete summary of the basic ideas which constitute it, by a text aimed at presenting in a clear and organized manner a very complex school of thought. Complex because of the importance of Lacan's own contribution, but also because of the preliminary knowledge it demands, a knowledge which constantly underlies his work and which relates to structuralism, linguistics and anthropology.

The basic document I have used is Lacan's book, *Écrits*; to this I have added articles not included in that volume and certain summaries of seminars held in France. This skeleton has been filled out with numerous readings which throw light upon the Lacanian school of thought in the strict sense and upon the broader school within which it is inscribed.

The present work constitutes 'a study of the work of Jacques Lacan'. Suffice to say that it represents one of the possible approaches, that this approach is relative, and represents an opinion and an attempt at explanation.

My study has met with some difficulties. I have frequently had to feel my way, to walk on tiptoe. Dr J. Lacan's literary style sometimes constituted an obstacle, as his writing is wilfully mysterious and plays upon a syntactic musicality which it is not always easy to decode. I have been helped in my labours by the works of Lacan's disciples, who were formed directly by his teaching: remarkable works which shed light upon the more complex ideas.

My own style may at times seem somewhat lapidary and schematic. Again, it must be remembered that I am seeking to put across the essentials of an immense subject matter without falling into a paraphrase. A paraphrase would bore the specialist and would lose the novice in a labyrinth of endless corridors. And I in no way pretend to be rewriting the work of Jacques Lacan. The most I attempt to do is to provide an introduction, to provide the reader with an approach to a source which is extremely rich but whose elements are complex and dispersed.

Jacques Lacan is a structuralist. He has underlined this fact in various interviews. His name marks the entry of psychoanalysis into this school of thought, a method of research applicable to various disciplines, but above all to the human sciences.

Claude Lévi-Strauss, the pioneer of structuralism in the field of social anthropology, provides us with the basic principles of structuralism in his *Elementary Structures of Kinship*. Following Lévi-Strauss:

behind the apparent and the tangible there lies hidden an internal logic: the structure. Thus, the Oedipus Complex is the underlying structure of the social and cultural forms of the organization of societies.

Theoretical research, which goes beyond the immediate experience, constitutes the means of access to these basic structures.

The structuralist method of research is modelled upon the methods of study adopted by structural linguistics.

As Émile Benveniste explains in *Problèmes de linguistique générale* (65), structural linguistics seeks to distinguish units of language at different levels (phonemes – monemes – words – phrases) on the basis of the different relationships they contract with one another at the same level and with units at higher levels. Structuralist method therefore privileges relationships to the detriment of the terms of those relationships. Linguistic analysis proceeds with the help of two basic dialectical operations: segmentation and substitution. The text is broken down into smaller and smaller portions until elements which cannot be broken down any further are obtained. The validity of the break-down is then verified at every level of segmentation by considering the possibility of creating a unit valid at the level above by substituting another element from the same level for the element which has been isolated. In other words, the 'functionality' of the isolated elements, its capacity for being integrated into a valid higher unit, is verified.

Using the same technique, linguistic analysis proceeds from minimal units to maximal units. The minimal acceptable units, those which are distinctive, oppositional and differential, form the lower level. A unit is further identified as distinctive at a given level if it forms an integral part of a unit at the level above.

To sum up, we can say that linguistic analysis takes as its guiding principle the relations between an element and those elements which are simultaneously present and those elements which may be substituted for it.

Such procedures result in the recognition of the laws of the arrangement of the formal features revealed. The different elements are organized in series at any one level and show the particular arrangements of the different levels in every language.

It is at this point that we discover the notion of structure itself, structure being nothing other than the organization of the parts of a whole in accordance with certain definite rules of mutual and functional conditioning. Structural linguistics will therefore define language (*la langue*) as a global unit containing its parts. These parts are formally arranged in obedience to certain constant principles. This mode of formal arrangement of the parts gives them a function. The constituent parts are units of different levels and the levels are hierarchical, each unit becoming a sub-unit of the level above.

In his turn, Jacques Lacan applies the linguistic model to the data of psychoanalysis.

He proposes an understanding of the subject in terms of a schema composed of layers of structures. These correspond to Freud's topographical distinction between conscious, preconscious and unconscious.

The unconscious is the second structure masked by an appearance of a conscious and lucid self-disposition.

The unconscious is composed of signifiers and is itself structured in the sense that, although distinctive and summable, its elements are still articulated in categories and sub-sets in accordance with certain precise laws of arrangement.

In this sense, the structure of the unconscious is identical with that of language in its synchronic dimension, the dimension in which it is layered within a single class of elements. Such a comparison obviously necessitates certain modifications and explanations; these will be introduced gradually into the text.

Jacques Lacan has himself made an exposition of his conception of the notion of structure:

I myself make use of the term structure in a manner which I think can be authorised by Claude Lévi-Strauss's use of the term. . . .

The category of the set, if it must be introduced, meets with my agreement in so far as it avoids the implications of the totality or refines them. But this does not mean that the elements cannot be isolated from the set or that they are not summable: at least if we seek in the notion of the set some guarantee of the rigour it has in mathematical theory. 'That its parts are themselves structured' would then mean that they are themselves capable of symbolizing all the relations which can be defined for the set. . . .

The elements are in fact defined there by the possibility of their being posited in function of subsets covering any relation defined for the set, the essential feature of this possibility being that it is not limited by any natural hierarchy. . . .

Now, as I have stressed elsewhere, structure is not form, and the question is precisely that only structure necessitates breaking thought into a topography. . . .

When Daniel Lagache begins by offering us a choice between a structure that is in some way apparent and a structure which he can describe as being at a distance from experience (since it is a question of the 'theoretical model' he recognizes in analytic metapsychology), the antinomy neglects a mode of structure which, for all it is a third mode, cannot be rejected, namely the effects which the pure and simple combinatory determines in the reality wherein it is produced. For is structuralism what allows us to posit our experience as the field in which it [*ça*] speaks or not? If it is, then the structure's 'distance from experience' vanishes, since it operates there, not as a theoretical model, but as the original machine which puts the subject on stage.

What Daniel Lagache puts down to the economico-dynamic point of view or, as he puts it, to the material and its interpretation is precisely where I see the beginnings of the incidence of the structure in our experience and it is there that structuralist research must pursue its effects. . . .

Why should we be surprised then if the genetic criterion meets with failure when put to the test of the Freudian topographies, in so far as their systems are structural? (*Écrits*, 29)

Linguistics introduces us to a layered structure of discourse: $\dfrac{S}{s}$ and thereby shows us one of the peculiarities of discourse: its relative autonomy in relation to meaning, concepts and ideas. Words do not in fact refer directly in their arrangement to the meaning which emerges from the totality of the sentence.

Psychoanalysis reveals a similar layering in the formations of the unconscious, in that these formations, which are articulated in an obscure language, manifest in their significant composition a heterogeneity with regard to the unconscious signification.

Let us take the analogies between the unconscious and language further.

The diachrony of discourse owes this relative autonomy from the global signification to two major stylistic effects: metaphor and metonymy. These two stylistic figures authorize substitutions of signifiers which make the meaning appear to 'float' somewhere without being literally contained in any one element of the sentence. Metaphor and metonymy follow precise and distinct linguistic laws: similarity of meaning between a signifier and its substitute in metaphor and displacement of meaning in metonymy. The presence of these stylistic devices in a sentence allows a vertical chain, so to speak, of contextual signifiers linked by rules of similarity or by connexions of meaning to be constructed for each discrete point in the sentence. And it is to these contextual references that the global signification owes its advent.

In the psychoanalytic register, according to Lacan, the formations of the unconscious owed their hermetic nature to the unconscious network of signifiers they keep suspended, as it were, at their apparent surface, a network which is structured in accordance with the very linguistic laws we have just discussed.

The apparent inadequacy or at least the hermetic character of the terms which alone accede to consciousness results, therefore, from the complex links between the apparent signifiers and other unconscious signifiers.

A further precision: the aim of this book is not to justify Lacan's adherence to structuralism, but to expound his theory as it is revealed by his *Écrits* and by his unpublished words.

In order to provide the reader with a brief indication of the line taken by this volume, these introductory pages are followed by a summary of the content of Lacan's work.

To avoid overloading the text, a numerical system has been adopted for bibliographical references: the figures in parentheses which follow the quotations refer to the numbered bibliography to be found at the end of the book.

Synthesis of Lacanian thought

Lacanian psychoanalytic theory is based upon the recent discoveries of structural anthropology and linguistics.

In order to enable the reader to grasp Lacan's implicit references to these new branches of knowledge, the beginning of the present work will be devoted to the exposition of some elements of structural linguistics and anthropology.

This summary at the outset situates the position of Lacanism in relation to these young branches of the human sciences from a panoramic point of view and allows the reader to understand the reasons for an exposition of the broad outlines of linguistics.

Lacan's originality consists in having placed the Freudian theory of the unconscious on the order of the day, in having analysed it, that is, in accordance with contemporary structuralist method and having brought the light of linguistics to bear upon it.

Lacan will insist upon the fact that socio-cultural and linguistic symbolisms impose themselves with their structures as orders which have already been constituted before the *infans* subject makes his entry into them.

The young child's entry into the symbolic order will fashion him in accordance with the structures proper to that order: the subject will be fashioned by the Oedipus and by the structures of language.

The symbolic order of language or of social organization is an order of interdependent signs bound together by specific laws.

The register of the signifiers, as opposed to the signifieds (the concepts), rejoins the register of the signifieds only through the mediation of the whole body of signifiers. This, schematically, is the meaning we can give to the Saussurian algorithm which inaugurates linguistics: $\dfrac{S}{s}$.

The relationship between a signifier and its signified is effected through the mediation of the whole body of the signs of the language.

According to Lacan's theories, the presence of this mediation will have a constitutive effect for the subject.

The intimate lived experience, which may be assimilated to the signified, will be mediated in thought by the interrelations between the signifiers which will be substituted for it increasing numbers as time passes.

The subject thus finds himself caught up in an order of symbols, and essentially median order which distances him from his immediately lived truth.

In this sense, language lends itself to every trap concerning the self and the lived experience. The promptness with which the unconscious can make its appearance can thus be glimpsed. There is in fact no common measure between what is spoken and what is lived, between the true essence and the manifestation of that essence in spoken discourse. In the discourse he pronounces on himself, the subject moves progressively away from the truth of his essence. This conception will be the basis of the Lacanian interpretation of the neuroses.

Lacan is indeed a structuralist then: the unconscious is the structure hidden beneath an apparently conscious and lucid self-disposition. Lacan will add that the unconscious is structured like a language. The repressed is of the order of the signifier and the unconscious signifiers are organized in a network governed by various relationships of association, above all metaphoric and metonymic associations. With the passage of time, a complex network of signifiers has been formed between consciousness and the unconscious in accordance with a linguistic model. This is shown by analysis of the formations of the unconscious: dreams, symptoms, forgetting of names, etc.

The prohibition of incest, on the other hand, is the structure underlying the apparent organization of societies: the young child who effects his or her entry into the order of social and cultural symbolism will henceforth encounter the Oedipal problem. His or her full or partial accession to society will depend upon the solution of that problem.

The phenomenon of the Oedipus and the phenomenon of language converge to ensure that the young child becomes totally conscious of his or her autonomy as a subject and a member of society.

In general terms, the symbolic order establishes mediate relationships between things; the relationship between man and man, between self and other is mediated, that is, by a symbol. It is not immediate, direct and without an intermediary.

It is the existence of the mediator which allows everyone to register himself in his distinct subjectivity. In an immediate relationship, on the other hand, the distinction between self and other is not clear.

In the Oedipus, the child moves from an immediate, non-distanced relationship with its mother to a mediate relationship thanks to its insertions into the symbolic order of the Family. The family institution distinguishes between parents and children, giving them names and places as singular subjects. In the Oedipus, the father plays the role of the symbolic Law which establishes the family triangle by actualizing in his person the prohibition of union with the mother.

Any serious fault in the Oedipus rivets the child to the immediate relationship, depriving it of subjectivity and rendering it incapable of making the symbolic substitution inherent in language.

Giving a name to a thing in effect presupposes that one can distinguish that thing as not being one's self, and that one therefore has at one's disposal a subjectivity and a signifier of that subjectivity.

According to Lacan, the failure of the Oedipus characterizes psychosis and differentiates it from neurosis.

Parallel to the Oedipus, the child acquires full use of language through the appropriation of the grammatical category of the 'I'. The young child, who at first designates himself by his forename followed by the third person singular of the verb, realizes in a second stage the full assumption of his personality.

Entry into the symbolic order is therefore the precondition of singularity.

PART ONE

Some elements and some problems of general linguistics

Linguistics has produced an extremely rich and varied amount of material. Tendencies and schools are numerous and, even within the same school, notions and terminology are not always the same.

There exist many works dealing with problems limited to certain languages or to certain categories of the facts of language, as well as more general works which frequently deal with problems of methodology.

I limited myself to some of these more general works and, while reading them, I was surprised at the immaturity of linguistic science. Authors do not agree as to the content of basic concepts, as to methods of study or as to the emphasis to be accorded to one or another notion.

A general uncertainty remains as to whether the categories of thought, meaning and concepts should be introduced into linguistic analysis, whereas, practically, it is admitted everywhere that the linguistic sign has two facets: phonic material and concepts.

Various linguists have criticized the use made of linguistics by Lacan on the grounds that he stresses certain aspects of language which they do not consider specific.

For the benefit of readers who are not linguists, I should like to point out that the Lacanian interpretation of linguistics finds, in every point, its verification by at least some linguists. The problem of the validity of certain linguistic conceptions adopted by Lacan is consequently a problem for the linguists themselves.

I will attempt here to bring out from within the heart of the controversy some constant principles of general linguistics. It must be emphasized that our task is not to resolve the problem of the validity of the theories expounded, but to show the theoretical struggles from within which Dr Jacques Lacan has derived the linguistic points he advances.

11

ONE

Debates as to the nature of the linguistic sign and their methodological consequences

The nature of the linguistie sign in F. De Saussure

In his *Course in General Linguistics* (58), Saussure, the pioneer of linguistics, designates the sign or linguistic unit as a double-sided entity. The sign unites, not a name and a thing, but a concept and an acoustic image, the representation of the word, that is, outside any actual use of it in speaking. The acoustic image is not the sound, but the psychical imprint of the sound.

The linguistic sign is, therefore, a relationship which may be represented as shown by Figure 1.1.

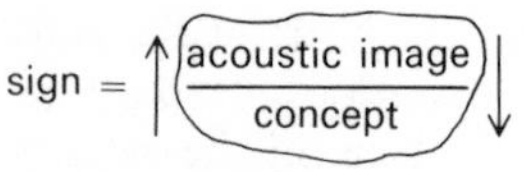

$$\text{sign} = \left\uparrow \left(\frac{\text{acoustic image}}{\text{concept}}\right) \right\downarrow$$

FIGURE 1.1

Saussure proposes that the acoustic image be termed the 'signifier' and the concept the 'signified'. Figure 1.2 shows the result of the substitution of these terms in Figure 1.1.

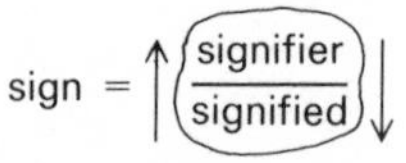

$$\text{sign} = \left\uparrow \left(\frac{\text{signifier}}{\text{signified}}\right) \right\downarrow$$

FIGURE 1.2

In its globality, the sign is the act of the unification of a signifier and a meaning, an act which engenders signification.

The discussions between linguists as to the arbitrary or non-arbitrary nature of the linguistic sign, as to the necessity of introducing the concept into linguistic analysis, and as to the pre-eminence to be accorded to thought or to language as a formal system which is closed in upon itself, may all be considered as having their origin in the Saussurian definition of the sign.

12

Saussure himself greatly modifies this definition with the introduction of the notion of *value,* one of the most productive notions in linguistics, and one which can be considered to be universally recognized, although it is at the origin of various controversies. In this new perspective, the sign is no longer a relationship between two things: a concept and an acoustic image. The sign also has a value which is not limited to its strict significance. The sign is no longer a union of a concept and an acoustic image in the sense that it could be isolated from the system of which it is part.

Only the entire system of the language gives it its specificity as opposed to the other signs.

Each element of the total sign, the signifier and the signified, is a value, a term in a system of interdependence, as is the total sign itself.

Thus, on the conceptual plane, value is an element of signification, but that is not all, otherwise language would be a mere nomenclature. Value results from the fact that language is a system whose terms are interdependent. The value of a word is the signification conferred upon it by the presence of all the words in the code, but also by the presence of all the elements of the sentence.

The value of a word thus results from the simultaneous presence of all the words in the sentence, as shown by Figure 1.3.

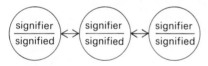

FIGURE 1.3

Here Saussure draws a comparison with the semiological system of money.

In order to determine the value of a five franc piece, one must first of all know what things of a different nature (such as bread) it can be exchanged for. But one must also know the relationship between a five franc piece and a one franc or a ten franc piece in the same system, or between the five franc piece and the elements of a comparable system, such as dollars.

Similarly, in order to determine the value of a word, one must know that it can be exchanged for an idea, as value always makes reference to the dissimilar, but one should also take into account its relationships with other words in the code and in the sentence. The French words *redouter* (to dread), *craindre* (to fear) and *avoir peur* (to be afraid) have value only because they can be opposed to one another.

We can now see how value differs from signification, which refers only

13

to the local correspondence of the signifier to the concept. When we speak of concepts, we imply that they are differential, that they are defined not simply by their content, but also, and primarily, by their oppositional relations with other concepts.

Ideas are nothing outside the system within which they derive their identity from their opposition to other ideas.

Similarly, on the material plane of the linguistic sign, what matters in the word for example is not the sound as such, but the phonic differences which allow that word to be distinguished from others. That signifiers are efficient is due, not to their external characteristics, but to their relative positions within the system. This is in the nature of all conventional signs. Thus, in itself a coin is simply a piece of metal and draws its value only from its correlates within the system.

Phonemes are above all 'oppositional', relative and negative entities.

Finally, the play of interaction is the same at the level of the total sign. In English, for example, the sign 'mutton' takes on its real value only because of the co-existence within the same system of the term 'sheep'.

It seems useful at this point to draw the reader's attention to the fact that by introducing the notion of value, Saussure is merely modifying his interpretation of the linguistic sign. He does not in fact deny the close correspondence of the signifier to its concept, a correspondence which is adequately stressed by the vertical arrows and the circles drawn around the terms of the sign in Figure 1.1.

In the second schema (Figure 1.3), which is meant to illustrate the notion of value on the conceptual plane, the interrelation between the signs of the sentence is represented by the bipolar horizontal arrows, but the signifier's relation to the signified is retained by the circles drawn around the terms of the sign.

In this schema Saussure clearly indicates that the local signification of an element in the sentence is determined by its correlations with the other elements, but he does not say that that signification does not exist as such, once the terms of the sentence have been related to one another.

This precision will be useful in the debate which follows. In it we shall see linguists in full polemic as to which of two conceptions should be given priority: that which stresses the relations between the signs in the 'process' of signification, and which sometimes leads to the signifier being considered as an order which is closed in upon itself and from which it is possible to exclude the signified, or that conception which recognizes an intrinsic designatory power in the sign.

The notion of value in general linguistics is one of the most widely recognized of notions.

It was established by Saussure, but his predecessor, the linguist Peirce, had already foreseen its importance.

For the sign to be understood, he says, there must be a speaker and a listener, but there must also be an interpretant, another sign or body of signs which is either concurrent with the sign in question or present in memory, and which may be substituted for it. For Peirce, the meaning of a sign is another sign by which it can be translated.

If, however, one blocks the notion of value by privileging relations between terms within one category (the signifier) or the other (the signified) to the detriment of the local correlation of signifier to signified, then one starts down a path which leads to extremist considerations.

Certain of Saussure's own expressions, which are correct, if debatable, open a crack in which error can take root. For example, the idea that:

> the final law of language is that nothing can reside in one term precisely because linguistic symbols are not related to the things they designate. 'A' cannot designate anything without the help of 'B', which is itself powerless without 'A'. They have value only because of their reciprocal difference. Things do not signify because of their concrete nature, but by virtue of the formal features which distinguish them from other things of the same class. To consider a term as simply the union of a certain sound with a certain concept is grossly misleading. (58, p. 113.)

Such phrases, which are, I repeat, correct in themselves, may lead to the conception of there being two radically different orders which are closed in upon themselves. What is more, they may give rise to linguistic studies from which meaning is partially or radically excluded.

Thus, in *Elements of Semiology* (56), Barthes will say that the notion of value leads to the conception of the production of meaning as no longer being the mere correlation of a signifier and a signified, but as an act of vertically cutting out two amorphous masses, two parallel floating kingdoms. Meaning intervenes when one cuts simultaneously into these two masses. The signs produced in this way are *articuli*, divisions. For my part, I would rather say that signification is born progressively from a permanent dialectic between grouped signifiers and grouped signifieds, rather like spiral loops uniting, at each discrete point of the spoken chain, a unit of signification extracted from the references thus actualized.

The notion of value is closely connected with that of the arbitrary character of the sign, a notion which is again proper to Saussure (and as litigious as the former notion).

The arbitrary character of the sign concerns only its choice in relation to the idea it represents. Saussure will say that the signifier *sœur*, phonetically translated as 's – ö – r', is not linked by any inner relationship to the concept *sœur*. The connexion between the sound and the concept is arbitrary. Saussure finds proof of the arbitrary character of the sign in the notion of value, according to which a given acoustic image has a designatory power only in relative terms and only in relation to some other acoustic image. It is the mutual relativity of values which proves that the signifier has in itself no designatory power.

He goes on to say that in semiological systems where the elements hold each other in place in accordance with fixed rules, the notion of identity fuses with that of value and is ultimately absorbed by it.

Saussure's exploitation of the arbitrary character of the sign has been criticized by É. Benveniste, R. Barthes and R. Jakobson.

Benveniste, for example, states that the sign is arbitrary only in relation to the thing, and that its connexion with the concept is 'necessary' and intimate, otherwise communication would be impossible. There is no thought without signifiers, therefore signifier and signified are indissociable. Before the appearance of language, there is nothing distinct in either the world or in thought.

The arbitrariness of the sign being justified only in relation to the thing, it is, according to Benveniste, relegated to the exterior of the linguistic sign, since the latter concerns only the signifier and the concept.

Benveniste even goes so far as to say that Saussure's thought led in this direction, although he did mistakenly speak of the arbitrary relationship between the signifier and the concept.

R. Jakobson, for his part, quotes examples of signifiers which have a diagrammatic relationship with their signifieds. Thus, the degrees of the comparison of adjectives show a gradual increase in the number of phonemes. He also invokes the presence of certain 'onomatopoeic' words in the English language in order to demonstrate the possible inner relationship between signifier and signified.

In fact would not *a conception of the sign as deriving its arbitrary nature from its difference in nature from the order of the signified,* as is the case in all symbolic systems, suffice to reconcile these authors, there being in effect no major reason of inner connexion for uniting a given signifier with one concept rather than another?

In the course of the construction of the language, however, certain analogies of formal configuration between signifiers come to represent an analogy between the corresponding signifieds. This is so in the following series in French: (i) *père, mère, frère*, where the analogy of form symbolizes an analogy of meaning – family proximity – without there being any homology of 'nature' between the order of the signifier and that of the signified; (ii) *poirier* (pear-tree), *figuier* (fig-tree), *cerisier* (cherry-tree), etc., where there is, we can see, no reason for attributing the radical *cerise* to the concept of that fruit rather than the radical *poire*. The similarity in the formal construction of these signifiers merely accounts for the identity of the thought-category: *arbre fruitier* (fruit tree).

I would also say that it is necessary for the unification of one signifier with one signified to remain stable, to become necessary for the mind if there is to be any ordering of the real and of thought without any risk of the signs encroaching upon one another and thus ruining communication. In saying that it is the oppositions and negative relationships between signs that makes them distinct entities, we come back to Saussure. A sign is a closed entity only because it is not the others and because the others reject it. The sign derives its designatory power, by which the concept is joined to the signifier in a necessary connexion, from its opposition to other signs. It should again be stressed that in other passages, Saussure insists upon the impossibility of separating the signifier from its signified without destroying the entity of the sign. 'A succession of signs is linguistic only if it supports an idea. The linguistic entity exists only through the associating of the signifier with the signified. Whenever only one element is retained, the entity vanishes.' (58, pp. 102, 103.)

We have been able to see how the Saussurian theories of the sign, of value and of the arbitrary character of the sign could, according to the interpretation given, lend themselves to a certain confusion.

Saussure is definitely one of the most determined linguists in insisting on the impossibility of disregarding meaning in the study of language.

Other linguists, such as E. Sapir of the American structuralist school, or Bloomfield who, although of the same school, is very different, do, however, attempt a study of language in which the orders of signifier and signified are more or less distinct.

We shall also have to mention Noam Chomsky, the revolutionary American structuralist, who is completely at odds with the above-mentioned linguists on this point.

American structural linguistics

For Sapir, there is a relative independence between form and linguistic function. Form must be studied from the point of view of types of configuration, independently of the functions associated with them. The formal methods used by a language (its grammatical processes) and the distribution of concepts must be distinguished in relation to their formal mode of expression (which concepts form the content of the formal configurations).

The principal grammatical processes are:
1 word order
2 composition of words

3 affixation

4 vocalic or consonantal mutation

5 reduplication

6 variation in accent

The world of concepts, which is reflected in the very structure of the language, is divided from a descriptive point of view into:

1 Basic concrete concepts, such as objects, actions and qualities. These are expressed in the language by independent elements or by radicals.

2 Derivational concepts: the verb 'to form' for example. These are expressed in the language by affixing a non-radical element to a radical.

3 Concrete relational concepts, which are expressed in the same way as derivational concepts.

4 Pure relational concepts which relate the concrete elements to one another and give the proposition its syntactic form. They are expressed through affixation, through modification of radicals or through isolated elements.

Bloomfield discusses language in terms of stimulus-response. Ideas, concepts and images are merely empty popular terms designating bodily movements.

The signified is the sum of practical events with which a speech-utterance is connected. The signified, that is, is as much the predisposition of the nervous system as the result of experiences or hereditary factors. It is impossible to account for it scientifically in the study of language.

To say that the signified of a word is the conception one has of it is not demonstrable, as one would have to use other words in order to speak of the concepts.

According to Bloomfield's *Language* (London: Allen & Unwin, 1969, ch. 12), 'the linguist must show in detail that the speaker has no ideas, and that the sound is enough for the words to act upon the nervous system like a trigger-mechanism'.

Bloomfield's conception is not far removed from the reality of things if one thinks of the way in which inter-human communication is effected. Linguistic signs act upon us immediately, without it being at first sight necessary to effect an inner return to ideas. Similarly, our speech almost pronounces itself, without its being possible for us to discern the site in which the signification is operating.

I think, however, that interpretation of language in terms of stimulus-response is limited to the most superficial aspect of the matter.

In my opinion, the human being has at his disposal the key principles and laws of grammar, as well as a host of associated and opposed terms, ready-made phrases and cultural contexts which allow him to grasp the global signification of a discourse with surprising rapidity.

The immediacy of the operations of thought does not provide

grounds for denying their existence. It is well known that scientific attempts to create translating machines have been fruitless. A machine will always remain incapable of creating, whereas every man is continually creating propositions with different structures and every man creates propositions different from those created by other men.

I will not dwell upon Bloomfield's theories, as this author in no way furthers the underlying aim being pursued in this study of linguistic controversies. I am trying to determine such a way of seeing things as would give a place to the Lacanian interpretation.

Far be it from me to have any intention of forcing things into what might be a Lacanian perspective. I am more concerned with showing the nuances of interpretation within which Lacan's use of contemporary linguistics is situated.

Sapir is, it seems to me, a linguist who has come to terms with the category of meaning. He even seems to be putting forward a structural analysis of concepts. But his linguistic analysis refers to the signified only in terms of categories of concepts and not to the signified in its true sense: the signified in its content.

In the following pages I hope to show why I think it impossible to disregard the content of concepts in any attempt at structural analysis in linguistics.

A. Martinet: A French linguist of the Prague School

Martinet draws the dividing line between the phoneme and the morpheme at the point where the criterion of meaning intervenes.

He puts forward the theory of the double articulation in language. The sentence can be analysed into units endowed with meaning and a verbal form.

e.g. *j, ai, mal, à, la, tête.* (I have a head-ache)

Each of these units could be found in another context and none can be divided into smaller units endowed with meaning. One cannot, that is, attribute to these syllables distinct meanings whose sum would be equal to the global meaning. The word *tête* (head), for example, cannot be divided into *tê te,* two syllables which, if added together, account for the meaning *tête.*

This principle of the division of the sentence into units endowed with meaning defines the first articulation of language.

At a second level, which determines the second articulation, the elements thus distinguished in the sentence can in turn be divided into smaller units according to their vocal form, but no longer in accordance with the criterion of meaning. Thus, the word *tête* can be divided into *t, ê, t, e.* The units can equally be found in other contexts: *tante, bête, terre.*

Like Saussure, Martinet defines the linguistic sign as an utterance or part of an utterance which has meaning. The signified is the meaning or value of the sign. And the signifier is that through which the sign manifests itself. It is, in other words, Saussure's acoustic image. The signifier of the sentence taken as an example is represented as follows: *z e mal a la tet.*

All the units of the first articulation are signs, monemes, because they cannot be divided by meaning. The units of the second articulation are phonemes.

As we can see, Martinet is in complete agreement with Saussure as to the nature of the linguistic sign. The French linguist will also adopt the notion of value in the full Saussurian sense.

For Martinet, the meaning of a sentence does not lie in the individual terms which go to make it up, but in the articulation of what goes before it and what comes after it, and in the relationship between these terms and their possible substitutes. The word *bois* (wood) does not for example correspond, says Martinet, to a single concept in French. Its meaning will depend on the context of the sentence and will refer to its value as a differential and oppositional term within the category: place planted with trees, matter, wood used as fuel, *bois de cerf* (stag's antlers). Martinet's position is nice; it does not lead, as a result of the notion of value, to the exclusion in linguistic analysis of the signifieds in favour of the organization of the signifiers, an organization considered as an autonomous and independent order.

The author does however discern a point at which the autonomy of the signifier as a closed system makes itself felt: 'The second articulation . . . makes the form of the signifier independent of the value of the signified.' (63, p. 27.)

At this level, the autonomy of the signifier is defined by the inter-relations between the signifiers without reference to the signifieds.

In *mal*, for example, what makes the signifier independent is the connexion between the *m* and the *m* of *masse*, between the *a* and the *a* in *chat*, etc.

In European structural linguistics, analysis of language is based upon the inter-relations of the signs amongst each other, but on the other hand delimitation of units is at every level effected with reference to the criterion of 'linguistic' meaning.

It seems useful to underline this point by making a detailed description of the process of analysis. I hope to prove that the concept retains pride of place, even in a method which, more than any other method, privileges relations between terms rather than the terms themselves and which gives a particular sense to the term 'meaning', as distinct from designation.

My formulation of the method of analysis in European structural linguistics is taken from *Problèmes de linguistique générale* by Émile Benveniste (65).

Structural method of analysis in European linguistics

In general terms, the linguist delimits the units of the language (phonemes, monemes, words, phrases . . .) with reference to the different relationships they contract with one another at the same level and with the higher levels.

The method consists of two operations which control one another:
1 segmentation
2 substitution

Segmentation consists of breaking down the text into smaller and smaller units until elements which cannot be further broken down are obtained.

In a parallel operation, the elements are identified by the *substitutions* to which they admit.

For example, the term *raison* (reason) is segmented into: [r], [ɛ], [z], [õ]. Each sound is taken individually and another (possible) sound is substituted for it. Thus, one can replace [r] by [b] by [s] by [m] by [t] or by [v]; similarly, one can replace [ɛ] by [a] to obtain *rason*, for example; one can replace [z] by [y] and [ɛ] by [a] to obtain *rayon*; or one can replace [õ] by [ɛ] to obtain *raisin*.

We can see from this that the phonemes are identifiable, not with the letters, but with the sounds or the acoustic images of the sounds.

I would, for my part, point out that the process of substitution is always closely connected with the process of 'integration'. The substitution of one sound for another, that is, is always effected within a unit from the level above in which the new sound has an integrative function. Substitution is meaningless unless it immediately gives rise to a higher unit already existing in the language or in the spoken chain. I point this out in order to show that the criterion of meaning plays a partial role at each level of identification, even at the most elementary level.

It is in fact only because a phoneme can be called upon to play an integral part in the unit above that it is identified as a unit of language. Substitution of [b] for [r] leads to the identification of [r] as a phoneme only because [r] is as capable as [b] of forming a unit at the level above: *rai* which could itself be integrated into *raisin*.

In the word *homme* (man), for example, one identifies the phonemes [ɔ] and [m] which form [ɔm] (the phonetic translation of *homme*) because (i) [m] can be replaced by [t] to give [ɔt] = *hotte*, or [s] to give [ɔs] = *os* and because (ii) [ɔ] may be replaced by [y] to give [ym] = *hume*.

By applying the same process to each sound in the sentence one can register all the phonemes in the language.

Each phoneme has thus been identified by its surroundings: its relations with those other elements which are simultaneously present (syntagmatic relations) and with those elements which may be substituted for it (paradigmatic relations).

21

Like Benveniste, however, we should note that if the minimal units are phonemes, we can still distinguish in them identifiable distinctive features capable of substitution, although they cannot be segmented any further. Examples of the distinctive features of phonemes are: occlusion, dentality, sonority, aspiration, etc.

To obtain higher-level units, the criterion of meaning comes into play.

Once the phonematic units have been picked out, an attempt is made to delimit a higher unit which can contain them. All possible combinations of phonemes are envisaged and one looks to see which of these combinations are effectively realized in the spoken chain or in the language. Those which have no meaning, which can neither, that is, be substituted for others, be recognized as free forms nor be posited in a complementary syntagmatic relation, are excluded.

A unit of any level is identified as distinctive if it forms an integral part of the unit at the level above.

[s] is a phoneme because it can be integrated with [al] in *salle* (room), with [o] in *seau* (bucket), or with [i] in *civil*. [Sal] is a moneme because it can integrate with [à manger] in *salle à manger* (dining room).

Benveniste underlines a peculiarity of the sentence as a linguistic unit: the words, he says, are not simply segments of the sentence whose sum would reproduce the whole. The word does not always have the same meaning when taken in isolation and when it is within the sentence. The meaning of the sentence is therefore distributed amongst the set of its components without its being possible to eliminate a single one of them or to discount their interdependence. Hence, Benveniste defines the word as the smallest free signifying unit.

It seems to me, however, that this analysis of the sentence is equally applicable to the word and to the syllable. What does Benveniste mean when he says that the word is the smallest 'free' signifying unit? If one goes back to his comparison with the sentence, this would mean that the word is the smallest unit which can signify independently of the inter-relations between its components and that the sum of the components reproduces the whole.

The signification or identity of a word arises from the distinctive oppositions of its constituent elements to other elements at the same level and from the inter-relations between them.

Martinet underlined precisely the fact that it is characteristic of the units of the first articulation that they cannot be segmented into units whose sum would reproduce the whole. We see, then, that if Benveniste is right in saying that the word is the smallest signifying unit, he is wrong in not extending the characteristics of the sentence to the word by stressing its inability to be segmented into units, the sum of which would reproduce the whole.

Let us make it quite clear, however, that it seems quite impossible for a linguist like Benveniste to propose an erroneous conception.

By the expression 'the word as the smallest "free" signifying unit' the author simply meant, in my opinion, that the sentence takes its general meaning from the oppositional references of the different signs, references which articulate them with other signs in the code which have been excluded as inadequate in the general context. In the word, however, the meaning is not dependent upon the segments of the word in their signification, but only upon their opposition to other segments at the same level. We know that the phoneme is not a level of signification and that the signifier is at that level independent of the value of the signified.

A further precision must be added.

Benveniste brings his description of structural linguistic analysis to a close by specifying that, in the delimitation of a unit, the criterion of meaning alludes only to the unit's function of integrating into the unit above, to the possibility of distinguishing it by opposing it to others. That the signifying unit corresponds to general or particular concepts, that the sentence corresponds to situations does not, he says, concern linguistics. Meaning in linguistics is in no way equivalent to designation.

In my view, it still remains indispensable to take into account the concept, the situations or the idea if we wish in our linguistic analysis to delimit a unit by its function of integrating into another larger unit. For me, the term 'integrating' means having a function in the whole, being able to be posited in a complementary syntagmatic relation. And in order to determine whether one form can complement another, one must know whether or not it corresponds to something at the level of the sign.

Thus [sal] is a moneme because it integrates into [salle à manger], which exists in the language and signifies something for the mind. [s] is a phoneme because it integrates with [al] in *salle*, and we can see that it is because of the concept evoked in us by the word *salle* that we know that it forms a unit at the level above.

There seems to be no point in playing indefinitely upon words because of a concern, which is quite legitimate on the part of linguists, to be perfectly scientific by excluding thought as being too psychological.

It is clear, at least to me, that the mind refers to a concept at every level of integration.

R. Jakobson: The Prague School

While we are discussing the re-evaluation of the category of thought in the field of linguistic analysis, mention should be made of Jakobson's article, 'Quest for the essence of language', in *Diogenes* (60).

In this article, Jakobson promotes ideas which in many ways belong to the same current of renewal which can be seen in the work of Chomsky. Chomsky, with whom we will close this debate on the nature of the linguistic sign and its methodological consequences, has effected a decisive historical turning point in linguistics, as can be seen from the resounding success of his recent work.

Jakobson's 'Quest for the essence of language' promotes the idea that the operations of the human mind are reflected in the syntactic form of the language.

To this end, he revives the distinction made by Peirce between three levels of signs according to the relations between signifier and signified, a distinction which had until then remained forgotten.

I   *The Icon*, which acts through a factual similarity between the signifier and the signified.

Within this category, he also distinguishes between:

(a) the image, in which the signifier reproduces the qualities of the signified, as, for example, a drawing of an animal represents the animal;

(b) the diagram, in which relations between signifiers represent relations between signifieds. For example, two rectangles of different sizes represent the differences in steel production of two great powers.

II   *The Index* acts through the lived, factual contiguity between a signifier and its signified. The signifier allows the signified to be inferred. For example, smoke allows the inference of fire, a footprint allows the presence of man to be deduced and the acceleration of pulse is an index of fever.

III   *The Symbol* acts through a learned, instituted contiguity between signifier and signified. The connexion here is a rule and does not depend upon any factual similarity or connexion.

Saussure, however, pointed out that many symbols do operate through factual similarity. For example: the scales are a symbol of justice because of a factual similarity. In this case the rule presiding over the imposed connexion has been aided by a factual resemblance. It is the same with onomatopoeic words.

Peirce also insists that the three qualities are often found mixed together within a single sign, every sign accentuating one tendency rather than the other two. The perfect sign would be that in which the three tendencies were most perfectly blended.

Peirce said that language is more diagram than symbol. For a sentence to be understood, the arrangement of the words must in effect function in the capacity of a diagram of the thought.

Jakobson points out by way of example that the conditional proposition, where the condition is given priority over the conclusion, shows the order of the concepts in its formal arrangement.

Similarly, in declarative sentences, the subject precedes the verb and the complement because it is the agent of the action and comes first with regard to the aim, the finality of the action.

The closeness or distance between the entities in a sentence, the central or peripheral character of the words, symmetrical or asymmetrical relations and elliptic suppressions all correspond to something in thought.

One of Jakobson's most striking examples is the following list of onomatopoeic words taken from Bolinger, words whose signifier resembles the signified and which themselves resemble one another, just as their signifieds may be assimilated to one another:

bash	dash
smash	crash
lash	brash
clash	rash

Jakobson quotes a further example: *star* means either a celestial body or a person – both of pre-eminent brightness.

Metaphor and metonymy, it will be noted, proceed by means of this type of affiliation.

The sparse ideas which Jakobson provides here are a prelude, as it were, to a new perspective in linguistics which it will fall to Chomsky to bring to maturity and render practical.

The option of meaning in practical linguistics as envisaged by Chomsky should, I think, put an end to the quarrel as to the preponderance of thought or of language, the quarrel, that is, over thought as determined by the categories of language and language as fashioned by the creative human mind and centuries of culture. One could in fact say that language creates our mode of perception of reality by imposing models, stereotypes and universal laws which have, in their turn, been fashioned in the course of man's philogenetic, sociogenetic and ontogenetic evolution. In other words, the mind has at its disposal a creative liberty actualized by the infinite forms of sentences it can construct on the basis of a few general principles. Conversely, these principles exist as germs innate in the child's brain, which gradually develop with the acquisition of language.

Noam Chomsky: A historical turning point in linguistics

The work of Noam Chomsky is still developing. It represents a historical turning point for linguistics.

Being an American linguist, he was formed by the American structuralist linguists Bloomfield and Sapir.

In *Syntactic Structures* (66), written in 1957, he attempts to denounce the lacunae of the analysis of language in terms of its immediate constituents according to the principles of structuralism. The work already announces his linguistic revolution against the schemas adopted until now. In it, Chomsky is in fact already elaborating the transformational model of surface utterances in terms of the simpler underlying utterances, a model which will constitute an extraordinary innovation in 1965.

Syntactic Structures, however, still shows a certain reluctance to break completely with learned principles. One feels that here the author is coming to grips with the important problem of the emphasis to be placed upon semantics in the analysis of language. Chomsky is still refraining from making any reference to thought-processes in the systematization of the rules of syntax.

In 1965 an article published in the review *Diogenes* foreshadows the remarkable volume published in 1966 under the title *Cartesian Linguistics* (68), immediately followed in 1967 by 'The formal nature of language' (69).

Let us briefly bring out the essence of the ideas contained in the latter two works.

The author questions the behaviourist conception of language as 'stimulus-response' as well as those conceptions according to which the constant production of new sentences is effected by analogy with previously learned phrases. He effects a return to what he calls the centuries of genius, namely the seventeenth and eighteenth centuries with their Cartesian linguistics, which issues directly from Descartes's principles concerning the supremacy of the creative power of the mind.

The human capacity for innovation in the face of situations which are always new is reflected in the creative aspect of language-use (novelty – coherence and pertinence of discourse).

Freed from any control exercised by identifiable external stimuli or internal physiological states, human language can serve as an instrument of thought; it can designate abstract properties or relations between speaker and listener. It cannot be reduced to a mere learned apparatus for the communication of information, requests and commands. Above all, language serves as an organ for the expression of thought, consciousness and reflection.

Recalling Schlegel, Chomsky quotes the phrase: 'everything which serves externally to manifest our interiority bears the name language'.

The creative aspect of language is directly perceptible in the frequently poetic character of the most ordinary language.

Humboldt had already said that 'words have a surplus of intensity, depending on whether they simply serve the practical or contribute to realizing the integration and unification of intellectual syntheses and affective values.' Humboldt adds that the use of language in poetry and in philosophy gives it an 'internal character' which should be distinguished from its simple 'form'.

The form of a language is the body of rules of syntax and word formation, the organized system of the sounds and the rules governing the system of the lexicon's concepts.

Without modifying the form of a language, the constant development of ideas, the resonance of the sentiments and human creativity give language things it did not previously have: modes of expression, stylistic devices, new meanings of words. It is in the colour and life taken on by language that one must look for the incidence of the creative aspect of mind.

Henceforth, any linguistic analysis using only the data actualized in simple direct statements and merely making an ordered representation of those objects will be unsatisfactory. Such an analysis would fail to take into account a whole aspect of language which can be perceived only by a reflexive analysis of the thought-processes presiding over the elaboration of apparently simple sentences.

Any utterance with a given construction (a surface structure) must, if it is to be understood, be analysed into the segments underlying that utterance.

In their transformation into surface utterances, these segments reveal a series of new grammatical rules which are consequently imperceptible to the adepts of the above-mentioned descriptive method.

The formation of the apparent phrase from its deep structure uses principles such as ellipsis, substitution and agglomeration. We can see that allusion is being made here to all the tropes present in the apparent structure of sentences which have until now been neglected by linguists; so many forms translating the creative aspect of thought and which have until now been missed by the linguists.

But let us go further into the analysis of Chomsky's principles.

The linguists and grammarians of Port Royal examined syntax by starting with the operations of the mind. Language thus has for them an external aspect (the sequence of articulated sounds) and an internal aspect (the signification).

This is the point which Chomsky, for his part, develops with the terms surface structure and deep structure.

The former concerns the organization of the sentence as a physical phenomenon, the latter the abstract structural substratum which determines its semantic content and which is present in the mind when the sentence is emitted or perceived.

The surface structure of the prototype sentence: '*Dieu invisible a créé le monde visible*' ('Invisible God created the visible world') indicates that we are dealing with a form of the subject-predicate type, with a complex subject and a complex predicate.

The deep structure reveals a system of three judgments: 'God created the world' (principal proposition), 'God is invisible' and 'the world is visible' (propositions incident to the principal proposition).

The inner structure, the substratum enclosing the semantic content, is a system of three propositions. Each of the three elementary propositions is, like the surface structure, of the subject-predicate type. The surface structure has been realized from the deep structure by a series of rules for grammatical transformation. In the example we are dealing with these transformations include an operation of relativization (God who is invisible created the world which is visible) and an operation of elimination of relatives.

The syntax of a language will consequently be described on the basis of two systems of rules: the basic system which generates the deep structures and the transformational system which allows them to pass into the surface structures.

We can now see that we place grave restrictions on the linguistic fact as soon as we neglect the inner connexion between thought and language.

A process of analysing the sentence into a hierarchy of levels, on the other hand, allows a new grammar to emerge from the links between the deep structures and the surface structures.

To sum up: *syntax consists of rules which generate deep structures and rules which transform the latter into surface structures.* That which generates deep structures will be termed a 'base component', and that which allows them to pass into the surface structures will be termed a 'transformational component'.

In the production of language everything takes place as if the speaker had assimilated into his own thinking substance this coherent system of rules, this genetic code which allows him to utter or interpret an indefinite number of sentences of varying forms. Everything takes place as though he had at his disposal a generative grammar of his own language.

Such a system of rules must allow man to give free rein to his creative faculty as, in the language, it is only the rules underlying the elaboration of sentences that are fixed. Conversely, this system must be able to account for the most peculiar phenomena of language.

The form of the language is not a 'mechanical' form imposed upon the subject from the outside, but an 'organic' form like an innate seed which develops from the inside and gradually acquires a full development of its potentialities. It is a generative system of rules and principles which offer finite means for infinite possibilities.

What is more, the study of language on the basis of deep structures will allow a universal grammar to be founded, as the deep structures, which are reflections of the forms of thought, are common to all languages.

The rules presiding over the transformation of deep structures into surface structures alone differ from one language to another and thus explain the diversity in the apparent structure of languages. The general features of the structures of grammar are, therefore, the same for all languages and reflect certain fundamental properties of the mind.

This succinct résumé of the main axes of Chomsky's thought allows us to glimpse the inadequacy of structural linguistics as it is practised today in that it limits itself to the surface layer of the utterance, to its physical dimension and to the categories brought to light by that dimension.

By evading the question of the processes of the transformation of deep layers into surface layers, linguistic analysis disregards the internal mechanisms of thought and its faculty for perpetual creation. The creativity of the mind enriches discourse, making it into an artist and giving it its metaphorical, imaged and elliptic character.

Chomsky's thought seems to promise much and shows, if there is still any need to do so, the necessity of taking the category of thought into account in linguistic analysis.

This first chapter has briefly traced the main methodological tendencies in structural linguistics and has connected them with the various possible interpretations of the linguistic sign.

Very schematically, tendencies are grouped around two poles: that which accentuates the autonomy of the signifying system to the extent of disregarding the signified, and that which recognizes a reflection of the activity of thought in the formal structure of the signifier.

The following chapter describes the organization of language on two distinct planes. We shall see that, in accordance with these planes, the organization of language corresponds perfectly to the notion of the value of the linguistic sign being a term which is referential to units at the same level and to units which are simultaneously present in the sentence.

Even though these facts may no longer seem to be of prime importance since the appearance of Chomsky's work, it remains indispensable to introduce them here, as Lacan will make abundant use of them.

It should be noted in passing that the innovations introduced by Chomsky are perfectly reconcilable with Lacanian psychoanalysis.

TWO

The two great axes of language

The essentials of this chapter are taken from Jakobson's *Essais de linguistique générale* (59). The data provided by this work is backed up with the help of Barthes's *Elements of Semiology* (56, 57).

Speech implies two fundamental operations: the *selection* of certain linguistic units in the Code or common lexical storehouse and the *combination* of those elements into larger units of a greater complexity, each unit integrating those which precede it into a higher level in the hierarchy: from phonemes to monemes, then to words, from words to sentences and from sentences to statements. These connexions of an increasing level of complexity are governed by phonological, grammatical and syntactic laws of decreasing constraint.

Selection

Selection is the choice of one term from amongst other possible terms and it implies the possibility of the *substitution of one term for another*, given the number of associations which may be made between words *on the basis of some similarity or other*.

Saussure said that, outside discourse, units having something in common are associated in memory, and thus form groups within which various relationships may be found.

For example: 'education' can be associated through its meaning (signified) to 'upbringing' or 'training' and through its sound (signifier) to 'educate', 'educator' or to 'application', 'vindication'.

Each group, therefore, forms a mnemonic series, a storehouse of memory.

Combination

The term *refers to the idea of link, context and connexion*: each linguistic unit serves as a context for simpler units and finds its own context in a more complex unit.

The combination of signs has as its support extension in space, as is perfectly clear from the spoken chain in which no two elements can be pronounced at the same time and in which each term takes its value from what precedes it and what follows it.

At the level of combination, the terms in the spoken chain are, as

Saussure puts it, united *in praesentia*; in selection, on the other hand, they are united *in absentia*.

The planes of selection and combination are in a close connexion which Saussure has explained by means of the following comparison: each linguistic unit is like a column in an ancient building. This column is in a relation of contiguity with other parts of the building: the architrave for example (illustrating the plane of combination). On the other hand, the column which may, for instance, be Doric reminds us of other architectural styles: Ionic, Corinthian (illustrating the plane of selection).

These two planes are connected in such a manner that combination can only advance by means of successive appeals to new terms drawn from the Code. We can see that the plane of combination is more closely connected with speech and the plane of selection with language as a system (*langue*).

In selection, the terms substituted are connected by varying degrees of *similarity* or *opposition*. This is the domain of synonyms and antonyms. Their figurative axis is the vertical: the 'vertical' associations of each signifier.

In combination, the terms combined have horizontal space as their support and stand in relations of *contiguity*, links of concatenation, to one another (see Figure 2.1).

horizontal dimension: relations of contiguity

⟶ a	b	c	d	↓
a′	b′	c′	d′	↓
				vertical dimension:
a″	b″	c″	d″	relations of
				similarity
a‴	b‴	c‴	d‴	

FIGURE 2.1

Obviously, *these two axes divide language in its totality* and not only discourse. As an example, let us apply this twofold division to various domains of language (see Table 2.1).

Jakobson has distinguished between two main types of aphasia, depending on which of the two great axes of the functioning of discourse is impaired.

Briefly, we can say that:

I aphasiacs suffering from *similarity disorder* have difficulty in finding their words; all that is left intact is the framework of the discourse and its connecting links. Naming objects, making associations on the basis of a single word (e.g. bachelor, unmarried) is always a difficult task for aphasiacs of this category. Essentially, the loss affects the symbolic or *metaphoric* function of language. Conversely, they readily associate by metonymy: the word 'fork' will be more easily associated with 'knife' than with 'pike', 'to smoke' will be associated with 'pipe' (by substitution of the thing for the use). These aphasiacs proceed, therefore, by sliding, by the displacement of one term by another which is contiguous to it.

TABLE 2.1

	Selection: relations of similarity	Combination: relations of contiguity
Clothes	Toque-bonnet hood. Garments which cannot be worn simultaneously on the same part of the body. Mutually exclusive in practice, but evoking one another in the mind.	Skirt-blouse-jacket. Juxtaposition in the same type of dress of different elements.
Food	Types of entrée or types of dessert. Sets of foodstuffs which have affinities or differences amongst which a choice must be made. Horizontal reading of a menu in categories: entrées, main dishes, etc.	Vertical reading of the whole menu at the entrance to the restaurant.
Furniture	Stylistic varieties of a single piece of furniture, e.g. a bed.	Juxtaposition of different pieces of furniture in the same space: bed, wardrobe, bedside table, etc.

II in *contiguity disorder*, on the other hand, it is impossible to combine elementary linguistic entities into greater entities, and the ability to put structures into a hierarchy is impaired, giving rise to the telegraphic style. But, whilst *contexture* disintegrates, the operations of selection continue: the patient uses metaphors and similarities. For example: spyglass for microscope, fire for light. Homonyms abound.

The terms of language can be associated, then, by similarity or by contiguity. Both types of relationship between the terms of language can be found in conversation, where one term leads to another either by similarity or by contiguity. These two forms of thought progression find their most condensed expression in *metaphor* and *metonymy* respectively.

In a psychological test, children are confronted with a word and are asked to express the first verbal reaction that comes into their heads. Two opposite predilections are invariably displayed: the response is either a *substitute for* or a *complement to* the stimulus. In the latter case, stimulus and response form a kind of syntactic construction, a kind of sentence.

For example, if the term 'hut' is proposed, two types of response are obtained:

1 burnt out
2 a little house.

The first of these responses creates a narrative context and the second is based upon a similarity. Another pair of children might respond:

1 thatch – straw – poverty.

These responses are based upon a contiguity of relations.

2 cabin – hovel – palace – den – burrow.

These responses are given by similarity or by contrast.

This associative test clearly shows that one topic can lead to another through a metaphoric train of thought, or, on the other hand, through a metonymic progression based upon a connexion of meaning between the terms associated.

Let us now try by means of two examples to see how metaphor is based upon relations of similarity between terms and metonymy upon relations of contiguity.

To begin with, we can take an example of metaphor drawn from Victor Hugo's poem *Booz Endormi*:

'Sa gerbe n'était point avare ni haineuse'
('His sheaves were not miserly or spiteful')

The signification generated by the metaphor is that of an advent to paternity, that of fertility. If a spark of fertility springs from the heteroclite arrangement of the terms: gerbe, haine, avare, it is because gerbe, the flower of summer, is associated by similarity with phallus, a symbol of fertility – or even with its outline – and with love and generosity.

One could certainly – and correctly – say that phallus and gerbe are metonymically connected with the father (the part for the whole), but the existence of some metonymic connexions within the 'vertical' associations in no way contradicts linguistic thought, so long as one remains within the same register of thought.

To take an example of metonymy: 'have a cup' (container for content). The substitution here is made because of the relation between the tea one drinks and the cup containing it. The contiguity expresses the leap, the displacement from register of thought to a neighbouring register.

A further precision may be usefully added to this chapter.

Certain linguists use the terms 'synchrony' and 'diachrony' to refer to the order of selection and that of combination respectively.

These terms are chosen because of a similarity between, on the one hand, so-called 'synchronic' linguistics (the study of a language at a given moment in its evolution) and the axis of selection, and, on the other hand, between 'diachronic' linguistics (the study of the evolution of the language in time) and the axis of combination.

Still other vocables may be found referring to the two axes of language. It seems, therefore, simpler to tabulate them in order to make it easier for the reader to locate quickly the axes referred to by these terminologies (see Table 2.2).

TABLE 2.2

Selection	Combination
substitutions ⎫ associations ⎭	context
paradigm	syntagm
oppositions	contrasts
similarity	contiguity
metaphor	metonymy
language (*langue*)	speech (*parole*)

PART TWO

Lacan's use of the general data of linguistics

Lacan's thought is very clearly influenced by linguistics, but his borrowings from that science are subject to an illumination which, although peculiar to Lacan, is necessitated by the subject he is dealing with: the human unconscious.

Lacan has elaborated his theories on the extremely rich basis of a knowledge of several domains: philosophy, linguistics, mathematics, anthropology, etc.

One would wish in vain for a detailed justification of the validity of the analogies drawn between the use of language at the level of consciousness and its use in the unconscious. Similarly, it would be impossible completely to explain Lacan's adherence to linguistic structuralism. Structuralism is a 'method' and it is applied in different ways in different disciplines.

The register of the innermost depths of the human soul will never submit to a rigorous analysis in the same way as rational phenomena. Consequently, every borrowing from the other sciences in psychoanalysis must bear the mark of the human, the mark of the irrational, the unexpected, the mysterious and the devious.

At the beginning of this second section we should none the less distinguish between Lacan's references to linguistics in the strict sense and a Lacanian philosophy of human ontogenesis which may be forged in the light of a certain conception of the effects of language upon man.

THREE

The Lacanian perspective in linguistics

In the *Proceedings* of the Congress held in Rome in 1953 (34), Lacan defines the signifier as the set of material elements of language linked by a structure; the signifier is the material support of discourse: the 'letter' or the sounds. It is no more the sign or the signal of the thing than the signified. The signified is the meaning of an experience related in discourse as understood by everyone: it is externalized in the globality of the successive signifiers and is not precisely situated anywhere in the signifier of the sentence.

Lacan's originality is to have wished to furnish proof that the signifier acts separately from its signification and without the subject being aware of it. As a constituent element of the unconscious, the figure, the literal character of the signifier, makes its effects felt in consciousness without the mind having anything at all to do with it. 'It' (*ça*) thinks in a place where it is impossible to say 'I am'.

For example, if a copulatory event takes place in the presence of a child who does not have a sufficient degree of biological maturity to give it its exact signification, it will be inscribed in the unconscious, but it will remain without its signification; it will be inscribed in letters, in pure signifiers.

Already we have here an interpretation of linguistics which it is impossible to detach from the human context in which it is inscribed and which consequently cannot be denied by the classic paths of scientific criticism.

Elsewhere in his *Écrits* ('The Freudian thing', 19) Lacan puts opposite the terms signifier and signified respectively, language as system, and speech or the spoken chain. He in fact assimilates signifier and signified to the opposed terms of the series: selection and combination; he also alludes to the notion of value.

He will consequently say that *signifier and signified are two networks of relations which do not overlap.*

The first network, that of the signifier, is the synchronic structure of the material of language in which each element takes on its exact usage by being different from the others. This applies at every level revealed by linguistic analysis from the phoneme to composite phrases.

For Lacan, then, the network of the signifier is specified by the relations of opposition between material elements at every level of structuration revealed by linguistics.

The second network, that of the signified, is the diachronic whole of discourse. It reacts historically upon the first network, just as speech influences language, but in reverse order, with the signifying network commanding the advent of speech through its laws of structure. A dominant characteristic of speech – signification – is born of taking the set of terms together and of the multiple interplay between signifier and signified.

Seeing signifier and signified in this way and relating them to paradigm and syntagm respectively in fact means adopting the notion of value as expounded by Saussure, insisting upon the fact that the signifier, the signified and the sign in its globality are at the same time terms and relations. The signifier is defined by its oppositions to the other signifiers in the code at a given level of possible comparisons. The signified, for its part, is given weight only by its correlations with the other elements of the sentence and all the elements of the code. The signification of the sign also derives from the other words in the sentence and in the code.

It is of little importance to us that Lacan should have preferred the signifier–signified terminology to that of syntagm and paradigm or any other terminology, although we should note that he does also speak of synchrony and diachrony. The important point for us is that the author of *Écrits* has adopted the linguistic notions of sign, value and division of language along two main axes.

His interpretation of the theory of value does, however, denote a very definite accentuation of relations between signs within the respective categories of signifier and signified to the detriment of the terminal unification of the signifier with its signified.

I have, I think, sufficiently stressed the risks involved here in the chapters on linguistics. Even if signification does progress by way of a detour through a complex network of criss-cross relationships between signifiers and signifieds, it is still possible, if the global context is taken into account, to pin down a circumscribed unit of signification at the local level of the word in the sentence. One will, of course, have sorted out the contextual networks and ultimately it will be thanks to them that the signification of a word will be determined.

It should not be forgotten, however, that discourse as experienced by Lacan as a psychoanalyst is very different from that experienced by linguists. In psychoanalysis, discourse shows its other face: that of 'overdetermination' in the Freudian sense.

For the psychoanalyst, discourse cannot be reduced to what is being said explicitly; like thought itself and like behaviour, it bears with it the weight of our 'other', the 'other' of which we are unaware or which we half refuse.

We should therefore not be surprised to see that Dr Lacan is fascinated by the stuff of the signifier, by the infinite symbolic detours of meaning. In the event, we would perhaps do better to draw from this a lesson which would be profitable to all the human sciences (social psychology, anthropology) and to linguistics itself. We should recall the perspectives opened up by the wider analysis of discourse as practised by Chomsky.

Let us, however, follow Lacan more closely.

In 'The agency of the letter . . .' (22), Lacan says that signifier and signified are two distinct orders, separated by a line which is resistant to signification, two parallel flows connected by slender dotted lines. 'It is in the chain of the signifier that the meaning insists without any of its elements making up the signification.' (22)

Lacan does not mean that there is no possibility at all of grasping the signification of a sentence.

In the *Écrits*, the recurrent spiral through which the signification of a sentence is apprehended is designated the anchoring point [lit. 'upholstery stud'], a point which is something like the button in the upholstery of a very psychoanalytic couch, as we shall see.

> The diachronic function of this anchoring point is to be found
> in the sentence, even if the sentence completes its signification
> only with its last term, each term being anticipated in the
> construction of the others, and inversely, sealing their meaning
> by its retroactive effect.   (*Écrits*, p. 805.)

What leads Lacan somewhat away from a purely scientific approach to language, as opposed to the science of handling the unconscious, is a philosophical conception of the phenomenon of inter-human 'understanding', and of man's 'impossible' grasping of Truth, the truth about himself, scientific truth.

As we shall frequently have to take into account Lacan's ideas about man's relations with the Truth, we shall only discuss them briefly here.

For Lacan, whose work proceeds from an enlightened reflection upon the history of science and philosophy, it is clear that the Truth shies away from language. The history of humanity is punctuated by valuable discoveries in what Lacan calls the 'conjectural sciences', but, although these 'anchoring points' point in the direction of truth, they always miss the important point, namely the impossible, the Truth, the Real.

What is more, these valid discoveries of *epistemè* are conveyed from mouth to mouth in the form of 'opinion' (*doxa*). And these forced marches of discourse chip knowledge a little more at every turn. As a result, discourse is a trap for inter-human understanding and above all for Truth.

This general philosophy of the truth-language relationship and of the *doxa-epistemè* relationship will obviously have its repercussions at the level of inter-human discourse in its narrow dimension. Temporarily pinned down at the level of the sentence, signification in fact always takes refuge in enigma. It generates new sentences which, piled up on top of one another in a chase after the mythical meaning-truth, give the impression that there is an irreducible distortion between signified and signifier.

We should add that the stress placed upon the separating function of the line in the Saussurian algorithm also operates for Lacan at the local level of the word. Each word in the sentence certainly acquires a meaning through the inter-relational play between the elements of the sentence, but, at the same time, this meaning is never fixed in a stable manner. The single word implies a series of references to the other words in the code, both synonyms and antonyms, so that one could go right through the dictionary and still come up with nothing but a tautology.

For here, too, in the synchronic structure of language, the anchoring point is mythical. The final signified for which one searches is radically excluded from thought as it concerns an incommensurable dimension, namely the Real.

To bear out his thesis of the autonomy of the signifier from the signified, Lacan quotes two lines from Paul Valéry. He demonstrates that the signifier can only serve our thought when it is taken as a whole, and even then only thanks to the connexions between the terms of the sentence and the contexts attested to on the vertical axis of each discrete point in the sentence.

–Non, dit l'arbre. Il dit non dans l'étincellement
    de sa tête superbe.
('No', says the tree. It says 'No' in the shower of
    sparks of its superb head.)

The signification which arises from these lines is that of majesty personified by a tree. No one part of the sentence has to itself the privilege of being the centre of this signification. Neither *arbre* nor *étincellement* for example supports the signification by itself. It arises, as if by magic, from a judicious arrangement of terms which hold appended to their vertical axis a whole cultural and 'linguistic' context of associations of signifiers and signifieds.

If the association of these few terms is in fact able to give the tree a human majesty, it is because *arbre* evokes 'plane tree' by association and evokes strength and majesty by metaphor. The word *tête* also

41

recalls concepts of authority and reflection which, when they are referred back to the line's initial *Non*, make the tree into a person.

The signification is, therefore, progressively born of a balanced and well-considered arrangement of terms which excludes some terms as being inadequate and which evokes certain other comparable terms.

These lines, Lacan goes on, also allow us to become aware of the obvious fact that language is used to say something very different from what it says if one takes it word by word, rather like a joke where a truth is heard between the lines thanks to the acrobatics possible with words. Thanks to man's metaphoric ability, words convey multiple meanings and we use them to signify something quite different from their concrete meaning. Thus the word 'arm' can, for example, metaphorically designate a deep inlet of the sea.

This possibility of signifying something other than what is being said determines language's autonomy from meaning.

Metaphor is the principal agent of this relative autonomy, but another equally important stylistic figure is used to the same effect. I refer to *metonymy*. The latter substitutes one term for another on the basis of a link of proximity, of connexion in meaning between the two terms. The expression 'I drink a cup' is metonymic and we perceive the correct meaning independently of the inexact nature of the signifiers used. It is clear that I am not drinking the cup, but its contents. The signification of the formula is nevertheless immediate thanks to the connexion uniting the cup with its contents.

One could multiply examples of these stylistic figures to infinity. I will give only a few examples to show how frequently they occur in the most everyday language: Thirty sail for thirty ships (the part for the whole); The town for its inhabitants (the container for the contents); He lives by his work for he lives by the fruit of his work (the cause for the effect).

I will take a few examples of metaphor from H. Wald (117): the word 'mouth' used of a cave or a river; the anatomical term 'tongue' to designate the vehicle of speech or as represented in the expression 'the tongue of a shoe'; the term 'heart' used of a forest, life or love. The author points out that many apparently banal terms were forged by metaphor: the expression *en haut* (above) comes from *ciel* (sky), *en bas* (below) from *terre* (earth), *phenomenon* from 'visible' and *essence* from 'invisible'.

In my comments on methods of linguistic analysis I reproached linguists with having neglected the creative aspect of language and with using only sentences aimed at simple communication in their analysis. When speaking of Chomsky, I emphasized the benefits for the progress of linguistic science of having recourse to poetic forms of speech.

It is easy to see that the stress placed by Lacan on stylistic devices rather than on the laws governing the syntactic organization of the surface sentence has given him a more rapid access to the mechanisms of thought. The formations of the unconscious: dreams, slips of the tongue, jokes, symptoms, are full of these stylistic devices. If it is to discover the unconscious meaning – cf. the insistence of the line which resists signification – psychoanalysis must proceed to veritable hermeneutics.

Hermeneutics is the art of the devious, the art of bringing out the contexts which underlie the statement and the apparent structure of the formations of the unconscious. It is the unconscious vertical chains which give the analytic technique of free association its value and its purpose. Lacan's insistence on the autonomy of the signifier and on the resistance to signification of the line in the Saussurian algorithm is, then, definitely influenced by his formation as an analyst. Lacan has taken from the teachings of linguistics, in a way which I find justifiable, whatever is capable of throwing light upon the strictly human phenomena he is analysing.

Thus, Lacan assimilates the metaphoric and metonymic processes of language to condensation and displacement respectively: the two mechanisms characteristic of the working of the unconscious in its formations.

In the aspect they present to consciousness, the formations of the unconscious are, like language, incomprehensible if taken word by word. They are to be analysed like a rebus, by reference to the contexts which lie beneath the utterance, contexts which unfold metaphors and metonymies or condensations and displacements.

> The psychoanalysable symptom . . . is supported by a structure identical to the structure of language. . . . This refers to the basis of that structure, the duplicity which submits the two registers knotted together in it to distinct laws: of the signifier and of the signified. The word register designating here two chains taken in their globality, and the first position of their distinction suspending a priori any possible eventuality of equating these registers term by term. (*Écrits*, 21)

It should again be pointed out that conscious language, and even scientific language, also contains many metaphors and metonymies fashioned on the basis of profound psychological experiences common to everyone. Sexual experiences belong within this category, and it is often these which are brought into play by humour; artistic experience belongs here too, and poetry takes it upon itself to relate them in a symbolism accessible to all, but by way of devious paths in which the line's resistance to signification is felt.

Dr Lacan cannot have had to go far out of his way in order to apply the discoveries of linguistics to psychoanalysis: he simply had to 'humanize' them a little. One could quite rightly say that the patient plays with words just like the poet, but with the important difference that the assimilations, comparisons or operations which he effects between signifiers are sometimes new and strictly private. If they already exist in the language, they will still be coloured by inner psychic motivations. We could ourselves assimilate a Citroen DS [déesse = goddess] to a woman, but the patient will do so because of an incommunicable personal experience which is incomprehensible to anyone.

In Lacan, linguistic theories are inevitably contaminated – or enriched – by coming into contact with the depths of the human soul.

In psychoanalysis, the Saussurian algorithm $\dfrac{S}{s}$ is understood to be of the dimension of the symbol rather than a sign restricted to its rational surroundings.

To put it simply: Lacan opens up to the general theories of the science of language all the human perspectives which linguistics owes it to itself to envisage. As an example, let me briefly indicate the mode of elaboration of the dream.

The latent dream material determines the manifest content in almost every last detail. Each detail derives, not from a single latent idea, but from several details borrowed from a common store.

Alongside the diverging threads leading from each detail to a store of latent ideas, there exist diverging threads which go from the latent ideas to the manifest in such a way that a single latent idea is represented by several details in the manifest. Finally, a complex network of crisscross threads forms between the manifest and the latent.

Here, as in the Saussurian algorithm, signification depends upon the articulations of the elements of the sentence and upon the vertical 'dependencies' of each elementary term.

In analytic terms, the signification of the dream is brought about by a dialectic between manifest and latent, with each stage englobing its predecessors in a wider synthesis.

The same technique of analysis is applicable to all the formations of the unconscious. The analyst arrives at it thanks to the free associations made by the analysand around each discrete element of the apparent phenomenon.

It will be noted that similar hermeneutics often apply when it is a question of extracting the substance of a poem.

Lacan considers the links inside this network as operating through the processes of metaphor and metonymy, *without the subject himself being aware of it.*

We should recall that the artist himself often has the sensation that another acts for him in his creation. Pathology, however, stresses the private nature of associations at the expense of their universality by introducing 'secret motivations'.

The interference of psychoanalytic data with the Lacanian interpretation of linguistics has, as I have already said, a further consequence which it is essential to recall. I shall come back to it in a more exhaustive manner once the first outlines of Lacan's global theory have been established.

Lacan develops at great length what he calls 'the autonomy of the signifying chain from the signified, the incessant sliding of the signifying chain over the waves of the signified'.

The notion of the anchoring point advanced in this connexion provides, as we have seen, only a very partial solution to the problem of the terminal hooking of the signifier to the signified, and the absence of any definitive hyphen concerns the relations between the real and thought as much as it concerns the relations between thought and symbolic signifier.

The psychoanalytic register bears out these facts. If one considers the return of the unconscious into the circuit of conscious discourse during the analytic treatment, one is confronted with phenomena parallel to those of conscious discourse. In psychoanalysis, the signified is reached only at the outcome of the analytic treatment. Placed in the circuit of consciousness, each layer of the unconscious which has been revealed takes refuge in 'mystery'.

If one then goes back in analytic time from layer to layer, from chain to chain, one eventually encounters the original text of the unconscious.

This text is a body of articuli, opposed syllables and elementary letters.

However, just as it is impossible to return across the initial divide separating the real from thought and the real from the symbol in conscious language, it would be impossible for psychoanalysis to locate with precision the connexion which mythically unites the original text of the unconscious with the subject's imaginary.

A fortiori, it would be unthinkable that one could 'in truth' make the connexion between the signifier and the subject's bodily and physiological lived experience.

We should also note that the separating line in the Saussurian algorithm which, according to Lacan, is operative at every structural level of possible connexions, has a further function, perhaps the most important of all, in the way Lacan conceives the connexion uniting conscious and unconscious language, the subject of thought and social symbolism and the subject of the unconscious discourse. Here, the separation is revealed at every stage of the analytic cure and is, of course, apparent in the original movement whereby the child's first stammerings are cut off from the first elementary signifiers of the unconscious.

For a clarification of these statements, the reader is referred to Part Four of the present work.

A critical comparison of linguistic and psychoanalytic symbolisms can be found in Benveniste's *Problèmes de linguistique générale* (65). We shall enter into debate with the author in order to go further into the possible points of similarity between the two symbolisms.

The symbolism of language is, he says, a learned symbolism co-extensive with the experience of the world: symbol and syntax are close to the experience of things.

Psychoanalytic symbolism, on the other hand, is characterized by its universality: the symbols which translate dream wishes or neurotic complexes are common to all peoples and, in this sense, they have not been learned by those who produce them.

Psychoanalytic symbolism also manifests a multiplicity of signifiers compared to the uniqueness of the repressed signifier. This is because, being repressed, the signifier can only give itself up under the cover of images. Furthermore, the multiple signifiers are united with the unique signified by links of personal motivation.

The author concludes that unconscious symbolism is at once supra- and infra-linguistic.

'Supra' because it uses very condensed signs which in conscious discourse would correspond to large units of discourse; because a dynamic of intentionality, of motivation, exists between the signs: the repressed desire which takes the most devious paths in order to manifest itself.

On the other hand it is 'infra-linguistic' because it has its source in a region deeper than that in which language has been installed by education and because it has recourse to the personal and the cultural.

Because of these divergences, the author suggests that it would be more reasonable to make the analogy between conscious and unconscious language on the basis of style rather than on the basis of symbolism itself. The rhetoric of the unconscious could in effect be assimilated to style in language, as both make use of euphemism, metaphor, metonymy, synecdoche ellipsis, allusion, etc.

Let us briefly recall Peirce's excellent classification of signs, thus continuing the debate on a more secure basis than that of a presupposition of knowledge of the exact nature of linguistic symbolism. This simple expedient will suffice to show how restrictive the conception of symbolism adopted by Benveniste is, limited as it is to arbitrary convention. Peirce distinguishes three tendencies in the relations a signifier may have with its signified, adding that the tendencies may be found together within the same sign.

First, the 'icon', in so far as it is a diagram, reflects the internal relations of the signified in the signifier. In so far as it is an image, it reproduces the factual qualities of the signified in the signifier.

Second, the 'index' infers the presence of the signified by a relation of connexion between signifier and signified.

Finally, the 'symbol' is closer to being a learned and imposed rule according to which such and such a signifier is linked with such and such a signified. A slight modification of the definition does, however, allow signifiers having some metaphoric similarity with their signifieds to be assimilated to symbols.

Obviously, there will never be a perfect similarity between the 'neurotic' symbol of a complex or a wish and the symbol of a conceptual signified in classical language or even in poetic language. The incidence of a motivation 'too personal' to be derived from universal human experience will always represent the dividing line between the two symbolisms, setting a limit to any similarity there may be between them.

The first level of the sign described by Peirce is often found in psychoanalysis, when, for example, the images of the dream or phantasy are the reproduction of identical images in the unconscious. These often emanate, however, from the uppermost layers of the unconscious, those which border upon the preconscious and in which 'transposition' is very weak. In general, these images overlap with other signifiers whose relationship with the signified is more ambiguous.

Language itself hardly ever functions with simple images. Onomatopoeic words where the phonic substance of the signifier is practically the image of the signified together with its sonic qualities are closer to the symbol than to the image.

The diagram, on the other hand, is more frequent in language and is more frequently encountered in psychoanalysis.

As an example of the diagram in language, Jakobson cited the order of propositions reflecting the order of priority in the schemes of thought. Similarly, the arrangement of the elements in the manifest content of the dream is not at all arbitrary, and reflects the way in which the unconscious contents are arranged in relation to one another.

A further point: the index is very common in both poetic and everyday language. Ultimately the index is not very different from metonymy, and Lacan has tried to compare this stylistic figure to the displacement proper to the formations of the unconscious.

All the formations of the unconscious, from the dream to the joke and the symptom, use these devices to outwit censorship, although they are still marked by it.

One of Freud's hysterical patients suffered from recurrent olfactory perceptions. It seemed to her that she had once smelt something burning and the return of these sensations weighted heavily upon her. The smell of burning was identified by analysis as being the index of a drama: a spoiled dish, a minor drama if it were not that it replaced in her memory the infinitely more painful drama of a letter breaking off an affair, a letter which the patient used to read over and over again at lunch time.

Ultimately, the smell of burning is the index of a *drame de cœur* with which it is metonymically connected.

Obviously, the case of the displacement in this symptom is more than metonymy, even if we recall that metonymy often operates by substituting the cause for the effect. Here, the relation between signifier and signified is, as Benveniste points out, motivated and determined by a quite personal experience. Because of the personal nature of the traumatic experience lived by the patient, a public allusion to 'a smell of burning' would not be accessible to anyone.

This is the line which divides the psychoanalytic sign from the linguistic sign.

To turn, finally, to the symbol in the full sense.

In language, the symbol is either a signifier whose nature and characteristics are unrelated to the signified – in which case it is conventional and learned – or a signifier whose nature is different from that of the signified, although their characteristics do show some factual similarity, as is the case with metaphors.

In languages, most words have only a conventional relationship with their signifieds.

The French word *poirier*, for example, designates the tree bearing that fruit (*poire* = pear) only because habit has decided that it will be so.

Similarly, there is no reason, apart from a common agreement as to the need for communication, why the German word *vögeln* should signify the act of copulation.

Language as a phenomenon, on the other hand, owes its mobility and its poetry to the personal creativity of the speaker and to the fact that human experience is to a large extent universal just as much as to the conventions of the academicians.

The film star owes her nickname to a metaphoric operation in thought which transposes the 'sparkling' and 'brilliance' significations of the word 'star' to the talented actress by virtue of an implied comparison between the signifieds. It is the same with the symbol of justice: the scales. In these cases, as in practically every case, language is merely ratifying the works of the human mind with its perpetual creations. In any case, each individual has his own language, expressions original to him, and is constantly making innovations in the field of metaphor.

Psychoanalysis, as I understand it, encounters both the above forms of symbol.

The first form of symbol, in which the signifier's relationship with its signified is totally arbitrary, is, however, never encountered in psychoanalysis without the underlying characteristics of personal motivation.

The unconscious can make use of sentences or words in everyday language, but their meaning will be reduplicated. There is no simple, naïve use of language in psychoanalysis. On the contrary, what is used by the unconscious is the frequent double meanings of words, the associative play between the sounds of the radicals. Which brings us back to the second category of symbols.

In the dream, nudity signifies moral shame; a staircase: an arduous task, effort; the departure of a missed train: failure or a desire to stay where one is.

Besides, these symbols with a psychological content have become part of tradition and anyone can grasp them.

Other symbols in language denote a direct borrowing from national culture or universal experience. The cross is the symbol of sacrifice and suffering; to be sick of someone or something is a metaphor for 'to be unable to tolerate'; to have one foot in the grave means being close to death; to be in hell means living through a nightmare and so on.

There is no need to underline how common these symbols are in psychoanalysis. The formations of the unconscious, especially dreams and jokes, are full of them.

These cultural references enter into the language, taking their place as signifiers like any others. Besides, the dictionary always takes the figurative use of terms into account, which shows that they do belong within the language.

In these cases of psychoanalytic symbolism, as in the cases dealt with above, the only peculiarity worth underlining is the incidence of a supplementary private motivation in the use made of the symbol. The human being enriches his vocabulary with personal psychological notes; the patient does the same but, first, he does so unawares and, second, his creations are sometimes unwarranted given the distortion he imprints upon his human experience. Slips of the tongue are the typical example: an incongruous word suddenly springs up despite the global context which rejects it, another word is called for in vain and refuses to come to mind, yet another word is deformed. These are so many cracks in conscious discourse which remain incomprehensible to their author without deep analysis.

The patient loses the reference signified by the symbol, short-circuits operate in his discourse without his being able to account for them.

This is why Lacan has always stressed that the line in the Saussurian algorithm is resistant to signification. *In language, the line symbolizes the mind's detours in search of meaning; in psychoanalysis, it symbolizes the repression of the signified* which remains inaccessible without the help of analytic techniques, as well as the private character of the signifier-signified link.

In conclusion, all that we need retain of Benveniste's criticisms are, first, those criticisms which stress the intentionality and motivation of psychoanalytic symbolism and then those which show that it has its source in a region deeper than that in which education installs language.

It should be pointed out that both language and psychological experiences install language. Our language is woven from expressions borrowed from our psychic experiences or other experiences which are part of the 'human condition'.

The lessons of linguistics are, then, fruitful for psychoanalytic theory and practice. I consider Lacan's borrowings both justified and welcome. Lacan certainly shows no signs of complete purism, but, as I said at the beginning of the chapter, one science is not another, and the complete integration of psychoanalysis is neither feasible nor desirable.

Lacan has not created a new psychoanalysis out of nothing, nor even a linguistic psychoanalysis; he has simply made use of a terminology which enriches the subject. And underneath this terminology, we still find the very substance of Freudian thought.

Lacanian theory is also based upon a philosophy of human ontogenesis which derives directly from contemporary understanding of language.

I will try to make a preliminary survey of this theory in a more philosophical chapter which will help us to understand the key-notions of Lacanism as expounded in the later chapters.

FOUR

Philosophy of language in Jacques Lacan

Adopting a phrase from Schlegel, Noam Chomsky said that animals and small children live in a world of 'states' and not in a world of 'objects', in a world, that is, without order or coherence. Language alone allows the order of the world to be instituted, and then allows acts of reflexion and of consciousness upon the world and upon sense impressions to be carried out. Language, he goes on, serves above all as an organ of thought, consciousness and reflexion. It thus provides the mind with an autonomy from the lived experience, allowing it to maintain a distance between itself and the lived experience.

As A. de Waelhens points out (79), one of the specific characteristics of language is that it evokes a thing, a reality, by means of a substitute which this thing is not, evoking, in other words, its presence against a ground of absence.

The word is the presence and the absence of the thing it designates and it posits it 'in itself' in its order of reality.

Two separate but referential orders are thus ordered by the act of designation: the *real* and *language*.

This act of substituting a sign for a reality is also an operation of mediation whereby the subject places himself at a distance from the lived experience and is thus able to locate himself as a subject distinct from his surroundings.

Let us recall the child's game recounted by Freud in *Beyond the Pleasure Principle* (8), where he shows how a child succeeds in dominating the cloudy lived experience of his mother's absence by replacing that experience with a symbol. A. de Waelhens has used this game to describe a child's accession to the metaphoric function of language.

The child, whose favourite game is recounted by Freud, had a cotton-reel with a piece of string tied around it. Holding the string, he would throw the reel over the edge of his curtained cot. While doing so he uttered a prolonged 'ooh', which was easily interpreted as being an attempt at the German *fort*, meaning 'gone' or 'away'. He would then pull the reel back into his field of vision, greeting its reappearance with a joyful *da* ('there'). It should be noted that the child's mother, busy outside, was in the habit of leaving her son alone for long periods.

The game thus had the signification of a renunciation. It allowed this 18-month-old child to bear without protest the painful lived experience of his mother's alternating disappearance and reappearance. By means of this game in which he repeated with an object – the reel and the string – the coming and going of his mother, the child assumed an active part in the event, thus ensuring his domination of it.

According to A. de Waelhens, this game with the reel and the string illustrates the birth of language in its autonomy from reality and allows a better understanding of how language distances us from the lived experience of the Real.

In a first act of symbolization, the child removes himself from the urgency of an event – his mother's disappearance and reappearance – by replacing it with a symbol – the appearance and disappearance of the reel.

By their alternation, the two phonemes O and A (*ooh* and *da*) will in turn symbolize the disappearance and reappearance of the reel. The distancing of the lived experience is effected in two stages: the child moves from the mother to the reel and finally to language.

Such an experience may be considered the inaugural moment of all future displacement, all metaphors and all language.

This game showed that language detaches itself from the Real and allows the subject to register himself by distancing himself from the lived Real. It should be noted in passing that the game illustrates Lacan's theory of the anchoring points. The symbol 'reel of string' is substituted for the primitive lived experience of the mother's absence and the reel is in its turn replaced in consciousness by a symbol of language: the alternation between two phonemes. This mechanism of access to language simultaneously constitutes both the unconscious and conscious language. But it is followed by the separation of the unconscious from conscious language, as the phonemes substituted for the child's imaginary lived experience have the universal meaning of the concepts 'gone' and 'present' as well as their subjective reference.

In *Le Discours et le Symbole*, Edmond Ortigues (71) makes the same observations about language as A. de Waelhens, and completes them by saying that 'expression individualizes'. It differentiates: (i) between the interior and the exterior; (ii) inside the self it differentiates between interiority and the expression of that interiority; (iii) furthermore, it causes itself to be recognized in itself by its form, which is related to other possible forms.

Signification does not proceed from a thought–language relation alone, but also from thought's relation to itself by means of a relation between signs.

To sum up: language re-produces reality. As there is no thought without language (*langage*), knowledge of the world, of others and of self is determined by *language* (*langue*). Lacan makes great use of this philosophy of language, which can be seen in his whole theory, especially in those texts dealing with the supremacy of the order of the signifier over man who makes his entry into it and finds himself subjected to it.

The philosophy which may be derived from the study of language will lead Lacan to promote the thesis that birth into language and the utilization of the symbol produce a disjunction between the lived experience and the sign which replaces it. This disjunction will become greater over the years, language being above all the organ of communication and of reflection upon a lived experience which it is often not able to go beyond. Always seeking to 'rationalize', to 'repress' the lived experience, reflection will eventually become profoundly divergent from that lived experience. In this sense, we can say with Lacan that the appearance of language is simultaneous with the primal repression which constitutes the unconscious. We will frequently come back to these theses in more detail and, for the moment, they need only be connected with the earlier chapters.

On the other hand language does have the virtue of providing the subject with a purchase, a possible point of reference for his own 'identity'. Lacan will frequently come back to the effects of language upon man, especially in his developments on the mirror phase and the Oedipus phase. For the moment, we shall analyse the grammatical categories which language puts at the disposal of the future 'singular subject'.

The awakening of consciousness in the child coincides with the linguistic apprenticeship which gradually introduces him into society.

The grammatical category of the 'I' is the index of individuality because it cannot be conceived without the Thou, without the He/it or without the listener to which it is opposed.

As Benveniste remarks in *Problèmes de linguistique générale* (65), it is in and through language that man constitutes himself as a subject because language alone founds the concept of Ego in reality: 'who says Ego is Ego'. And because consciousness of self is only possible if it is felt in contrast to the Thou which actualizes the concept of non-me. It is the I–Thou dialectic, defining the subjects by their mutual opposition, which founds subjectivity. By actualizing relations between persons, language therefore allows the self to turn back upon itself as a distinct individuality, thus allowing inter-human communication.

The philosophy of language expounded in these lines cannot, of course, deny that there may be a possible first intuition of individuality before any intervention on the part of language, but language actualizes and realizes this innate intuition by providing the grammatical categories for that individuality.

In psychoanalysis, one finds cases of children whose peculiar experience of relationships with their parents have destroyed this intuition of individuality, thereby barring access to language and to the 'I'.

I refer here to cases of psychosis, and in psychotics one does observe a frequent use of he/it for self-designation. Unable to circumscribe himself, the psychotic sees himself as another, as a thing in the world on which he pronounces utterances in the third person.

It is also important to point out that proper names do not take the place of the I and the Thou, but rather the reverse. Proper names designate the subject, but they do so by excluding the I–Thou relationship. Besides, young children who have not yet fully acquired the notion of 'I' speak of themselves by using the third person together with their forenames. In this way they reproduce the language of their parents, who talk among themselves about children in a communication from which they are still excluded. Children of this age have not yet assumed language as a means of communication between distinct individuals in the same society.

Language is thus the precondition for *the act of becoming aware of oneself as a distinct entity*. It is also the means by which the individual keeps his distance and autonomy from the world of real things which he posits 'in themselves' as being different from the concepts which convey their meaning and different from the words or symbols which actualize concepts in the social relation of communication.

An intermediary is necessary between man and the world, between man and man, between self and manifestation of self. The intermediary is the necessary and sufficient condition once men wish to come to an agreement with one another on general principles and wish to exchange something in common.

But the presence of the intermediary, it will be recalled, is also what engenders unconscious human conditioning. Language is the vehicle of a social given, a culture, prohibitions and laws. The child who enters into this symbolic order with its multiple dimensions will be fashioned by this order and will be indelibly marked by it without being aware of it.

If, for example, the prohibition of incest is, as Lévi-Strauss asserts, the underlying structure of societies, then the taboos and laws it subtends will be present in language, in the organization of the rules of society, and the child will have to pass through it if he is to become a social being, a member of society.

We can consequently say that social and linguistic symbolism interpenetrate one another to form a third order, a three-dimensional order of self, intermediary and society (the other or the world). The order of symbolism occupies pride of place in the thought of Lacan, as it is from this order that the virtues and dangers of the act of becoming aware flow. Without access to this order the child will not in fact acquire his or her individuality or the status of a member of society, but, on the other hand, entry into the symbolic establishes a distance with regard to the lived real and organizes the web of the unconscious in everyone.

It remains for this chapter on the philosophy of language in Lacan to show the homology between the linguistic fact and the social fact, a homology which brings the two symbolic orders together in a single body of signifiers which is determinant in human ontogenesis.

Once the orders in question have been related to one another, I shall try to give a better understanding of the opposition between the imaginary register on the one hand and the symbolic register on the other.

From linguistic symbolism to social symbolism

Edmond Ortigues (71) tells us that symbolic thought is a conceptual thought without any empirical intuition; it in fact releases the concept from all intuition of an object. Symbolism has only a formal significa-tion; its signification, that is, depends upon the coherence of its re-lations. A symbol is only an operator in a structure, a means of effecting the distinctive oppositions necessary to the existence of a significant structure. It is essentially an indirect expression. Its condition is that of not being what it represents.

In language it corresponds to the operation which transforms the natural given, negates it and which generates mediate, formal values.

Symbolism is, then, an order of values which is different from all reality: the order of the signifiers.

At the level of symbolism we will distinguish between: the principle of symbolism, which is the mutual relationship between distinctive elements whose combination is significant, and the effect of symbolism, the effect of a pact, an alliance or a convention as a token of mutual recognition between subjects.

The three major symbolic orders we know of are:
logico-mathematical symbolism
language
social and cultural symbolism
The last of these attests to our adherence to an order of values (philo-sophy, fatherland, religion). It introduces something more than life, something like a vow, a pact or a law.

The homologous character of linguistic symbolism and social symbolism derives from the fact that both are structures of oppositional elements capable of being combined, that both establish a possibility of recogni-tion between subjects and, finally, that both necessitate the passage from an immediate 'dual' relationship to a mediate relationship through the intervention of a third term: the concept in language, and the Ancestor, the Sacred Cause, the God or the Law in society.

On the other hand social symbolism is inseparable from discourse in so far as it implies rules, taboos and beliefs which must be formulated.

Where the passage from the dual relationship to the mediate relationship, from the Imaginary to the Symbolic, is more closely concerned, it should be remembered that a term in a symbolic order may be imaginary when considered absolutely or symbolic when it is a differential term correlative with other terms which delimit it. It is the understanding of the lateral correlations which stays the Imaginary, because this understanding founds the concept.

Nevertheless, as Ortigues shows in the same volume, the process of symbolization, in the sense of engendering, unfolds between two poles, the first of which – the minimum threshold of opening – is the imaginary, and the second of which – the threshold of accomplishment – is the social relation recognized in discourse.

Each threshold is defined by what lies before it and what lies beyond it.

The threshold of opening: the imaginary:
before it we have the fascinating realism of the imaginary.
Consciousness is the captive of its double and does not distinguish itself from it. This is the level of phantasy.
beyond it we have material imagination, the fetish or the emblem which already cuts across the symbolic organization of a system of significant values. The image stands for a relation to the overall structure to which it belongs.

the threshold of accomplishment: symbolism:
before it the symbolic social tradition, for example, the framework of kinship, the rules of authority.
beyond it social symbolism assumed by speech.

By means of this schema, Ortigues succeeds in clarifying the nature of the homology between the linguistic fact and the social fact; a homology which brings them together in a single order: that of the Symbolic in its opposition to the imaginary.

Dual relationship and mediate relationship
(The imaginary and the symbolic)

It transpires from the preceding chapters that the symbolic order has the power of effecting distinctions essential to the subject's registration of himself in the surrounding world. Spoken discourse in fact differentiates between: the self and the other or, more generally, between the interior and the exterior; inside the self, it differentiates between our psychic individuality and the manifestation of that individuality through discourse; and finally, it differentiates between discourse in its autonomy and reality. Social symbolism exercises a parallel action through different means.

The first of the distinctions effected by the symbolic register of language – *the distinction between interior and exterior* – is particularly vital for the 'subject'. One of the great movements in contemporary thought – a movement in which Lacan participates – is to accord prime importance to language in the constitution of the singular 'subject' distinct from the world into which he is inserted and distinct from the others with whom he might otherwise merge. As I have just shown, language in effect establishes mediate relationships as opposed to immediate relationships in which there is no distance between the self and things, between self and others. As a mediator, therefore, it situates the subject in his distinctive place.

Socio-cultural symbolism effects an identical registration of self on the part of the subject. For example, when the child takes his place in the family constellation on an equal footing with a forename and a surname as well as the third party position he occupies with regard to the parental couple, he recuperates himself as a distinct entity as opposed to the primary merging of himself with his mother. For the Lacanians, access to socio-cultural symbolism, to a socialized existence, is realized by going beyond the Oedipal drama. We will look more closely at this in Part Three.

As far as the second distinction made by symbolism is concerned – that between subjectivity and the manifestation of subjectivity or in other words the distinction between the self and the social 'I' of speech and behaviour – it will be the object of a second fundamental thesis of Lacan's.

The making of such a distinction within the subject is particularly apt to make us see the rapidity with which the unconscious springs up. Reference to the self, to desire or to life can only be made through language, through the symbolic register and is never direct or immediate. Hence it is susceptible to every alienation or lie, wilful or not, susceptible to all the distortions inscribed in the very principles of the 'symbolic', conventional dimension of group life.

I will use the example of sexual life in order to make myself understood.

Born of the appeal of the senses, humanized by affects and phantasies, sexuality only finds its behavioural and ideational expression within culture.

Because of the human condition of group life and the psycho-intellectual activity characteristic of man, there is an automatic filtering of life.

At the outcome of this process, life has acquired a radically other dimension which de-natures it in the true sense of the word.

All that remains of desire, of natural reproduction, of the physiology of bodies is symbols, laws, concepts or even ideologies. Marriage, Family, stereotypes of heterosexual relations, Fidelity, etc., are, at the symbolic level, the inevitably reductive and partially arbitrary preferential crystallization of lived biological and physiological experiences which are infinitely numerous and which are henceforth inaccessible as such. For, on the one hand, the child has his vital experience in the melting pot of a culture and in accordance with its norms and, on the other hand, the symbolic catches him unawares in its nets, short-circuiting any possibility of a naïve return to the roots of his soaring flight.

It is therefore a question of conditioning together with misrecognition. If symbolism is then a human dimension or even a positive human condition in that it socializes and organizes man, it also presents the disadvantage of formalizing the vital individual experience. What is more, symbolization is human, it is the work of human minds, which implies from the start: imperfection, reduction, arbitrariness, submission to external constraints and a partial failure to recognize its own mechanisms. The impossible task of symbolization in the broadest sense of the word is to organize at its own level the multiplicity of 'vital human conditions'. Each type of social organization has only been able to respond to these necessities in a partial way, accentuating certain aspects of life at the expense of others and therefore effecting repression.

Thus, for example, our occidental, patriarchal societies have given what is universal in the Oedipal drama a particular dramatized form which leads to the male and female types of castration complexes with which we are acquainted.

Knowing with Lacan the mechanisms and paths of our conditioning is, therefore, the precondition for any possible progress.

Freud discovered the discontent inherent in any civilized form of life, calling the cultural knots in which the unconscious returns for us occidentals the Oedipal and castration complexes. Following Freud, Lacan denounces human conditioning, but grasps its mechanisms more closely. Broadened by the new knowledge of linguistics and cultural anthropology, his point of view is no longer restricted by a spatio-temporal situation. Raised to the level of general principles, it allows his analysis of the occidental Oedipus complex to avoid the Freudian failure to recognize the relative nature of its 'form'. What follows must therefore be read in a certain spirit.

Lacan has recourse to the occidental Oedipus and castration complexes because his practical experience derives from them. His analysis does, however, arrive at a general philosophy of the socio-genesis of the individual. It reveals not the spatio-temporal 'contents' of the unconscious, but the universal existence of an unconscious, an unconscious whose content is certainly closely linked to existing social interdictions, but also and above all to a psycho-intellectual functioning which is inherent in all humanity.

To take an example: Lacan will say that what corresponds in the unconscious to any possible imaginable form of sexual relation is an individual 'lack', an original and chronic state of self-insufficiency. He will say that it is in this that the universality of the castration complex lies. He will say that, whatever cultural influences may accentuate or limit its manifestations, its modes of expression in the two sexes relate precisely to the symbolic function inherent in human beings.

If the 'Phallus' in fact takes on the symbolic meaning of absence of lack, if it leads to the idea that the woman has been castrated, it is because of its form, because of its erectile power, because of its function of penetration. It is that which denies the lack, that which fills the empty space. And as the human is specified as suffering from incompleteness, the two sexes will spontaneously organize their love and hate relationships around possession and non-possession of the phallus. For a psychoanalysis with a firm theoretical basis, the important thing is, Lacan will say, to make it known and understood that none in fact has this mythical phallus which will exclude lack. That on the contrary, man has a penis, an organ which has been elected to the function of a 'phallic' symbol of non-lack and which consequently engenders the conflicting forms of the male and female castration complexes.

Knowing these things is therefore the secret of the reduction of the castration complex. But it also unfortunately means stating that, aside from purely cultural conditioning, there exists a kind of spontaneous human self-intoxication. This is at the origin of social institutions and is, at this stage of human evolution, responsible for the facility with which we undergo cultural influence. It is responsible for the slowness with which we reach consciousness in theory, for the difficulties we have in conceiving sexual relations in a healthy way, this, together with the appropriate physiological means, being the way to help our deficiency while taking stock of it.

These clarifications as to the Lacanian use of linguistic and anthropological data appear indispensable.

The reader will, I think, be able to see more clearly the direction taken by this study. It situates the contemporary ideas on language which Lacan uses, and then expounds the Lacanian theses on the philosophical understanding of the human subject, on neurosis and on psychosis.

For the moment we shall look, as promised, at the imaginary and bring out the characteristics distinguishing it from the symbolic.

The text referred to in this passage is *Le Discours et le Symbole* by Edmond Ortigues (71).

The image given back to us by the imagination is characterized by its dissimulation of the system of reference, by its fusion of figure and ground and, in that sense, it will be impossible for us to recall it in detail.

The imaginary object will either repeat itself indefinitely, remaining identical to itself – in which case consciousness clouds over and sinks into the automatism of repetition – or it will submit to a discontinuity of aspect through continuous qualitative changes – in this sense imagination really is our faculty of creation. Each image is, however, a blind alley in which subjective intention drowns in its own creation, collapsing into its object and failing to keep its distance from its own internal vision.

The imaginary hides consciousness's own operations and attitudes from it: *in its representation, consciousness sees something other than itself, whereas there is nothing in this other except what consciousness has put there*. In other words, consciousness dissimulates itself from itself in this other.

Lacan defines the essence of the imaginary as a dual relationship, a reduplication in the mirror, an immediate opposition between consciousness and its other in which each term becomes its opposite and is lost in the play of the reflections. In its quest for itself, consciousness thus believes that it has found itself in the mirror of its creatures and loses itself in something which is not consciousness.

Henceforth, a certain self-presence is possible only through the genesis of a third term, a mediating concept which determines each term, ordering them and distinguishing between them. We have arrived back at the dimension of symbolization, since this consists in the passage from the dual relationship to the ternary mediate relationship.

Relations between men will be mediated by discourse or, to be more precise, by the concepts it engenders. In the domain of social symbolism, the third term which mediates between the living will be the Ancestor, the Dead, God, the Sacred Cause, the Institution, Ideology, etc.

These considerations are correct, but they are also very abstract.

What is the imaginary at the human level of life?

This book is designed to reflect its aspects progressively, but as it begins with an attempt at rapidly situating the problems, I will now give a more concrete example.

A moment ago we took the castration complex as an example; we will use the same example again, but this time in order to define the imaginary.

The imaginary is an infinitely supple conceptual category. It covers everything in the phantasy which is an image or representation of a lived experience pertaining to the castration complex before its formalization – forever incomplete, of course – becomes petrified in the symbol of the 'Phallus'. At the level of our example, the imaginary concerns the intuitive lived experience of the body (the receptive hollow, the erectile form, for example), of the affects (dependence, welcome, gift, etc.), of activity, of passivity, of the will to power, etc., lived experiences which overlap, accumulate and overflow into infinite successions of sensorial, emotional and conceptual jugglings.

In the castration complex, the Imaginary is the insatiability with which roles and modes of being are sought to compensate, together with sex, for the profound ill of human incompleteness. It is also the uninterrupted rotation of reflex adaptations to styles and functions of being which prove themselves by experiment to be adequate to the unconscious wish which produces them. In short, the Imaginary is everything in the human mind and its reflexive life which is in a state of flux before the fixation is effected by the symbol, a fixation which, at the very least, tempers the incessant sliding of the mutations of being and of desire.

The imaginary is the psychoanalytic register *par excellence*, but psychoanalysis has taught us to find traces of it in language, where words overlap with symbols multiplied a hundredfold, and where organization ultimately depends upon such a slender thread that it is not aberrant to wonder whether language really is the agent of inter-human dialogue. At the same time, the imaginary is pertinently reflected in socio-cultural symbolism, as much by the multiplicity of thoughts it implies as by the number of thoughts it neglects.

If this is so, then any symbolic order presupposes in and for its constitution a rupture of the inaugural continuity (non-distinction between consciousness and the other, non-distinction between the image and consciousness).

It presupposes a power of heterogeneity which will establish it as an order of distinctive and significant values extracted from all reality and which will situate it beyond immediate life.

E. Ortigues has described this power of heterogeneity, which is the foundation of the law, for traditional social symbolism. This power is twofold:

1 the Forbidden
2 the Sacrifice

The Forbidden

In order to express the concept of the Forbidden, Ortigues adopts the analysis of the prohibition of incest made by Lévi-Strauss in *The Elementary Structures of Kinship* (trans. J. H. Bell and J. R. von Stormer, London: Tavistock, 1970).

What is forbidden is coincidence between kinship relationships (blood relationships) and relationships of alliance (marriage relationships) on pain of abolishing the Family. The Family appears as a symbolic structure which is irreducible to any natural structure: animal promiscuity. It is also irreducible to awareness of the psychological relations actualized by reproduction on the one hand and by love on the other hand.

This means that the family structure manifests a transcendence of all natural order by the establishment of Culture. It alone allows each and every one to know who he or she is. In total promiscuity no one could in fact be called father, son or sister and no one would be able to situate himself or recognize others by the particular place they occupied. In this sense, the name, in so far as it is an element conveying relations of proximity, is a token of the recognition of individuals by one another.

The interlocutory relations of the persons (I – thou – he) are mediated by reference to the Other (the Ancestor, the Absent, the Dead), a fact underlined by the custom of naming a new-born baby after his grandfather.

The Forbidden is, therefore, the first of the forces which establish culture or the symbolic order (in this case relationships of kinship and alliance) and which furthermore establish the subject in his singularity by designating him and giving him his place in the family constellation.

We now turn to the second manifestation of the force of heterogeneity which establishes the socio-cultural symbolic order.

The Sacrifice

Like the Forbidden, the Sacrifice manifests the rupture through which the symbolic establishes itself as an order distinct from the natural or profane material given. In the case of the establishment of the family structure, the prohibition of incest is duplicated in the sacrifice of sexual relations with the mother or the sister. It is also duplicated by the law of exchange, the obligation to take a wife from another family in order that relationships of alliance may be established. Sacrifice is, therefore, equally a precondition for the transition to the symbolic order. And what a subject sacrifices here in order that he may designate himself and situate himself by entering into the symbolic order is incest.

Ortigues adds that sacrifice is also always present in the domain of language. Thus, for example, the fact of naming a foodstuff 'bread' imposes the sacrifice of the thing, as the word 'bread' cannot be eaten.

Unlike the imaginary, symbolism conquers mediate relationships in which each term is a differential, relative and negative value.

The Forbidden and the Sacrifice are terms which correspond, grosso modo, to what we call 'repression' in psychoanalysis. I say 'grosso modo' because it would be a logical error to associate term for term the conceptual and imaginative vagueness underlying the symbolic with the psychoanalytic repressed on the one hand and socio-cultural and linguistic symbolism with what comes to the surface of consciousness in the form of a symptom on the other hand.

Interdisciplinary contacts in the human sciences are, and continue to be, of the order of dialogue rather than of agreement.

This can be seen by reading, for example, Lévi-Strauss's *Elementary Structures of Kinship*. Here we have a scientist who has attempted to analyse a phenomenon as pluridimensional as the prohibition of incest, and who has voluntarily restricted himself to the spirit and the letter of anthropological science alone. Whilst trying to universalize what is forbidden in the most varied forms of control over incest, he has in fact expressed himself in sociological terms and in sociological terms alone. It is, he says, a question of forbidding coincidence between relations of alliance and relations of kinship by creating a link of solidarity, of widening the agreement between members of a large or closed group.

It is now up to the psychoanalyst to attempt a comparison between this social law and the psychical phenomena which constitute the sphere of his experience. It is up to him to discover what psychic conflicts, what feelings and what imaginings are covered by the three symbols: alliance, kinship and the forbidden which, in its turn, presupposes an order, namely exogamy. It is also up to him to discover what is aleatory in all this and what, on the other hand, belongs to the universal 'human condition'.

The task of the psychoanalyst is becoming clearer and more complicated. The contribution of ethnology and anthropology now makes him aware that he must distinguish between the repressed of one civilization and the repressed of another civilization, between the repressed of individuals belonging to the same civilization and hence between what is individual and what is collective in the repressed.

Between psychoanalytic repression and cultural prohibitions, between adaptive psychology and social rules there is a kind of crescendo of blindness – witness the conceptual and historical vacillation of symbols and of the 'power' of thought. This is why I am inclined to bring together what knowledge we have of the respective fields of psychoanalysis and anthropology.

But we must guarantee that our conceptualizations have the nicety demanded of us by the facts: in the unconscious of an individual there are as many elements which derive strictly from private experiences as there are elements attributable to the social instance or elements proper to the 'human condition'.

Finally, what appears to justify the great movement towards interdisciplinarity in our time is the as yet confused but growing perception of a sort of principle of human activity whose mechanisms could be synthesized under the heading of 'symbolization'.

This process runs through phylogenesis, ontogenesis and sociogenesis. As I understand it, the process of symbolization is what ensures the passage from nature to culture via the psychic in the above three movements of humanization. It is, in short, the difficult and tortuous emergence of thought, a thought which filters life through the prism of sensation, affectivity and intuition and which pushes it towards a beyond of a quite different order. During this journey, it is in the nature of thought to omit, since it organizes and synthesizes. It has as a further characteristic a partial ignorance of its own faults, as it in part fails to recognize its own activity. Thus a child localized in time and space simultaneously realizes ontogenesis and sociogenesis. His cognitive syntheses of experience will be made within a culture which has already thought for him, but which, because of the variety of its members, does nevertheless leave him a certain margin for personal creativity. He will then continually remake these syntheses in the course of his own historicity, and in a world which is continually changing. These syntheses show the human tendency to question things, one example of which is the psychoanalytic cure, another being theoretical research.

Thanks to the general term 'symbolization' what we must henceforth begin to see is the inextricable tangle, rather like the mode of construction of the dream, which separates the two mythical poles of the universal unconscious and the ideal society. If we could explain what happens between these two poles on the basis of the multiple knowledge of the human sciences, we would have brought the task of research to completion. This dream is only a dream, for how could the human mind, characterized as it is by its imperfection (as the process of symbolization itself shows), grasp the multiplicity of existences?

This chapter has consisted in the setting out of notions indispensable to the understanding of what Lacan calls the *Spaltung* (splitting) of the subject or the division of the subject which results from the fact that he speaks and from the fact of his insertion into the symbolic order. By mediating himself in his discourse, the subject in effect destroys the immediate relation of self to self, and constructs himself in language (Lacan's *refente*) as he wishes to see himself, as he wishes to be seen, and thereby alienates himself in language.

This is the best way of conceiving the establishing of an unconscious. If the image a subject makes of himself for himself is a lure, then his desire will be lost in its real implication to his consciousness and will be conveyed in a demand (that is, in spoken discourse and in accordance with the exigencies of Culture) in which it will be only a metonymy of itself. The task of making this clear can be left to later chapters.

PART THREE

The constitution of the subject by accession to the symbolic – the Spaltung – the role of the Oedipus in this transition

FIVE

The Spaltung

The Spaltung (from the German *Spalte* = split) is the division of being revealed in psychoanalysis between the self, the innermost part of the psyche, and the subject of conscious discourse, behaviour and culture.

This division, which for Lacan creates a hidden structure inside the subject – the unconscious – is due to the fact that discourse, or, more generally, any symbolic order 'mediates' the subjects and thus lends itself particularly well to a rapid turning away from truth.

The symbolic order can in essence be supported only by itself; it cannot, that is, be referred directly to the real. Besides, the term 'order' designates a dimension apart, defined and specified only by its internal articulations.

According to Cassirer, the symbolic function is the mediation which confers sense upon the sensuous.

The symbolic order is a third order, which means that it is organized between the subject and the real world and that it is possible to make use of it without any direct empirical reference.

Conversely, the real acquires a certain order in the mind which releases it from a primary confusion. To be precise, concepts undertake to organize things which were at first sight confused.

In his article, 'La suture' (95), J. A. Miller designates the relation between the real and the symbolic by the name 'suture' and specifies the nature of this relation: that of a lack in the structure (the symbolic), a lack which is not, however, completely absent from the structure, since it is 'represented' there in the form of a stand-in.

In the first two parts of this text we said that the human being acquires his individuality only on condition of being inserted into the symbolic order which governs and specifies humanity.

All we were doing there was defining one of the conditions of human existence. What does this mean. 'Singularity' is not equivalent to originality or liberty. The term means that man – existentially a being by and for the other – can only reconcile the necessity of his condition with its drawbacks by recuperating himself through exchange. The symbolic is the agent and guarantor of this step. It is the field, the common ground in which individuals assert themselves, oppose each other and find themselves again.

Accession to the symbolic is, however, balanced with what Lacan calls 'the division of the subject', with the loss of an essential part of himself, since, in the symbolic, the subject can be no more than represented or translated.

The symbol is different from what it represents, this is its condition; thus, if the subject who is called 'John' or who translates himself in discourse as 'I' saves himself through this nomination in so far as he inscribes himself in the circuit of exchange, he becomes, on the other hand, lost to himself, for any mediate relationship imposes a rupture of the inaugural continuity between self and self, self and other, self and world.

In the article cited (95), J. A. Miller also applies the term 'suture' to the subject's relationship with the symbolic.

> The suture names the subject's relationship with the chain of his discourse; we shall see that he figures there as a missing element, in the form of a stand-in for it. For although he is lacking in it, he is not purely and simply absent from it.

It will perhaps already be possible for us to understand the enigma proposed by Lacan in the expression: 'The signifier is that which represents the subject for another signifier.'

The subject is in effect represented in symbolism by a stand in; a signifier which may be the personal pronoun 'I', the forename which devolves upon the subject, or the denomination 'son of . . . .' What is more, the order of the symbol, of the signifier, an order supported only by its collateral relations – relations between the signifier and other signifiers – has definitively captured the subject in its nets. Mediated by language, the subject is irremediably divided, because he is at once excluded from the signifying chain and 'represented' in it.

We begin to see the importance of such a situation for the constitution of the subject. In the perspective being developed here, the human being can no longer be said to be the 'cause' or 'origin' of linguistic or cultural symbolism in the sense of creating this symbolism and reducing it to being a means for his projects as an absolute master.

In our societies, rich heirs to traditions and culture, modes of expression and legends, the young child submits to symbolism as a homogeneous and all-powerful mass into which he must insert himself with no hope of gaining a total mastery of it.

One could, therefore, say that *the human being is an effect of the signifier rather than its cause.* Insertion into the symbolic world is a mimesis, a collage. It fashions a being of 'representation' for us.

The young child submits to society, to its culture, organization and language, his only alternatives being to constrain himself to it or to fall ill.

What remains of the most truthful and the most important part of the personality is the underside of the mask, the repressed, Nature, in short, life, bowed before a superior force. Whereas, in the mask, in discourse, ego and social behaviour, the subject proliferates in the multiple forms he gives himself or has imposed upon him.

These forms are nothing but phantoms, reflections of the true being which reveal to analysis a temporal and logical organization that is completely distinct from the 'self'.

It results from this phenomenon of division that consciousness and reflection are to be situated at the level of discourse, whereas the unconscious is to be placed on the side of the true subject. It also follows that, henceforth, the unconscious will be accessible only by way of a long and laborious analysis, as all the forms in which the subject believes in all good faith that he will rejoin himself belong to the autonomous order of symbolism which holds him prisoner.

> Thus, the subject's bad faith, such a constituent part of this intermediary discourse that it is not even absent from the avowal of friendship, is reduplicated by the misrecognition in which these mirages establish it.
>   This is what Freud designated in his topography as the unconscious function of the ego before demonstrating its essential form in the discourse of denegation (*Verneinung*). If, therefore, the ideal condition imposed upon the analyst is that the mirages of narcissism become transparent to him, it is in order that he may become permeable to the authentic speech of the other, the question now being how to know it through his discourse.   (*Écrits*, 15.)

But let us go back to the division of the subject, the division between the 'I' of the utterance and the psychic reality it represents by the alternation of presence and absence. It will be noted that it is the exteriority of the subject to the Other (language for Lacan) which will institute the unconscious. 'It is in the reduplication of the subject of speech that the unconscious finds the means to articulate itself' (*Écrits*, 26).

In her article, 'Communications linguistique et spéculaire' (86), Luce Irigaray explains the phenomena we are dealing with in other terms. (In the passage which follows, the use of parentheses indicates that it is a question of the protagonists of the enunciation. Inverted commas, on the contrary, indicate the insertion of the term into the utterance of the discourse.)

As the epithet indicates, the *infans* does not yet have language at his disposal. In the circuit of exchange between the parents, permutations of the 'I' and the 'thou', the subject is designated by a 'he' which is equivalent to the lack of which Miller speaks. This 'he$_0$' is a blank, a void, the negation which allows the structure to exist: it is simply the precondition for the permutations of the 'I' and the 'thou'.

The Spaltung

The subject will be inserted into the linguistic circuit of exchange only by being named in his parents' dialogue and by receiving a forename.

It is by being named in the father–mother dialogue that, from being zero, the subject becomes 'he', but it is also by being designated as 'son' or 'John' by the word of the father. The name is the best illustration of the paradox of the generation of one from zero.

Once named, the subject enters into the circuit of exchange as $\dfrac{he_1}{he_0} = \left(\dfrac{S}{s} \right)$.

This death is the pre-condition of the subject's insertion into the chain, of his appearance in the order of the signifier. Thus, the subject is born into his singularity. But the constitution of 'he' also allows the disjunction between the 'I', subject of the utterance, and the (I), subject of the enunciation. This is precisely what defines the Spaltung: 'It operates in any intervention by the signifier between the subject of the enunciation and the subject of the utterance' (*Écrits*, 30). The (I) can absent itself from the 'I', or can disguise itself in 'thou' or 'he'; better still, it may figure in the 'one'. The path lies open to all the lures and deceptions of discourse engendered by the impossible co-incidence of the (I) with the 'I'. Thus, the utterance is never to be taken as it stands, but as an enigma, as a rebus in which the subject is concealed.

A moment ago I began to explain what Lacan calls the splitting (*refente*) of the subject, the alienation of the subject in his discourse. This is a direct consequence of the first Spaltung he undergoes on entering into language. I will bring this explanation of the Spaltung to a close with two quotations which sum up its essence perfectly. The first is taken from P. Martin, *La Théorie de la cure d'après Jacques Lacan* (Documents, Recherches et Travaux, no. 2).

In this quotation, the author gives an interpretation of the sentence already quoted from Lacan—'the signifier is that which represents the subject for another signifier':

> The signifier, materiality invested only with the power of the appeal for recognition, represents that part of the other's presence which is found again in so much as I recognize it as being irremediably lost, as being out of the power of all the forms in which it would wish to be pinned down in an adequate representation of itself.
>
> Functionally, it refers back by association to another signifier in the very quest it promotes and in the bottomless chasms of its interchangeable relays. It is organized like a concatenation.

This quotation does, however, require further clarification.

What is meant by the expression 'the signifier represents that part of the other's presence which is found again, but only as a representation'?

Martin's sentence coincides exactly with the explanation I have given of Lacan's enigma, if we recall that, in this sentence, the author is putting himself in the place of the analyst and that the 'other' therefore designates the patient.

The second quotation is taken from Lacan (39):

The register of the signifier is established because a signifier represents a subject for another signifier. It is the structure of all the formations of the unconscious and it also explains the primal division of the subject. Being produced in the place of the Other (the symbolic), the signifier causes the subject to arise there, but at the cost of becoming fixed. What was ready to speak there disappears, being no longer anything more than a signifier.

SIX

'Splitting', otherwise known as 'Separation' (Introduction to the alienating identifications, the imaginary and the neuroses)

With the introduction of the notion of Spaltung, Jacques Lacan marks out the beginnings of his theory of the human being. We may assume that we have grasped the meaning of the victory which insertion into the symbolic world of his parents and the assumption by his little person of the title of member of society represents for the young child.

We have not, however, developed the problem raised by this unavoidable transition. For the child also goes into exile when he takes this path.

If accession to the logos and to the symbolic in general is salutary in that it provides the subject with an identity, the impossible coincidence of the (I), the subject of the enunciation, with the 'I', the subject of the utterance, begins the dialectic of the subject's alienations. The subject becomes set in his utterances and social roles, and their totality is gradually built up into an 'ego', which is no more than an 'objectification' of the subject.

> The ego is not the subject, it is closer to the persona, to appearance, to a role than to consciousness or subjectivity. The ego is situated on the side of the Imaginary, whereas subjectivity is situated on the side of the symbolic. *The ego is the site of the subject's imaginary identifications.* (S. Leclaire, 45)

The subject responds to the imposition of a proper name, which constitutes him as $\dfrac{\text{one}}{\text{zero}}$, with a masked and fleeting appearance in discourse.

> *The drama of the subject in the verb is that he faces the test of his lack of being.* It is because it fends off this moment of lack that an image moves into position to support the whole worth of desire: projection, a function of the Imaginary. (*Écrits*, 29)

The ego is that which opposes itself most surely to the truth of the being. The ego concentrates in it all the person's ideals, all the person wants to be or thinks himself to be. The ego is the other of our self, assimilated and stuck on to the self, rather like an inadequate mould.

The subject gradually fashions himself and lives himself in accordance with his phantasy and his dreams, he conceals himself from himself and from others. Once on this slope, it is difficult to return and, with time, the distance separating the subject from his truth becomes greater. This outcome is fatal, but, as Freud himself thought, the degree of gravity varies and it is this which divides the healthy man from the sick man.

Splitting, to use the term chosen by Lacan, therefore masks the subject from himself in the utterances he makes on himself and on the world. But Lacan also tells us that in discourse the subject experiences his lack of being, as he is no more than represented in discourse, just as his desire is no more than represented there.

The truth about himself, which language fails to provide him with, will be sought in the images of others with whom he will identify. Children say 'I would like to be like . . .', and adults say, 'I have my mother's temperament', to give only examples which have no connexion with pathology. Lacan is thus in the right when he says:

> The only homogeneous function of consciousness is the imaginary capture of the ego by its mirror reflection and the function of misrecognition which remains attached to it.   (*Écrits*, 32)

> The ego is absolutely impossible to distinguish from the imaginary captures which constitute it from head to foot: by another and for another.   (*Écrits*, 17)

Alienation of this type leads Luce Irigaray to say that the discourse of the patient in analysis can be taken only as a rebus, as an enigma. In the various modes of their relations, the patient always imposes upon the other an imaginary form of himself which bears the superimposed seals of the experiences of impotence in which this form, his ego, was modelled. Discourse becomes fixed at this level and the end of analysis is situated at the point where the subject, having found once more the origins of his ego through regression and stripping and thanks to the frustration imposed upon him by the analyst's refusal to be caught in his game, finally recognizes that this ego was never anything more than his work in the imaginary. In analysis he finds once more the alienation which made him construct his ego as another and for another.

It may be useful at this point in the exposition to raise a problem of understanding. The first part of this study of Lacan put forward the view that accession to language and to the symbolic order was a transcendence of the dual relationship, which is truly imaginary, and, as a corollary, a process of individualization of the subject, the subject's registration of himself.

How, then, can we resolve the enigma of this relapse into the imaginary, which ultimately seems to be all the subject gains from his promotion into language? Is 'splitting' a question of the same imaginary trapping as is found in the dual relationship, or does accession to the mediate relationship represent, despite everything, a progress, even if it is truncated from the start?

It seems to me that Vergote provides a solution to the problem in *La Psychanalyse, science d'homme* (116). In substance, he says that the symbolic and the imaginary are at once connected and distinct.

Symptoms and the other formations of the unconscious are mnemic symbols of past lived experiences of a traumatic character. But in the formations of the unconscious, symbolism is reduced to the level of the imaginary because it is not decoded.

The symbol is an imaginary figure in which the truth of man is alienated. The intellectual elaboration of the symbol cannot de-alienate it. Only analysis of the imaginary elements taken individually can reveal the meaning and the desire the subject has enclosed in them.

The cure is the transition from the non-symbolized imaginary to the symbolized imaginary. It is, in other words, the access to the truth of the patient's personal code. Restored to its essential status of a symbol, the symbolized imaginary stands opposed to the alienating imaginary.

It appears, then, that, carried away despite himself by the play of the signifier as soon as he accedes to the symbolic, the subject ends up by losing the signifier's reference to the first repressed signified. Trapped by the imaginary, the alienation of the subject is the loss of distance from the signifier, from the representative in so far as that is precisely *all* it is: *representative*. The subject believes in his delirium, he believes in his symptom, retaining only its literal signification, independently of its reference to the repressed signified.

Coming back to the question of splitting, let us now talk about Freud's *Verneinung* (translated as negation or denegation), the essential form of the ego's unconscious function, of the alienation of the subject.

The subject's bad faith, such a constituent part of this intermediary discourse . . . is reduplicated in the misrecognition in which these mirages establish it. This is what Freud designated in his topography as the unconscious function of the ego before demonstrating its essential form in *Verneinung*. If, therefore, the condition imposed upon the analyst is that the mirages of narcissism become transparent to him, it is in order that he may become permeable to the authentic speech of the other.

(*Écrits*, 15)

The analysis which follows has its sources in 'Commentaire parlé sur la *Verneinung* de Freud' (J. Hyppolite, 85), and Lacan's introduction and reply to this commentary by Hyppolite (18, 19).

In his article 'Negation' (11), Freud defines *Verneinung* in these terms:

> The subject matter of a repressed image or thought can make its way into consciousness on condition that it is *denied*. Negation is a way of taking account of what is repressed; indeed it is actually a removal of the repression, though not, of course, an acceptance of what is repressed. It is to be seen how the intellectual function is here distinct from the affective process. The result is a kind of intellectual acceptance of what is repressed, though in all essentials the repression persists.

To take the examples of *Verneinung* cited by J. Hyppolite:
1 'Now you'll think that I mean to say something insulting, but really I've no such intention.'
  read: 'I want to insult you.'
2 'I saw someone in a dream. It was certainly not my mother.'
  read: 'It *was* my mother.'
Negation is a mode of presenting what one is (or what is) in the mode of not being what one is (or negation of what is).

The essential characteristic of this form of resistance in the return of the repressed is clearly illuminated by this passage from an article by the linguist Benveniste (75):

> Linguistic negation can never annul what has been stated or explicitly posited. *A judgment of non-existence always has the formal status of a judgment of existence. Negation is always firstly an admission.*

> This *Verneinung* . . . demonstrates in itself the avowal of the signifier that it annuls.

> The *Bejahung* (affirmation; judgment of existence, primary process by which the judgment of attribution is validated) is a necessary condition for any possible application of *Verneinung*.
>
> (*Écrits*, 23)

It follows that *the phenomenon of* 'Verneinung' *demonstrates the possibility of the ego's retaining the unconscious while at the same time refusing it*.

It is, in Hyppolite's phrase, an *Aufhebung* (negation – suppression – conservation) of the repressed. That is to say that, in one sense, as Freud says, it removes repression, as the repressed signifier is always present in the negation, but, in another sense, it retains the repression through the 'not'. In analysis, interpretation of the *Verneinung* provokes a recognition or an admission on the part of the patient, but this remains purely intellectual, as it is only the negation of the negation, 'a kind of intellectual acceptance of what is repressed, though in all essentials the repression persists'.

Verneinung is therefore a manifest form of the function of misrecognition into which the ego is drawn by the imaginary.

I shall now try to summarize the preceding paragraphs. In order to do so, I shall quote a passage from Lacan which seems to give a perfect synthesis of
1 the primal division of the subject resulting from the fact that he speaks
2 the division resulting from the fact that he is no longer anything more than a signifier:

> Two fundamental operations in which the causation of the subject should be formulated:
>
> First: alienation is the doing of the subject. To start with, let us take it as given that the subject has no reason for appearing in the Real, apart from the fact that speaking beings exist. . . . This division proceeds from nothing other than the play of the signifiers. . . .
>
> The register of the signifier is established because a signifier represents a subject for another signifier. It is the structure of all the formations of the unconscious, and it also explains the primal division of the subject. Being produced in the place of the Other (the symbolic), the signifier causes the subject to arise there, but at the cost of becoming fixed. What was ready to speak there disappears . . . being no longer anything more than a signifier. It is, therefore, not the fact that this operation starts out from the Other which qualifies it as alienation. That the Other should be for the subject the site of its significant cause merely motivates the reason for which no subject can be said to be its own cause. . . .
>
> The alienation resides in the division of the subject from its cause. To go further into the logical structure. This structure is that of a *vel*. . . .
>
> It (the *vel*) must be derived from what is termed, in so-called 'mathematical' logic, a union. This union is such that the *vel* of alienation, as I call it, imposes a choice between its terms only by eliminating one of them. . . .
>
> Our subject is faced with the *vel* of receiving a certain meaning or being petrified. But if he keeps the meaning, it is this field of meaning which will be eaten into by the non-sense produced by his being changed into a signifier. . . .
>
> To come to the second operation, in which the causation of the subject comes to a close.

We call this operation: Separation. In it we recognize what
Freud called the *Ichspaltung* or splitting of the subject. . . . The
subject realizes himself in the loss from whence he sprang forth as
an unconscious.
Here *separare*, separate, ends in *se parere*, to engender oneself.
This sliding from one verb to another is based upon their common
pairing with the function of the *pars*. . . .
Here, it is from his partition to his parturition that the subject
proceeds. *Parere* is firstly to procure. This is why the subject can
procure what concerns him here, a status which we will qualify as
civil (*état civil*). Nothing in anyone's life unchains a greater
determination to arrive. He would sacrifice a great part of his
interest in order to be *pars*. . . .
Separare, se parere: in order to deck himself out (*se parer*) in
the signifier to which he succumbs, the subject attacks the chain,
which we have reduced to a simple binarity, in its interval. The
interval which is repeated, the most radical structure of the
signifying chain, is the site haunted by metonymy, the vehicle of
desire. In any case, it is to the extent that the subject experiences
something Other than the effects of meaning solicited of him by
discourse motivating him in this interval that he effectively
encounters the desire of the Other.
What he will place there is his own lack. But what he thus
fills in is the constituent loss of one of his own parts, because of
which he finds himself constituted in two parts.   (*Écrits*, 32)

In order to make the indispensable link between all this and Part Four
of this book, it should be noted that the double phenomenon of the
division of the subject engenders the unconscious.

Just as it has been said that the word brings about the murder of the
thing, and that the thing must be lost if it is to be represented, so the
subject loses himself in his truth or his reality by naming himself in his
discourse and by being named by the speech of the other. This leads
Lacan to say that:

'I am what I think', therefore I am: divide the 'I am' of
existence from the 'I am' of meaning. This splitting must be taken
as being principle, and as the first outline of primal repression,
which, as we know, establishes the unconscious.   (*Écrits*, 37)

And 'The reduplication which discourse provokes is what Freud calls
Urverdrängung (primal repression)' (*Écrits*, 26).

SEVEN

The role of the Oedipus in accession to the symbolic

Taking up his place in the symbolic register of language and of the family represents for the young child a circumscription of his individuality within the family group and within the global society. It means taking a grip upon himself, a personal realization.

The accession in question occurs, grosso modo, during the Oedipal period, if what should be termed a universal phenomenon of transition or an inaugural and decisive turning point can in fact be referred to as a period or historical moment.

Regardless of its variable forms, the Oedipal phenomenon is, as a structure, a radical and universal transformation of the human being; it is the transition from a dual, immediate or mirror relationship (all these terms are used by Lacan) to the mediate relationship proper to the symbolic, as opposed to the imaginary.

The first dual relationship between the child and his like – another child, his own image reflected in the mirror, the mother herself or her substitutes – does not provide the child with 'subjectivity' in the sense of 'singularity' given above to that term. According to Lacan, the most this relationship can do is to constitute a registration of the totality of a body previously lived as fragmented.

In the other, in the mirror's image, in his mother, the child sees nothing but a fellow with whom he merges, with whom he identifies.

A child who remained fixed in this state of affairs would be incapable of situating himself and others in their respective places. He would be reduced to the level of animal life, he would not, that is to say, have at his disposal the common symbolic ground through which any human 'relationship' passes. This is what has happened with the psychotic.

Psychotics are frequently observed to be confused about those around them, calling in turn upon the same people to play the role of persecutor and then that of preferential object.

In the Lacanian perspective, accession to the mediation of the symbol is, therefore, indispensable if the ordering of the world, of things, beings and of life is to be effected.

The dual relationship, which, as we know, opens up the dialectic of alienating identifications does, however, persist in man despite the assumption of subjectivity through entry into the symbolic. As we know, this is a matter of splitting, which is nothing but the loss of a good part of the symbolic references through repression. In cases of neurosis, it is always possible to restore the forgotten relations by analysis, whereas the outcome is more doubtful in psychosis. It is much easier to remind someone of things he once knew than to impress symbolic relations upon a patient who never established them in the first place.

When Lacan speaks of the dual relationship, he often refers to the so-called 'mirror' stage, a stage he was the first to put any special stress on.

Taking this to be the corner-stone of his work, some critics have seen fit to use the 'factual' insubstantiality of the phase in an attempt to invalidate his work as a whole.

If Lacan attaches great importance to this phase, as he certainly does, it is because it reveals the immediate dual relationship proper to the imaginary and because observation of this stage reveals the crucial importance of the transition to the three-dimensional register of the symbolic.

Self-recognition in the mirror takes place somewhere between the ages of six and eight months. At the same time, a child of this age shows definite attitudes to another of the same age. Confronted with another child, he will be aggressive towards him and will try, by imitating him, to situate himself, to have himself accepted or even impose himself upon him.

A kind of social relativization of the two children takes place, a prelude to the registration of the self as an entity, but as an entity in the form of an image in the mirror.

Furthermore, such games show a mutual identification in which the dual relationship itself can easily be recognized: a mirror relationship, a relationship of the merging of self and other.

In Lacan's own words:

Experience of oneself in the earliest stage of childhood develops, in so far as it refers to one's similar, from a situation experienced as undifferentiated. Thus about the age of eight months, we see in these confrontations between children (which, if they are to be fruitful, must be between children whose age differential is no more than two and a half months) those gestures of fictitious actions by which a subject reproduces the imperfect effort of the other's gesture by confusing their distinct application, those synchronies of spectacular captation that are all the more remarkable in that they precede the complete co-ordination of the motor apparati they bring into play. Thus the aggressivity that is manifested in the retaliations of taps and blows cannot be regarded solely as a lucid manifestation of the exercise of strengths and their employment in the mapping of the body. It must be

understood in an order of broader co-ordination: that which will
subordinate the functions of tonic postures and vegetative
tension to a social relativity. . . .

Furthermore, I believed myself that I could show that on such
occasions the child anticipates on the mental plane the conquest
of the functional unity of his own body, which, at this stage, is
still incomplete on the plane of voluntary motility. What we have
here is a first capture by the image in which the first stage of the
dialectic of identifications can be discerned.   (*Écrits*, 13)

Occurring as it does at the age mentioned in the above discussion of the
relationship between the child and his fellow, self-recognition in the
mirror (the true mirror stage) is even more important when it comes to
the establishment of an alienated ego.

This jubilant assumption of his specular image by the little man,
at the *infans* stage . . . would seem to exhibit in an exemplary
situation the symbolic matrix in which the I is precipitated in a
primordial form, before it is objectified in the dialectic of
identification with the other, and before language restores to it, in
the universal, its function as subject.   (*Écrits*, 12)

The mirror stage is interesting in that it manifests the affective
dynamism by which the subject originally identifies himself with
the visual *Gestalt* of his own body: in relation to the still very
profound lack of co-ordination of his own motility, it represents
an ideal unity, a salutary *imago*; it is invested with all the original
distress resulting from the child's inter-organic and relational
discordance.   (*Écrits*, 12)

Henceforth, between the ages of six months and two years, the behaviour of a child faced with his fellow will be dominated by the
trapping of the being by the image of the human form. This behaviour
will be one of identification: the child who strikes will say that he has
been struck, the child who sees his fellow fall will cry.

But the most important point is that, from the outset, the mirror
stage situates the instance of the ego in a line of fiction, of alienation.

The ego will crystallize in the ensuing Oedipal conflict, which at
first reproduces the dual relationship (with the mother) and the aggression, now directed against the intruder: the father as competitor.
From the outcome of this conflict arises the triad of other, ego and
object. The Oedipus determines a refashioning of the subject in his
identifications, a secondary identification through introjection of the
imago of the parent of the same sex. This identification, however, is
possible only if the first of these identifications has actually been realized
by the structuring of the subject as his own rival.

It would, however, be a mistake to consider the ego as being definitively constituted by the outcome of the Oedipal drama:

Each instinctual metamorphosis . . . will again challenge its
delimitation. . . . This is why . . . man's ego can never be
reduced to his 'lived identity'.

This narcissistic moment in the subject is to be found in all the
genetic phases of the individual, in all the degrees of human
accomplishment in the person, in a before in which it must
assume a libidinal frustration and an after in which it is
transcended in a normative sublimation.   (*Écrits*, 13)

To sum up: the mirror stage is the advent of coenaesthetic subjectivity
preceded by the feeling that one's own body is in pieces. The reflection
of the body is, then, salutary in that it is unitary and localized in time
and space. But the mirror stage is also the stage of alienating narcissistic identification (primary identification); the subject *is* his own
double more than he is himself. The whole drama of the dual relationship is played out here: consciousness collapses into its double without
keeping its distance from it. There is an immediate opposition in which
each term becomes its opposite:

Only one moment separates Narcissus from the echo. Let the
distance die, let time end; desire for love becomes desire for death,
my other is my fellow, my fellow is my other.   (Ortigues, 71)

In Lacan's thought, the dual relationship covers the human being's
initial way of life before he becomes involved in the dimension proper
to his humanity, namely the symbolic organization.

The imaginary-symbolic opposition has an anthropological meaning
for Lacan, who articulates his views on humanization in these terms. He
is, therefore, to be numbered amongst the numerous researchers who
bring together the problematics of various sciences, such as ethnology,
anthropology, social psychology, etc., in their interrogation of man.

But Lacan is inscribed amongst them in a very special way. It has
been said that the views he articulates on humanization are structuralist.
This is correct. Bringing the whole genesis of the little man down to a
transition, a metamorphosis – from the imaginary to the symbolic –
gets him out of the problem of ethnological and historical relativity.
For Lacan, the relative form of the Oedipus complex or of the family
does not exclude the essentials of what they represent for humanization
in structural terms: the obligation every child is under to submit his
or her sexuality to certain restrictions and laws; the laws of organization
and exchange within a sexually differentiated group.

Lacan's terminology places him beyond psychoanalysis itself. Lacan
assumes knowledge of Oedipal and pre-Oedipal lived experiences. He is
addressing himself to psychoanalysts and this allows him to omit a lot
of explanations.

It follows from these two comments that I will neither stop short of
what Lacan says nor go beyond him by entering into a discussion with

our whole epoch on anthropogenesis. To imply or to develop always means interpreting, if not presupposing that the thought of the author of *Écrits* can be delimited. Once again, this book is an introduction and nothing more. It gives a clear, articulate form to Lacan's thought in the form of an evocation, an overall view. Lacan is working with a microscope on the most secret area of human life, and what is least visible in this life is precisely that which can only be spoken abstractly, by means of a trace and by panning across it.

As I do not wish to suggest to the future reader of Lacan any interpretation not explicitly contained in his work, I have at least taken it upon myself to respect the abstract form of his work.

We shall now look at the meaning given by the author of *Écrits* to the *mother–child dual relationship at the outset of the Oedipus*.

In his seminars on *Les formations de l'inconscient*, which have been summarized by Pontalis, Lacan articulates three periods in the development of the Oedipus. The first coincides with the mother–child dual relationship.

At first, he explains, the child does not merely desire contact with his mother and her care. He wishes to be everything to her, to condition her life, he wishes, perhaps unconsciously, to be the complement of what is lacking in her: the phallus. *He is the desire of his mother's desire and, in order to satisfy that desire, he identifies with its object, with the phallus.* If the mother's attitude even slightly favours this attitude, the child is ripe for alienation.

One could say that at this stage the child, identifying with the object of the other's desire, passively submissive and subjugated, is not a 'subject', but a lack, a nothing, because he is not individually situated or registered in the symbolic circuit of exchange. He merges with the object of the other's desire and, fusing with his mother as a mere extension of her, presents himself as a nothing, as a blank. Having no symbolic substitute for his own self, he is deprived of individuality, subjectivity and a place in society. This is the period of imaginary possession (identification with the mother *by way of identification with the object of her desire*) and *the realm of primary narcissism*.

This brings us to the *accession to the symbolic through the Oedipus*.

In this second movement, the father intervenes as the privative agent in two ways: *he deprives the child of the object of its desire and he deprives the mother of the phallic object*. His attitude, literally that of a spoilsport, could be translated as a double commandment:

thou shalt not sleep with thy mother

and, to the mother:

thou shalt not reappropriate thy product.

The child comes up against the Forbidden (the power of heterogeneity, the basis of the symbolic order), he encounters the Law of the father. This encounter shakes the very foundations of the child's position. This second stage, both transitory and of capital importance, is what permits the third stage of *identification with the father* and registration of the self through relativization.

But if the father is to be recognized as the representative of the law which founds humanity, his speech must be recognized by the mother. It is speech alone which gives a privileged function to the father, and not the recognition of his role in procreation.

The existence of a symbolic father does not depend upon the recognition of the connexion between coition and childbirth, but upon something corresponding to the function defined by the Name-of-the-Father.

And, further on,

The father is present only through his law, which is speech, and only in so far as his Speech is recognized by the mother does it take on the value of Law. If the position of the father is questioned, then the child remains subjected to the mother. (Lacan, 35)

If, then, the father is recognized by the mother both as a man and as the representative of the Law, the subject will have access to the 'Name-of-the-Father' or 'paternal metaphor' (Name-of-the-Father, the signifier of the paternal function or installation of the father in the place of the Other, the symbolic order), which gives the symbolic law of the family its basis.

If the child does not accept the Law, or if the mother does not recognize this position in the father, the subject will remain identified with the phallus and subjected to the mother's desire.

If, on the contrary, the child does accept this, *he identifies with the father as he who 'has' the phallus.* The father reinstates the phallus as the object of the mother's desire, and no longer as the child-complement to what is lacking in her. *The child's identification with the father announces the passing of the Oedipus by way of 'having' (and no longer 'being').* He is either he who has the phallus or he who does not have it, or he who can give or receive it in a full sexual relationship. At the same time, a symbolic castration takes place: the father castrates the child by separating it from its mother. This is the debt which must be paid if one is to become completely oneself and have access to the order of the symbol, of culture and of civilization.

The resolution of the Oedipus liberates the subject by giving him, with his Name, a place in the family constellation, an original signifier of self and subjectivity. It promotes him in his realization of self through participation in the world of culture, language and civilization.

> By internalizing the Law, the child identifies with the father and takes him as a model. The Law now becomes a liberating force: for, once separated from the mother, the child can dispose of himself. He becomes conscious that he is still in the making and, turning towards the future, integrates himself into the social, into Culture, and re-enters into language. Three components must be distinguished in the Oedipus: (i) the Law, (ii) the Model, and (iii) the Promise. The father is he who 'recognizes' the child, giving him a personality by means of a Speech which is Law, a link of spiritual kinship and a promise. (A. Vergote, 115)

In order to clarify how acceptance of the Law of the father introduces the 'subject' to the order of social symbolism, culture, civilization and language (for it is this which makes him a subject), it is indispensable to recall what was said above about the problem of symbolization through the intervention of a twofold power of rupture: the Forbidden and the Sacrifice (chapter 4).

In *Le Discours et le Symbole* (71), Ortigues designates the problem of symbolization as the transition from a dual opposition – the register of the imaginary – to a tertiary relationship through the intervention of a third, median term. This is as valid for the order of language as for that of social symbolism and the domain of individual life (desire, the subject). The advent of the symbolic order always presupposes a rupture of the inaugural continuity (dual relationships where one thing is the other and vice versa), the intervention of a power of heterogeneity. This power, the foundation of the Law, is, as we have said, twofold: the Forbidden and the Sacrifice.

Precisely what is forbidden in the Oedipus is coincidence between relationships of kinship and relationships of alliance (sleeping with one's mother and having a child by her). If these relationships do coincide, the symbolic family institution is destroyed, the register of culture, interdependent organization and peace is replaced by that of nature, dedicated to the law of mating without any criterion, the law of unbridled competition in all things.

The prohibition of incest superimposes the realm of culture, whatever its local forms may be, upon that of nature by means of sexual restrictions and by the creation of links of solidarity.

Accession to the symbolic order of the family (Alliance and Kinship) alone allows everyone to know who he or she is, what his or her exact position is, what limits are placed upon his or her rights in the light of respect for the others; in total promiscuity and in the absence of a minimal organization of the group life, no one can situate himself or herself in relation to everyone else. Name and place are signs of recognition. They give the subject his individuality, his place and his role in the system.

The primordial law is therefore that which in regulating marriage
ties superimposes the kingdom of culture on that of nature
abandoned to the law of mating. The prohibition of incest is
merely its subjective pivot. . . . This law is revealed clearly
enough as identical to an order of language. For without kinship
nominations there is no power capable of instituting the order of
preferences and taboos. (*Écrits*, 16)

Sacrifice is realized in the Oedipus through the symbolic castration
which legislates the use of the sex through the death of the father by
the fact of his accession to the place of the Other: this is the paternal
metaphor. We know that the word is the murder of the thing and that
this death is the condition of the symbol.

It is now much clearer how the paternal interdiction, reiterating for
each subject the inaugural, mythical principle of the transition from
Nature to Culture, makes the father the representative of the Law and
a protagonist in the subject's entry into the order of culture, civilization
and language. 'It is in the Name-of-the-Father that we must recognize
the symbolic function which identifies his person with the figure of the
Law' (*Écrits*, 16).

In the course of the Oedipal phenomenon, the child gains access to
the Law (whose basis is the Name-of-the-Father itself) by symbolizing
the paternal reality, by acceding, that is, to the 'paternal metaphor'
(Name-of-the-Father, something named in so far as it performs the
function of prohibition and can castrate the subject).

If some light has been thrown on the link uniting *the Oedipus with
accession to culture* in Lacanian theory, the link which makes *the
Oedipus coincide with accession to language is still obscure*. Let us attempt
to clarify this somewhat.

A. de Waelhens defines primal repression, which is simultaneous with
accession to language, as:

The act whereby the subject – or, to be more precise, he who will
by this act constitute himself as 'subject' – withdraws from the
immediacy of a lived experience by giving it a substitute which it
is not, no more than the subject is the lived experience, and which
will constitute the real as the real, the symbolic as autonomous
and the subject as subjectivity.

Primal repression is only possible if the subject posits himself as no
more being the thing or the lived experience than the substitute he
gives to this lived experience. This repression is therefore only possible
if the subject has at his disposal an original signifier of self which he
can posit as the negative of his coenaesthesia and which will allow him

85

to effect the negation inherent in primal repression: the thing is no more its substitute than it is the self.

We have just seen that a happy outcome to the Oedipus complex placed this original signifier of self at the disposal of the subject (the name) by giving him his singularity. The Oedipus does, then, allow the transition from the imaginary register to that of the symbolic: language.

A further remark is called for here. For Lacan, the phenomenon of *foreclosure* is what distinguishes psychosis from neurosis. It is defined by the failure of primal repression and hence by the failure to enter into the symbolic or language. The subject remains riveted to the imaginary, which is taken for real, to non-distinction between signifier and signified: either the signifier is privileged and is taken in the literal sense, outside of any operation referring it to its symbolic dimension, or the signified prevails.

The cause of this incapacity to distinguish between signifier and signified is the absence of an original substitute for self, itself due to an unfavourable outcome of the Oedipus.

The distinction between neurosis and psychosis touched upon here will be the object of a special chapter at the end of this volume.

Let us now look at the significant value of the Phallus in the Oedipal phenomenon. This is a very badly understood term, but it is, however, of fundamental importance. I shall try to bring out the concept from the numerous texts written on the subject.

The term 'Phallus', as used by Lacan, is not to be confused with the real, biological sex, with what is called the penis.

It is an abstract signifier, which, like any symbol, goes beyond its materiality and beyond what it represents. Adopting a phrase from S. Leclaire's 'Les éléments en jeu dans une psychanalyse' (51) we can say that: 'It is a copula, a hyphen – in the evanescence of its erection – *the signifier par excellence of the impossible identity.*'

Lacan says that the Phallus has a signification which is evoked only by the paternal metaphor, and in his article, 'On a question preliminary to any possible treatment of psychosis' (23), he suggests a formula which allows its symbolic meaning to be grasped.

In general, metaphor is realized through the substitution, in the signifier–signified relationship, of one signifier for another, S', the first signifier falling to the level of the signified, as in the formula:

$$\frac{S'}{S} \cdot \frac{S}{s} \rightarrow S\left(\frac{1}{s}\right)$$

When applied by Lacan to the paternal metaphor, this formula is transformed into:

$$\frac{\text{Name-of-the-Father}}{\text{Desire of the Mother}} \cdot \frac{\text{Desire of the Mother}}{\text{Signified for subject}}$$

$$\rightarrow \text{Name-of-the-Father} \left(\frac{0}{\text{Phallus}} \right)$$

Let us try to understand something of what happens in the child who arrives at the paternal metaphor.

Originally, the *infans* subject wishes *to be* the Phallus, the object of his mother's desire. This means that, in order to ensure himself of his mother's presence and her complete affective support, the child unconsciously seeks to be that which can best gratify her. He seeks to make himself exclusively indispensable. This affective wish is tinged with eroticism, and the multiple phantasies elaborated by the child, who is, in a confused way, awake to his parents' sexual relations, are grouped around the phallic symbol, around the general idea of the 'Father', all the more so because the father renders the mother–child fusion impossible by his interdiction and marks the child with a fundamental lack of being. Castrated, that is, removed from his mother by the paternal interdiction, the child must renounce the omnipotence of his desire and accept a Law of limitation: he must assume his lack. Through the paternal metaphor, the child names his desire and renounces it. His true desire and the multiple phantasmatic forms it took are pushed back into the unconscious. This is the primal repression which determines accession to language and which substitutes a symbol and a Law for the Real of existence.

What does the alienation of desire which results from accession to language consist in? By assuming the Law of his father the child passes from the register of being (being the all-powerful phallus) to the register of having (having a limited and legitimate desire which can be formulated in an utterance) and enters into a quest for objects which are further and further removed from the initial object of his desire. Parallel to this, he follows a dialectic of identifications in which his Ego constitutes itself and in which the ideal of the self takes shape. We can see that it is in the transition from being to having that the subject's Spaltung is situated, the division between his conscious being and his unconscious being. The desire to be the phallus which is lacking in the mother, the desire for union with the mother, is repressed and replaced by a substitute which names it and at the same time transforms it: the symbol. If the Name-of-the-Father fulfils this function of symbolizing desire, if being 'a' father henceforth replaces the desire for fusion, it is because the father reveals himself as he who *has* the desired phallus and as he who is able to use it in a socially normalized relationship.

The phallus is the privileged signifier of that mark in which the role of the logos is joined with the advent of desire. (But) it can only play its role when masked, that is to say, as itself a sign of the latency with which any signifiable is struck, when it is raised to the function of signifier. (*Écrits*, 24)

I do not think it false to say that if the subject 'crosses himself out' in the Spaltung, if he effaces himself to the profit of a signifier, it is in so far as he is the phallus that he is crossed out. The lack of being engendered by the imposition of the Law explains the eternalization of the desire, which is metonymically displaced from signifier to signifier in the 'demand', that is, for Lacan, in the traditional forms of culture.

The phallus is the signifier of this *Aufhebung* itself, which it inaugurates (initiates) by its disappearance. . . .
 Thus, a condition of complementarity is produced in the establishment of the subject by the signifier and the movement of intervention in which it is completed.
 Namely:
 (i) that the subject designates his being only by barring everything he signifies. . . .
 (ii) that the living part of that being in the *Urverdrängt* finds its signifier in receiving the mark of the displacement (*Verdrängung*) of the phallus (by virtue of which the unconscious is language).
 The phallus as signifier gives the *ratio* of desire. (*Écrits*, 24)

It should be noted that the terms in the formula for the paternal metaphor are to be taken simply as models, as abstract symbols for phenomena actually lived in infancy.

The paternal metaphor is no more than a symbolization which is useful in conceptualizing things. The exact nature of this 'Name-of-the-Father' or of the 'Phallus' remains obscure, but can be thought of as corresponding for the child to his confused and varied intimate experiences which go to make up Freudian thought.

Considered as the transition to the symbolic, the Oedipus is a phenomenon which cannot, on the other hand, be located precisely in time. I am of the opinion that the transition from dual relationship to tertiary relationship is effected progressively and begins at the age of less than four years, the age at which the child's characteristic feelings towards his mother are generally observed. Besides, a child of this age has been able to speak for a long time.

I have found an article by C. Stein (113) which comes close to my way of seeing things. According to Stein, the unconscious is initially 'structured' on the conflicting model provided for it *a posteriori* by the Oedipus complex.

At the time of this complex, the author goes on, linguistic communication has already been established, and logically, therefore, the complex itself cannot bring about the primal repression which establishes language.

The structure of the unconscious can be called Oedipal only by analogy; it is in fact the form which gives the repressed Oedipus complex its structure *a posteriori*: the structure of metaphor.

If the Oedipal drama is subsequent to the advent of language, what then, according to Stein, is the element which ensures the simultaneous establishment of language and the unconscious in accordance with the process of metaphoric substitution?

> The phantasy of the primal scene is the imprint, as it were, upon which the Oedipus will be structured. Precipitated into the unconscious by primal repression, this phantasy can be named by the Name-of-the-Father, as it is none other than the phantasy of the desire of the mother.

Stein in fact says that, existentially, the relationship between desire and the mother can only be repletion or lack, absence or presence, as can be seen in the game with the cotton-reel referred to in Part One of this study. The game, which occurred at the age of only eighteen months, may be considered in this particular case, as the first accession to language on the part of the child in question. This first pair of phonemes (*Fort* and *Da*, as will be recalled) are connected in the unconscious with the phantasy of the desire of the mother. At this time, they represent the Name-of-the-Father which can only later come to have all the symbolic content seen in it by Lacan.

In subsequent developments, *Fort* and *Da* will, according to Stein, be integrated in their turn into a fragment of unconscious discourse whose only worth is its individual and unique value as a substitute-sign for the same eternal phantasy of desire. The elementary structure of the unconscious will, therefore, be supported by a pair of linguistic signs denoting the positive and negative sides of accomplishment of the original instinct.

The Oedipus complex will then complete the subject's entry into the symbolic order through a metaphoric process similar to that suggested by Lacan.

Let us see if such a thesis can find a place in the context of Lacan's *Écrits* themselves.

In 'Les formations de l'inconscient' (35), Lacan says:

> Even before the acquisition of language, there is, in the child's very first relations with the maternal object, a process of symbolization. As soon as the child begins to be able to oppose two phonemes, there is sufficient in the four elements introduced: the two vocables, he who pronounces them and he to whom they are addressed, to contain virtually the whole combinatory from which the organization of the signifier will arise.

89

When Freud makes his first model of the psychical apparatus, he admits that the type of mnemic inscription which corresponds in hallucinatory fashion to the manifestation of need is a sign (letter to Fliess, no. 52), not the kind of lure which can arouse need but not fill it, but something which, in so far as it is an image, is already situated in a symbolic relationship. Witness the play of presence and absence linked with discrete signifying elements.

It would appear, then, that understanding the Oedipal phenomenon as an essential structural moment of humanization requires one to distance oneself from the precise existential content covered by it in Freudian thought.

The moment at which the Oedipus, in the broad sense, and all its structural implications for the formation of a human being occurs cannot be fixed at any definite age.

In Lacan, the Oedipus complex is not a stage like any other in genetic psychology; it is the moment in which the child humanizes itself by becoming aware of the self, the world and the others.

In addition to the above remarks, I would like to make a further point.

The Oedipus owes its status as the maker of the human subject to its age-old inscription in the very structures of society. It underlies the symbolic organization of the Family and one could therefore say that if the child lives it, it is precisely because he must become socialized.

In *L'Oedipe africain* (102), Edmond Ortigues points to the necessity of a reversal of perspectives concerning the Oedipus: basically, he says that we must beware of psychologizing the Oedipus. We must beware of limiting the Oedipus to the existential lived experience or to a genesis of facts and events which can be objectivized from the outside. The Oedipus, in the broad sense, is radically other and constitutes the fundamental structural moment in the history of a 'subject'. Its articulations are conveyed by the cultural structures of societies, by language, and it is by entering into these that the subject lives them. The Oedipus is not, therefore, of the order of an anecdote on the sidelines of history, but a cultural phenomenon: the prohibition of incest is inscribed in the social code which pre-exists the individual existence, and it is in growing up within these pre-established social structures that the child will be faced with the problem of the difference between the sexes, of his third party role in the parental couple and with the prohibition of incest. It is through language that he will progressively assume the Oedipal drama from the inside as an ancestral heritage in which he situates himself before there is any possibility of the act of becoming aware.

The individual who lives them is unaware of the full implications and meaning of the institutions and the language which convey the Oedipal structures.

The members of a society, for example, are not aware of the meaning of its social structure or the reasons for the triad: relations of consanguinity, of alliance and of descent which gives the family its symbolic dimension. Science has made some progress by advancing that the meaning of this triad is the impossibility of making relationships of kinship coincide with relationships of alliance on pain of preventing the mutual recognition of beings. The child who is not situated amongst the other members of the group, who is not designated by a particular name or by a role, cannot become a 'subject' or a full, complete member of society. Thus, it is the question of the subject as relative individuality that is posed in these 'social' structures.

If this is so, then it is correct to say with Lévi-Strauss that: as a concept, the Oedipal unconscious is homologous with this structuring of existence by Culture, and that the problem of the unconscious is that something natural manifests itself in the significant forms of a civilization (*Structural Anthropology*, 92).

Finally, the unconscious arises as a problem of the nature–culture, life–language divorce.

How then can we understand a myth like that of the primal horde or that of Oedipus? In *The Elementary Structures of Kinship*, Lévi-Strauss explains that these myths do not correspond to any event occupying a given place in history. They translate, in symbolic form, man's most ancient and most permanent dream.

> Their prestige arises precisely from the fact that the acts they evoke have never been committed, because culture has opposed them at all times and in all places. Myths, said Freud, are symbolic gratifications in which the incest urge finds its expression. They do not commemorate an actual event.

We can add that they are:

> The permanent expression of a desire for disorder, or rather counter-order. Festivals turn social life topsy-turvy, not because it was once like this, but because it never has been and never can be any different.

We can now see the points at which the concepts unconscious – Oedipus – Culture tie up.

The Oedipus is articulated in the forms of the social institutions and of language of which the members of the society are unconscious – unconscious as to their meaning and, above all, to their origin. The Oedipal unconscious is homologous with these symbolic structures. The Oedipus is the drama of a being who must become a subject and who can only do so by internalizing the social rules, by entering on an equal footing into the register of the symbolic, of Culture and of language; it is the drama of a future subject who must resolve the problem of the difference between the sexes, of the assumption of his or her sex and of his or her unconscious drives by means of a development which presupposes the transition from natural man to man of culture.

Society and its structures are always present in the form of the family institution and the father, the representative of the law of society into which he will introduce his child by forbidding dual union with the mother (the register of the imaginary, of nature). By identifying with the father, the child receives a name and a place in the family constellation; restored to himself, he discovers that he is to be made in and by a world of Culture, language and civilization.

In conclusion we can say that the Oedipus is the unconscious articulation of a human world of culture and language; it is the very structure of the unconscious forms of the society.

Like Lévi-Strauss in anthropology, Lacan does not take the question 'why the prohibition of incest?', 'why the family?' to extremes. His point of view consists simply in seeing the Oedipus complex as the pivot of humanization, as a transition from the natural register of life to a cultural register of group exchange and therefore of laws, symbols and organization.

Neither Lacan nor Lévi-Strauss will ever provide us with the detailed existential web which makes obligatory the universally observed transition to the laws of organization which, despite the particular forms they take in various societies, make up the family or the prohibition of incest. We know that individuality, sexuality, the differences between the sexes, inter-individual rivalry, concurrence of positive and negative feelings between the two generations play a part, as do reciprocal interests of survival, commerce etc. But we shall never know precisely how and why the plurality of the conditions of human existence crystallize into these cultural forms. To reply to these questions would be equivalent to putting an end to the necessity for research in the human sciences. For ultimately, the mystery of the human is the life-culture duality and the absence of parallelism between cultural signifier and existential signified.

Faced with the contemporary radical questioning of the Oedipus and of the Family, the position of Lacan and Lévi-Strauss is that of the statement pure and simple. This is the way of society, this is what anthropology and psychoanalysis have discovered in the course of their structural analysis. The question of the humanly conceivable margins of a revolution would require much more information about the nature-culture link than science possesses. The revolution is, after all, the task of politics rather than that of science.

PART FOUR

The engendering of the unconscious by primal repression (or accession to language) in accordance with the process of metaphor

The insertion of the subject into the symbolic order underlying the social organization by the Oedipus is simultaneous with a division between the I of existence and the I of meaning.

These few words sum up the object of Part Three of the present work.

Continuing our investigation of Lacanian thought, we will see how the division in question engenders the unconscious.

By forbidding dual union with the mother, the resolution of the Oedipus forces the subject's original desire, together with all its accompanying phantasies, into the position of something misrecognized, and substitutes a symbol for them in accordance with the process of the 'paternal metaphor'.

In other words, *accession to the symbolic order is simultaneous with and indissolubly connected with primal repression* which, for the Lacanians, is effected in accordance with the formal process of metaphor.

Here are a few quotations from Lacan which set out what is to be discussed:

> In the quest for the phallus, the subject moves from being it to having it, it is here that is inscribed that last Spaltung by which the subject articulates himself to the Logos. (*Écrits*, 24)

> The psychoanalyst spots the subject's Spaltung in the simple recognition of the unconscious. (*Écrits*, 33)

> The reduplication which discourse provokes is what Freud calls *Urverdrängung* (primal repression).
>
> It is in the reduplication of the subject of speech that the unconscious finds the means to articulate itself. (*Écrits*, 26)

EIGHT

The constituting metaphor of the unconscious

The thesis we are concerned with was developed by J. Laplanche and S. Leclaire in 'The unconscious: a psychoanalytic study' (48), an article which has since become famous.

Read in 1960 at the sixth Bonneval Conference under the direction of H. Ey, the text was not published until six years later.

Until today (January 1970), Lacan has never made a written statement on the caution with which the theoretical content of this article is to be approached.

The Preface written by Lacan for the present work represents only a brief summary of the numerous reservations he expressed to me in a conversation in December 1969 (41).

I therefore propose first to expound the substance of the essential chapters of the article (chs 1, 2 and 4), the chapters for which Laplanche is responsible, and then to formulate the development of Lacan's criticisms.

In 'The unconscious: a psychoanalytic study' (48), J. Laplanche demonstrates that the formula for metaphor given by Lacan in 'On a question preliminary to any possible treatment of psychosis' (23) is an exact representation of the processes of primal and secondary repression.

Metaphor, writes Lacan, consists in the substitution in a signifier–signified relationship of a new signifier, S', used as the signifier of the original signifier S, which now becomes a signified. The formula is:

$$\frac{S'}{S} \times \frac{S}{s} \to S'\left(\frac{I}{s}\right) \tag{I}$$

Laplanche then shows that the signifier S has been repressed, that it has fallen below, that it has been simplified out in the algebraic sense.

To make this clearer, Laplanche reasons as follows:
as, in algebraic terms, it is permissible in the formula:

$$\frac{A}{B} \times \frac{C}{D} = \frac{\dfrac{A}{D}}{\dfrac{B}{C}}$$

so Formula I can be written as follows:

$$\frac{S'}{S} \times \frac{S}{s} = \frac{\dfrac{S'}{s}}{\dfrac{S}{S}} \qquad\qquad (II)$$

We can in fact observe that in Formula II, S has fallen to the rank of signified or, to be more accurate, to the rank of latent signifier.

Form II of the formula for metaphor, Laplanche goes on, is none other than the schema for repression, be it primal repression (*Urverdrängung*) or secondary repression (*Verdrängung*). More exhaustively, Formula II will account for three things: repression; the relation between the repressed unconscious and the preconscious; the nature of the unconscious chain.

Speaking of the mechanism of secondary repression, Freud basically tells us that an instinct-presentation is repressed by the action of a rejection by the preconscious and an attraction on the part of the unconscious (or that which has already been repressed). This action of rejection is itself effected in two stages: withdrawal of cathexis, or the breaking of the connexion which existed in the preconscious, and counter-cathexis, the replacement in the signifying chain of the repressed term by another term.

If we apply the Freudian definition of secondary repression to Formula II for metaphor, we do in fact see a similarity in the mechanisms, and we see that the formula for metaphor can rightly be considered an effective symbolization of secondary repression.

On the other hand, things seem less clear where primal repression is concerned.

In his *Papers on Metapsychology* (11), Freud posits the necessity of conceiving the existence of a primal repression which establishes the unconscious in order to be able to account for the mechanism of secondary repression, as the latter is effected mainly by attraction on the part of an already-fashioned unconscious.

According to Freud, primal repression consists of 'a denial of entry into consciousness to the mental (ideational) presentation of an instinct. This is accompanied by a fixation: the ideational presentation in question persists unaltered from then onwards and the instinct remains attached to it' (ibid.).

The object of primal repression has thus never been conscious. Laplanche points out that, as on the other hand it was not unconscious either, given that the unconscious did not yet exist, one must admit the existence of a sort of primitive, mythical state in which the differentiation between the preconscious and unconscious systems does not yet exist.

Freud also makes it clear that, as the repressed idea was never conscious, one cannot speak of withdrawal of cathexis with regard to primal repression: one must therefore speak, he says, of counter-cathexis, the one and only mechanism of primal repression.

Laplanche goes on to describe two stages in primal repression, the process which introduces the subject into the symbolic universe and which at the same time brings about the constitution of the unconscious.

At a first level of symbolization, he says, the network or web of significant oppositions is cast over the subjective universe, but no particular signified is caught in any particular mesh. What is introduced with this system is simply pure difference, scansion, the line: the edge of the cot in the '*Fort–Da*' gesture for example. Here, it is a question of a purely mythical stage, although the phenomena of psychotic language show that it can reappear 'secondarily' in regression, which cannot be mastered by a pair of differential elements.

At a second level of symbolization, again according to Laplanche, the process of the engendering of the unconscious is realized in perfect accordance with the mechanism of metaphor. This second level of symbolization is the only one really to create the unconscious: it acts by metaphor upon certain oppositions and produces a kind of un-conscious ballast: elementary signifiers known as key signifiers, which fix the instinct. With this fixation, the signified (the lived psychical dimension of the instincts) becomes caught in particular symbolic meshes, and the indefinite oscillation of the terms of the previous oppositions (the + and the −, the 0 and the A, the good and the bad, the right and the left) comes to an end.

We can see that it has been necessary for Laplanche to split the process of the engendering of the unconscious by primal repression into two stages in order that the process might take place in accordance with the schema adopted for metaphor.

S. Leclaire does not share his collaborator's conceptions of this point. According to him, the first level of symbolization already has the power to engender the unconscious. For Leclaire, primal repression does not, then, conform to the mechanism of metaphor. On the contrary, it is primal repression which will later allow metaphor to function.

Continuing our analysis of Laplanche's text, let us see what he has to say about the lower storey of the metaphoric relation (Formula II).

According to Laplanche, the second graphic representation of the formula for metaphor gives us an idea of the nature of the unconscious chain.

The $\frac{S}{S}$ in fact represents the unconscious and makes clear its com-

position: the unconscious is composed of signifiers.

These signifiers do not, however, have the status of our verbal language and are reduced to the dimension of the imaginary – notably the visual imaginary. According to Laplanche, they correspond to the term *Imago*, taken in the broad sense.

For, at the level of the unconscious, there is no distinction between signifier and signified; the signifying image refers to nothing but itself as signified, and is both open and closed to all possible meanings.

Laplanche claims that in his description of the unconscious he is in agreement with Freud.

We should, then, recall the distinction made by Freud between the unconscious and preconscious-consciousness systems.

> It strikes us . . . that now we know what is the difference between a conscious and an unconscious idea. The two are not . . . different records of the same content situate in different parts of the mind . . . but the conscious idea comprises the concrete idea plus the verbal idea corresponding to it, whilst the unconscious idea is that of the thing alone. (11, pp. 133–4)

It should, nevertheless, be pointed out that the term 'thing' comes under the linguistic category of the signified (the concept) and therefore includes the imaginary dimension of the psychical presentation of the thing in the Lacanian sense. With his metaphoric formula, Laplanche clearly brings out the signifying aspect of the sign in the unconscious and at the same time makes it clear that, here, it is only a matter of *images*.

In short, it is still unclear whether the unconscious englobes the signifier in its materiality, as an acoustic image or a letter, or whether it englobes the signifier as the presentation in thought of the thing, or even whether both elements of the linguistic sign are present, but without having, as they do in conscious language, at least a certain fixed relationship which restricts the 'floating' of the meaning of the symbols.

It should also be noted that Freud's own thinking is not always consistent in this chapter, since the analysis he gives of 'unconscious formations' refers at times to a purely literal play of the signifier in the unconscious and at other times to an interlacing of thoughts, ideas, concepts and thing-presentations.

The whole problem arises, I think, from the fact that these formations of the unconscious are not the unconscious itself, but its expression through censorship and consciousness and that the original content of the unconscious comes to us already modified. Henceforth, it is practically impossible to reconstitute the unconscious as such and, consequently, to describe it. The thinker becomes lost in conjectures which, as the mind never admits defeat, are certainly agreeable both to make and to read, but which are impossible to prove.

The problem still remains, therefore, as to whether the unconscious functions with both signifiers and signifieds, with signifiers alone, or with signifieds alone.

Formulated in this way, with all the characteristics of rigorous logic, Laplanche's theses appear simple, acceptable and in conformity with Lacan's thought.

All the more so as, in 'On a question preliminary to any possible treatment of psychosis' (23), Lacan suggests the following schema, which is designed to account for the terms of substitution in the paternal metaphor in the Oedipus:

$$\frac{\text{Name-of-the-Father}}{\text{Desire of the Mother}} \cdot \frac{\text{Desire of the Mother}}{\text{Signified for the subject}}$$

$$\rightarrow \text{Name-of-the-Father} \left(\frac{0}{\text{Phallus}} \right)$$

It should, however, be noted that Laplanche's reflections concern stages prior to the development of the Oedipus, as accession to language should be situated at an earlier age.

For authors like Laplanche, Leclaire and Stein, the imaginary lived experience of the desire of the mother, translated into the primal scene phantasy, into the perception of alternate maternal presence and absence, or into the lived experience of alternating repletion and emptiness, is replaced in the mind by elementary signifiers.

This is a question of a first rough sketch of the paternal metaphor, in which the symbolic law obliges the child to refract his desire through the defile of the signifier.

In his commentary on Lacan's theses, Laplanche is, then, merely making a hazardous interpolation: making a literal use of the metaphoric formula and bringing out all the algebraic usages it implies.

Lacan for his part only resorts to this type of schema for didactic purposes. It should be stressed how dangerous it can be to go too far with something which has only an allusive and comparative value. Between 'it is as if . . .' and 'it is this . . .', there is all the distance between intuitive suppleness of thought and rigid reflection.

Laplanche's method is tendentious because it applies the simple play of mathematical logic to the study of man.

In the same way, when we hear of people rejecting Lacanian formulae such as 'the unconscious is structured like a language', or 'the unconscious is a discourse' in the name of a purist adherence to the principles of linguistic science, we can consider them as dismissing, with too hasty a stroke of the pen, the richness of such analogical recourses.

As we have just said, it is quite obvious that language at the level of the unconscious cannot be assimilated to our verbal language. We are also obliged to admit to a certain inability to specify the relations between these two languages, as thinking and unfolding the unconscious in analytic discourse means denaturing its essence.

I am convinced that Lacanian psychoanalysis, like Freudian psychoanalysis itself, is as much an art as a science and that it requires a great deal of receptive intuition, openness of mind and intellectual subtlety on the part of the thinker.

Any formulation of statements relating to a domain as complex as the human mind will always be somewhat intuitive, if not irrational. Just as Freud came up against, and still comes up against, 'logical incomprehension', so *a fortiori*, Lacan lends himself to criticism and to blind alleys. This does not prevent one from having a definite sensation of finding something true, something which conforms to the 'unthinkable' reality of man while reading Lacan, even though his language is complex and often metaphorical.

To come back to Laplanche's 'deviation', to which, according to Lacan, his later writings bear witness. In a quite understandable intellectual effort to make connexions everywhere and to fill in the gaps in our understanding, Laplanche is led in his article to draw a 'heretical' conclusion, a conclusion radically opposed to certain of Lacan's statements, namely: 'The unconscious is the condition of language.'

To begin with, Laplanche tries to specify the origin or cause of the cleavage and the formal difference between the unilinear language dedicated to the *primary* process of the unconscious and the organized language of the *secondary* conscious process.

We know that analysis of the unconscious confronts us with a free, almost frantic circulation of cathectic energy which, by way of condensations and displacements, follows a very illogical path from *Vorstellung* (presentation or idea) to *Vorstellung*. At the level of the unconscious, the instinctual energy does not appear to be very closely bound up with any one of its presentations.

From a descriptive point of view, the primary process of the unconscious is close to the paradox noted by Frege in language: the eternal flight of meaning, which can never be grasped, as any attempt to pin it down constantly sends us from one signifier to another.

At the level of the unconscious, it seems as if the instinctual energy can never hook itself on to a signifier which could represent it in a stable manner. There is no fixed binding of a signifier to a signified in the unconscious, but an almost frantic sliding of pure energy from one signifier to another. The unconscious meaning, the instincts and desire borrow significant representations with an irrational flexibility authorized by constantly changing criteria.

On the side of verbal language, however, we can see a certain limitation of this primary process. We have the feeling that our signs are reasonably adequate to what they express and that speech is a source of mutual understanding. In short, we have the impression that there is a certain join between thought and language.

This impression, it will be recalled, is not endorsed by Lacan. Lacan insists upon the meaning to be given to the line in the Saussurian

algorithm: $\dfrac{S}{s}$, namely a separation which excludes *a priori* any possibil-

ity of seeing a term for term equivalence between the signifying chain and the flow of the signified.

His theory of the anchoring point, as we have seen it expressed in the article (27), does, nevertheless, locate the knot which closes signification in the sentence. The sentence closes its meaning only with its last term. Such is the *diachronic* function of the anchoring point which cannot, however, interrupt the chase after signifiers at the level of inter-human discourse or intellectual human exchanges at the level of science. According to Lacan, the process is never closed at the level of science, of intellectual human exchange; witness the human science and philosophy, vainly seeking throughout the ages for truth refused by language.

In the same article we are also told that the *synchronic* function of the anchoring point refers us back to the source of language, to the moment in which the child effects the cleavage between the thing and the sign connoting in thought both the thing and its absence. Here, the disjunction between the thing and the sign is a one-way process; in other words, language is radically excluded from thought as soon as it enters into it in one way – by way of the sign which alienates it. Looking for the signified of a given signifier brings us to the dictionary, and we can explore the whole dictionary by way of synonyms and antonyms without ever being able to avoid tautology at the end of our search.

Having clarified this, we can pursue Laplanche's idea. He is looking for that which puts a stop to the primary process at the level of conscious language, that which accounts for the connexion between signifier and signified and a 'certain' fixity of meaning.

His search seems justifiable to me, whatever Lacan, preoccupied as he is by the problem of inter-human incomprehension, may think of it. Conscious language makes use of catalogued and conventional signs which do have a partial efficacy as regards understanding, whereas the unconscious can, for example, play as it likes upon the sonic materiality of the symbols of language without regard for their real meaning, and can use them to express a quite different unconscious 'meaning'.

It therefore seems quite legitimate to look for that which founds the basis of the difference, at least in intensity, between the primary process at the conscious level and at the unconscious level.

Given the extreme complexity of the debate we are entering into, we should be more precise, if such is possible.

Lacan is right to stress the existence of a certain primary process at the level of conscious language. Language is 'padded' with multiple strata of signification. The very essence of the symbol and the very function of the concept (from the Latin *concipere*) imply this. Thought and understanding leap from one vocable to another, from one phrase to another, unable to grasp them all at once.

He is even right to compare the mechanisms of this phenomenon to those governing the unconscious: the mobility of psychic energy, which makes the meaning fluctuate through the infinite metaphoric and metonymic associations of signifiers and signifieds.

But Laplanche, too, is right when he establishes, as does Freud, a crescendo of organization between unconscious and conscious language. Preconscious-conscious language is governed by the secondary process, which limits the remaining effects of the primary process. Consciousness is the site of our rational efforts to find a join between thought and language. And if, as Laplanche says in the postscript to his article, poetic language is close to the form of unconscious language, it forms a kind of intermediary layer between the latter and the discourse of reason. Ultimately, the divorce between the two authors focuses upon the question of the intensity with which the primary process affects conscious language. Their divergence over various theoretical points becomes greater and is finally concerned with the central point of Laplanche's thesis, contained in the assertions that: the fixation of a few key signifiers to the drive during primal repression (i) is what founds (ii) the relative fixity of the signifier to the signified in conscious language.

I do not in fact really see how this can be possible. In a moment I will develop the reasoning which leads Laplanche to make these assertions, but not without adding that something of the order of creative intuition can be seen in the thinking which leads him to this untenable local deduction.

Having found the binding of the signifier to the signified in primal repression, in the inaugural moment of language, Laplanche then advances the thesis that the fixed chain of signifiers in the unconscious is 'responsible for the secondary process of conscious language' because it represents a 'ballast', rather like an anchor which prevents the boat from pitching too much.

What prevents one term from sliding – endlessly – into another is not its empirical relation to a thing, but the fact that it is not

univocal and includes several definitions, that it is the whole
group of meanings *b*, *c*, etc., which prevents word *x* flying out of
the door opened by meaning *a*.   (48, p. 155)

If a global meaning is to be retained and fixed at the level of a conscious signifier, all possible definitions of the vocable and the metaphoric process which multiplies its meanings must be taken into account.

Metaphor, Laplanche goes on, is precisely the process through which
repression is effected. Metaphor preserves what was simplified in the
preconscious discourse in another line, another chain.

As the layered structure of the formula indicates, metaphor constitutes hierarchical layers of signification. By going back from metaphor
to metaphor, from signifying chain to signifying chain, one eventually
arrives at the elementary signifiers of the unconscious, which were put
in place during primal repression.

According to Laplanche, these form the final ballast which puts an
end to the primary process of conscious language and puts a full stop to
our search for meaning. Unconscious language, with its elementary or
original layer of signs, 'is' the hidden meaning of all conscious language.
Hence it is the condition for the possibility of conscious language. It
gives the secret reason for its fixity.

> It is the 'thesaurus' of various definitions that fall into place for
> a given word that we must look for the path to that which limits
> the primary process. A thesaurus of metonymies, according to
> J. Lacan, to the extent that the signifier thus finds itself included in
> a number of chains. But at the same time, we would say, a
> thesaurus of past metaphors.   (48, pp. 155–6)

> In the formula for metaphor, it is necessary here to conceive of the
> existence of certain *key signifiers* placed in a metaphorizing
> position, and to which is assigned, because of their special weight,
> the property of ordering the whole system of human language.
>   (48, p. 160)

> It is indissolubly because of the existence of this unconscious
> signifying chain that preconscious language possessed a certain
> fixity of meanings, the stability (*capitonnage*) that characterizes the
> secondary process – and because of the existence of a preconscious
> chain with the characteristics familiar to us that the unconscious
> chain has taken over, so to speak, the characteristics of the
> primary process . . . as characteristics of a signifying chain
> reduced to a single dimension.   (48, p. 161)

Laplanche's thesis asserts that there is a link of reciprocal conditioning
and dependence between unconscious language and preconscious
language; his thesis mixes the discourse of reason up with unconscious
discourse, as though it were at any moment possible to establish a

junction between the two languages. For Laplanche, the underlying padding of our conscious discourse is thus necessarily connected with the unconscious, which is ultimately the reason for the commonly understood meaning. As I understand it, Laplanche's proposition is based upon a false interpretation of the Lacanian notion of the anchoring point.

When Lacan speaks of the anchoring point in the synchronic dimension of language, he certainly does go back to the source of language, but there it is a question of conventional, learned language, and not of individual symbolism of a psychoanalytic character. There is no question of confusing conventional language and unconscious language either at the level of primal repression or at any other, later level. On the contrary, it is a question of asserting that there is a division between them.

I think for my part that, at the source of language, signifiers with a strictly personal content reflecting the profound psychical experience of the young child mingle with signifiers completely free of any psychical or traumatic taint.

To take the example given by Leclaire in the article we are studying: I would willingly admit that the 'Poôr (d) J'e-LI' (the elementary signifying chain of Philippe's unconscious) meshes through some metaphoric process with signifiers like Lili, Georges, Je, etc., which have, on the one hand, an unconscious resonance but are, on the other hand, inscribed in everyday speech without those resonances and are connected in the mind with the persons they evoke.

This brings us back to the problem of the double inscription in a way which does, I think, conform to Lacan's thinking. We will return to this question in more detail in a moment.

In short, I think it *a priori* out of the question that a metaphorical search for the multiple meanings of a given vocable would directly and necessarily lead us to the elementary signifiers of the unconscious rather than to the signifiers which first inscribed these object-things in thought.

On the other hand, I would be much more likely to be influenced by other of Laplanche's statements, such as the following:

> It is because of the existence of a preconscious chain with the characteristics familiar to us that the unconscious chain has taken over, so to speak, the characteristics of the primary process.
>
> (48, p. 161)

> What conditions the transition from the primary process to the secondary process is precisely the constitution and maintenance of the unconscious as a separate domain. (48, p. 178)

In these formulae, we are closer to the point which Lacan sees it as a priority to maintain: that it is language which conditions the unconscious, creates it and keeps it in its proper place. 'The unconscious is the logical implication of language', says Lacan in his Preface to the present book.

In my view, it is then more likely to be a process of censorship, a cohesion supported by thought or imposed by the rules for the application of language which keeps the primary process within certain limits and, more importantly, prevents it escaping into the unconscious through free association or through poetry.

To sum up: in so far as the primary process of conscious language encounters certain limits, I do not agree with Laplanche that its origins should be sought in the stable fixation of the unconscious signifying chain to the instinct.

On the contrary, I would explain these limitations by the maintenance of the unconscious in its proper place, a maintenance ensured by a certain diachronic anchoring – in the Lacanian sense – within the sentence, by respect for convention in the use of linguistic signs, by coherence of thought and by the necessity of maintaining the repression of the private sphere.

This does not mean neglecting the existence of a certain interaction between conscious and unconscious languages. Such interaction can, for example, be observed in the formations of the unconscious, or in the fact that certain symbols in our language have overdetermined relations with the repressed instincts.

But these cases of convergence between conscious and unconscious betray such discordance with the rest of the text that unconscious language can be spotted at once.

Stressing, as we have done, the impossibility of the unconscious conditioning the relative order of spoken discourse brings us gradually closer to the problem of the 'double inscription'.

At the limits of the possible join between conscious and unconscious language in, for example, the case of repression or, conversely, in the return of the repressed, the following problem arises:

Is there a duality of inscription – conscious and unconscious – in the phenomena in question, or is it rather a question of the same inscription suddenly receiving a different illumination as it returns to consciousness – the illumination of lucid consciousness?

In the article we are analysing, Laplanche gives a personal interpretation of this problem.

We will therefore bring this chapter on Laplanche's theses to a close with an exposition of his views on the double inscription problem. The following chapter will make the necessary comparison with Lacan's views on this point and on the article's fundamental thesis, which we have just studied.

In his *Metapsychology*, Freud poses the problem of the double inscription in these terms:

> If we wish to take seriously the notion of a topography of mental acts, we must direct our attention to a doubt which arises at this point. When a mental act (let us confine ourselves to an act of ideation) is transferred from the system Ucs into the system Cs (or Pcs), are we to suppose that this transposition involves a fresh registration comparable to a second record of the idea in question, situated, moreover, in a fresh locality in the mind and side by side with which the original unconscious record continues to exist? Or are we rather to believe that the transformation consists in a change in the state of the idea, involving the same material and occurring in the same locality?
>
> (11, pp. 106–7)

In Freud's view, if one wishes to stress the topography of the psychical apparatus, the hypothesis of two different inscriptions is the cruder, but it is certainly easier to handle. According to him, the second hypothesis of a simple change in the functional state of the presentation or idea is more probable, but not so easy to handle.

The hypothesis of a second inscription would, at first sight, seem to be confirmed by the facts of analytic practice.

Thus, according to Freud, when analytic interpretation communicates a repressed idea to the patient, the effect is sometimes slow to be seen. There is no immediate lifting of repression, but a phenomenon of negation. At this point in the treatment, the patient seems to have the same idea in two forms and in two different places in his mental apparatus. On the one hand, he has at his disposal the conscious memory of the 'auditory impression' of the idea communicated to him by the analyst, but on the other hand he simultaneously bears within him the unconscious memory of what has been lived.

As Freud puts it, 'To have listened to something and to have experienced something are psychologically two different things, even though the content of each be the same' (p. 109).

The lifting of repression only comes about when the connexion is made between the unconscious mnemic traces and the conscious idea by *Durcharbeiten* [working through].

Here, Freud avoids the question of the choice between the two options, as his example seems to him rather to be a sign of an imperfection in the analytic work.

But in Section Four of *The Unconscious* ('Topography and Dynamics of Repression'), he returns to the question left in suspense and proposes another explanation:

Repression can consist here only in the withdrawal from the idea of (pre) conscious cathexis which belongs to the system Pcs. The idea then remains without cathexis, or receives cathexis from the Ucs, or retains the unconscious cathexis which it previously had.

(11, p. 113)

In such a view of repression, Freud continues, the passage of an idea from one system to the other is purely functional and does not necessitate a new inscription.

At this point in the *Metapsychology*, the hypothesis of the double inscription is given a negative solution. But it is consequently necessary for Freud to posit the existence of a process of counter-cathexis designed to ensure the maintenance of repression and to protect the preconscious from the pressure of the unconscious idea. For the functional hypothesis is infinitely less qualified to account for the solidity of repression than the topographical hypothesis.

Finally, on pp. 133–4 of the *Metapsychology* (11), Freud thinks that he has been able to solve the question of the double inscription. This, then, is the third aspect of his thinking on this point:

It strikes us all at once that now we know what is the difference between a conscious and an unconscious idea. The two are not, as we supposed, different records of the same content situate in different parts of the mind, nor yet different functional states of cathexis in the same part; but the conscious idea comprises the concrete idea plus the verbal idea corresponding to it, whilst the unconscious idea is that of the thing alone.

At the same time, Freud adds that the concrete idea is hypercathected in consciousness by the presentation of the verbal ideas corresponding to it and that these hypercathexes introduce the secondary process as opposed to the primary process.

As far as I am concerned, it appears that, on reflection, none of Freud's attempts to clarify the double inscription problem is complete in itself, although not one of them is completely erroneous.

First, the initial statement (11, p. 108) which asserts the simultaneous and parallel existence of two different inscriptions in two different places appears necessary if we are to retain the topography of the psychical apparatus and the functional difference between primary and secondary processes in the two respective systems.

The second thesis of a change in the state (conscious or unconscious illumination) of a single content is valid if understood in a particular sense, which, although it is certainly not the sense intended by Freud, cannot be rejected. One could in effect assume that the *same* signifier undergoes a change in state due to the general context in which it is found, depending on whether it is present in one or the other system or whether it is simultaneously present in both. The whole problem lies in the terms; what is to be understood by the expression 'the same signifier'? Is it a question of its content or, on the contrary, of its literal character alone, or is it both? If we pose questions like this, it is of course because there is an interaction between content and state and because the characteristics of the primary process are still not well known to us.

As far as the description of repression or of the return of the repressed given by Freud (11, pp. 133–4) is concerned, it does not seem to me to exclude the topographical hypothesis and the double inscription in favour of the functional hypothesis, whatever Freud may say about it.

Preconscious withdrawal of cathexis does not in fact mean that the idea is completely excluded from the preconscious-consciousness system, even if there is countercathexis on the part of the unconscious.

It certainly is excluded in so far as it is an idea invested with libido, as the existence of counter-cathexis confirms, but it is not excluded in so far as it is a simple idea pinned down by the global context of conscious discourse.

For example, when Hans represses a particular presentation of his father and substitutes a horse (countercathexis), the same 'father' remains conscious, but decathected, freed from its pathogenic character and integrated into the normal circuit of verbal exchange. But, as Freud expressly states, this preconscious withdrawal of cathexis is accompanied by countercathexis which, in our example, takes the form of the representative 'horse' which will henceforth support the whole weight of the complex.

The repressed paternal representative to which the instinctual problematic is attached will, for its part, be caught in an unconscious signifying chain upon which the instinct can operate.

A brief allusion to affect is necessary to make my reasoning clear. We know that in his *Metapsychology*, Freud relates it closely to cathexis itself. Like the representative, it is a form in which cathexis (dynamism of the instinct) becomes psychically palpable.

Matters may be made clearer if we recall that when an idea is repressed, its affect is discharged and is transposed to the counter-cathected conscious substitute for the idea. Caught in an unconscious chain, the repressed idea is neutralized at the conscious level, because the fact that it has been countercathected means that the affect which was bound up with it has been transposed. Having been neutralized, this same idea can then persist in the field of everyday conscious language and at the same time be present in unconscious language.

In psychoanalysis, the return of the repressed proceeds from the same mechanism, but in reverse order. Here, the unconscious idea is cathected consciously; the affect returns to it and is either abreacted in analysis or short-circuited. On the other hand, the idea in question may still persist in the unconscious system, as it differs from the conscious idea by virtue of the global context of the complex surrounding it. It persists, then, in the unconscious, but as the analytic work unfolds a major part – but never all – of the unconscious associative system surrounding it, this idea is neutralized for the advance of the instinct.

Finally, the last hypothesis suggested by Freud (11, pp. 133–4) reinstates the topographical difference between the inscriptions and provides a further possibility for understanding the nature of their difference: conscious and unconscious inscriptions differ in that the former include concrete ideas together with the corresponding verbal ideas, whereas the latter include only ideas of things.

Although its formulation is not perfect, the last hypothesis is in my opinion the most complete because it simultaneously asserts the duality of inscriptions and attributes the reason for this duality to the functional differences between the two systems in which it is caught up.

Whatever the nature of this functional difference, the important thing for the moment is to assert that it does exist, thus removing all possibility of equivalence between the two ideas.

As Freud himself said, 'having heard and having understood' are two completely different things. One could also add that an idea caught up in the configuration of the interdependencies of the unconscious cannot be identical to the same idea caught up in conscious existence.

Let us now consider Laplanche's remarks, remarks which divert him into a rather personal conception of the problem in question.

Being an adept of the double inscription theory, Laplanche bases his criticism of Freud's 'functional' hypothesis (according to which, we recall, a term's passage into one system abolishes its presence in the other) on the necessity of establishing a distinction between systemic cathectic energy and libidinal energy. Systemic cathectic energy is peculiar to each system and is not transmitted. It works upon the representatives and these alone pass from one system to the other, from consciousness to the unconscious and vice versa. Laplanche stresses that, being connected with presentations, libidinal energy on the other hand will be sometimes conscious and sometimes unconscious and is in any case mobile.

According to Laplanche, Freud confuses the two energies in his functional description of repression and of the return of the repressed. He consequently has great difficulty in accounting for two well-known psychoanalytic phenomena: the conscious representative which is to be repressed is attracted into the unconscious, and the repressed forces its way towards consciousness.

It is not very clear, says Laplanche, whether Freud sees cathexis acting as a system of cohesion or as a propulsive force which constantly tends to make its derivatives emerge into consciousness.

Laplanche thinks he has solved the problem by separating out systemic cathectic energy and libidinal energy. The whole process of the passage from one system to the other is effected through the play of the systemic energies, whilst libidinal energy is responsible for unconscious ideas pressing their way into consciousness and for conscious ideas being attracted by the repressed.

The phenomenon of the passage from one system to the other is produced as follows: one representative at a time passes from one system to the other. Systemic cathectic energy could be compared to the pregnancy of a good shape, rather like

> those puzzle-drawings where a certain perceptual attitude suddenly makes Napoleon's hat appear in the branches of a tree that shades a family picnic. But if this hat is able to appear, it is because it can be related to an entirely different anecdote which is not at all present in the rest of the drawing: the Napoleonic legend. In this model, what Freud calls cathexis is the relation of the detail in question (the hat) to the system which corresponds to it (the Napoleonic legend). The anti-cathexis is found in the same detail's relation to the term which evokes it in the other system (that is, the leaves of the tree): it is the pragnanz of the conscious system (the picnic) which keeps the tree and its leaves in existence and maintains the hat in a latent state.

It seems to me that Laplanche is correct to make a distinction between libidinal energy and cohesive systemic energy. Libidinal energy is more mobile and, above all, more dynamic. In so far as it is cathectic energy, it is as much the motor of repression as of countercathexis, during which operation it splits, with one part devolving upon the counter-cathected idea (substitution) and the other part devolving upon the repressed idea. As libidinal energy makes its way from idea to idea, it provokes the return of the repressed in the substitutive form of the formations of the unconscious.

Systemic cathectic energy is such a different mode of functioning for each system that it acts as a cohesive force, as a context. But if Laplanche's reasoning is correct, his gestaltist image does not, as we will see, account too well for the phenomena in question, as, except in the formations of the unconscious, the return of the repressed does not have such a discordant character in analysis. But this is a minor reservation.

We now come to Chapter 9: a critical examination, following Lacan, of the theses put forward by Laplanche in the article I have just introduced. The sources for this are: (i) a private conversation with Lacan in December 1969 on the themes dealt with in Part Four—this was typed up on the basis of a complete tape-recording made at the time. (ii) the Preface written by Lacan for the present book.

NINE

Critical study of the article, 'The unconscious: a psychoanalytic study' by J. Laplanche and S. Leclaire. Clarifications as to Lacan's thought

Following on from the discoveries of Freud, Dr Lacan's psychoanalytic experience has enabled him to reformulate in new terms the status of the human subject. This status, he will say, is one 'of representation'. The stress placed upon man's symbolic conditioning is proper to Lacan's thinking.

Each period in scientific history accumulates a given from which there emerges an original thought which can without doubt be called a step forward for science.

We must, then, recognize an advance in the domain of the human sciences in the contribution made by Dr Lacan. Lacan extends Freud with the support of the new discoveries of structural linguistics and structural anthropology.

The author of *Écrits* has rethought and reformulated the structure of the subject by means of a basic intuition of the primary role of symbolism and its determination of man.

Lacan's work, which began years ago, also includes a cleaning up, so to speak, of contemporary philosophy. In order to introduce a new mode of reflection into the common consciousness, Lacan has been obliged to take 'polemical' measures. The denunciation of deeply rooted presuppositions, the outwitting of some of the directions taken by psychoanalysis since Freud, the elimination from within psychoanalysis of the limitative incidence of philosophy; so many slow and wearying stages in the work of Lacan.

In the course of his years of teaching and in connexion with this epistemological labour, Lacan has pronounced certain axioms with regard to psychoanalysis. His intellectual approach, which he himself qualifies as 'ironic' – having, that is, an interrogative import – includes an underlying layer of trenchant assertions that are collected together in his *Écrits*.

According to Lacan, however, the *Écrits* merely point the way to his thought: the articles collected together in that volume form the punctuation, as it were, of the unpublished teachings of his seminars. Each separate text represents the cornerstone of a year's seminars, and places particular emphasis on those points resisted by the common consciousness. As a result, and despite its 900 pages, *Écrits* cannot, according to Lacan, serve as a basis for a complete enclosing of his thought.

To this we can add, as Lacan himself says, the extreme complexity of his discourse, both spoken and written, a complexity which he attributes exclusively to the importance of the subversion of thought being realized and to the inevitable resistances due to the very nature of the domain in question, namely the unconscious and the analytic discourse.

Lacan claims, therefore, not to have put forward 'theories'. His 'utterances' or 'writings', seeds scattered among the thorns of traditional philosophy and psychology, in no way lend themselves to anything resembling a closure.

'One is either taken by what they formulate or one leaves it.' (J. Lacan, Preface)

For Lacan, then, any attempt to unify his scattered statements into a whole runs the risk of making erroneous interpolations.

He says, for example, that the 'academic discourse' of his followers translates into a didactic whole statements in which truth 'spells itself out' – as Lacan wishes it to – from which it springs forth, despite the treachery of a vehicle whose function of lure is precisely what Lacan is denouncing here.

It is advisable here, in order to place Lacan's reservations correctly, to take due note of his own very personal philosophy of science.

In substance, he says that academic discourse retransmits for each generation the knowledge (*savoir*) conveyed by history; it accounts for its slidings and modifications through time, it decants and . . . re-creates.

Everything conveyed in this way by discourse, everything which is inscribed in the rising generation, is of the order of *doxa*, opinion. The basis of truth underlying this discourse, the thought of the Masters, represents the *epistemè* or knowledge. The latter stands, however, in a circular relation of interaction with *doxa*. Lacan seems in fact to think that, ultimately, it is always in the heart of discourse that knowledge slides, because it is precisely within the cracks in discourse that it is inscribed. Knowledge is that which denounces error and the mistakes made in the agreed usage of the signs of language. A term which is more efficient, more fruitful and which produces a better result at the level of practice is a term of knowledge. It is still not a term of truth, as truth is the Real, the very thing which no one has been able to attain since humanity began to express itself.

In the more specific field of the teaching of psychoanalysis, Lacan goes on, one is confronted with distinctions different from those revealed in the transmission of knowledge by discourse: these differences have only an analogical relationship with *epistemè* and *doxa*.

As a practitioner, Lacan will say that there is no question of psychoanalytic discourse itself being exempt from 'symptomatic' propositions. What an author seeks without knowing it, what motivates him in his scientific quest without his being aware of it, is a substitute for (a), the forbidden object of his desire, which has now entered into the imaginary and which has been transformed into a quest for social status.

In conformity with the knowledge acquired from his human experience Lacan therefore mistrusts science when it asserts itself 'in truth'.

As he also says in his article, 'La science et la vérité' (33), the cogito is a fundamental moment for the subject because it divides the subject between truth and knowledge; it follows that the unconscious is an effect of language and of the cogito. The truth is repressed by primal repression and as such it returns into the unconscious. The subject of the unconscious itself is represented in a signifier of the order of language, but this signifier does not signify it: it represents it erroneously.

On the basis of Saussure's teachings, Lacan establishes a separating line at three levels of the human being: (i) between what lies before the unconscious (and this is impossible to know); (ii) between the unconscious as a language and conscious language; (iii) between signifier and signified at the level of conscious language itself.

Man can therefore seek to know himself only from within a position in which he finds himself radically divided from himself. What psychoanalysis is then able to study is 'the subject of science', that is the subject revealed as being conditioned by language and all it conveys of an inter-human symbolic play.

As to the question of a join connecting the three levels of division actualized above, Lacan considers it to be out of reach, for this link can only be seen in desire, which carries with it a minimum of binding with antique knowledge, for this link is object (a), which can never be pinned down, but which is always present everywhere, having repercussions at every level and in changing forms throughout an individual's history.

Is this philosophy of language and of the limitations of science pessimistic? It is not, because Lacan himself is pursuing his quest for knowledge. But in his eyes it is without doubt pessimistic as regards us, the adepts, pupils and mere vehicles of the Master's thought. We are for him, during our brief lives, at least the clumsy links of history in which the golden ears are threshed. And if a little bran becomes mingled with the flour, that will not prevent a future genius from making bread if he uses the sieve carefully.

As to the transmission of Lacan's thought, the rule to be followed in this very particular case is, obviously, the permanent collation of his texts with the texts of the authors who translate him and an exact redistribution of what belongs to those authors and what belongs to Lacan himself.

It is this concern which has guided me throughout the present work until now, when we can try to see what it is in Lacan's utterances which does not lend itself to Laplanche's inductions.

Obviously, every author has the right to criticize and to innovate, so long as he makes it clear what belongs to him and what he is borrowing from elsewhere.

Perhaps Laplanche's only error is to have sinned by omission in this necessary redistribution.

When Laplanche tries to define what puts a stop to the primary process in conscious language and what accounts for certain effects of meaning in our discourse, he neglects Lacan's trenchant position in this domain.

According to Lacan, the limit of the perpetual sliding of the signifier over the signified, which he also calls 'Frege's paradox', cannot be reduced to a phenomenon of inter-human understanding. As he told me in our recorded conversation of December 1969, what is habitually called comprehension is not the positive outcome of an initial misunderstanding, but rather the success of that misunderstanding. To be more precise, what one notices in the discourse of the other, what is to be understood, is the mistake itself, a mistake which is meant not to be resolved.

'The more closely one grasps things, the more clearly one sees that, somewhere in the discourse made by the other, there is a mistake in the agreed usage of the signs.' As one looks for terms which conform more closely to a truth which cannot be reached, since it is of the order of the Real, one notices that something 'arranged in a certain manner operates in a more satisfactory way, has a positive result, but still leaves out what one does not understand: the Real'.

Such assertions are obviously connected with (i) Lacan's philosophy concerning the division between knowledge and truth; and (ii) the status of the human subject as apprehended in the psychoanalytic experience. The 'I' of discourse is no more than the indicative of the speaking subject: it designates the subject of the enunciation without being able to signify it. As we saw above, this is a 'fading' effect.

Lacan has however put forward a theory of the 'anchoring point', a hypothesis relative to the essentially mythical join between signifier and signified.

He makes it clear (Seminar 22/1/1958, Archives de la SFP) that no one has ever been able to pin a signification on a signifier in a definitive way. If one attempts to do so, one in fact merely succeeds in pinning another signifier on to the first signifier, thus giving rise to a new signification and so on.

One could then go through the entire dictionary in thought without ever emerging into the real, this being the final signified one is looking for.

As Lacan says in 'On a question preliminary to any possible treatment of psychosis' (23), if it is articulated in the *synchrony* of language, the anchoring point does bring us back to the source of language in the child, but without ever rejoining the Real. With the first metaphorical attribution, such as that whereby the child disconnects the thing from its name, the animal from its cry, etc., the division between real and symbolic, between thought and signifier, is established without any possible return. If we refer now to the level of the sentence, the anchoring point has its role here too, a role which, according to Lacan, is still mythical. Here the anchoring point comes into play in *diachrony*, through a principle of recurrence.

The sentence, says Lacan, only closes its signification with its last term, each of the terms being anticipated in the construction of those going before, and its meaning being sealed only by the retroactive effect of the terms following it.

> The diachronic function of this anchoring point is to be found in the sentence, even if the sentence completes its signification only with its last term, each term being anticipated in the construction of the others and, inversely, sealing their meaning by its retroactive effect. But the synchronic structure is more hidden and it is this structure that takes us to the source. It is metaphor in so far as the first attribution is constituted in it . . . by which the child, by disconnecting the animal from its cry, suddenly raises the sign to the function of the signifier, and reality to the sophistics of signification. (*Écrits*, 27)

To come back to Laplanche, we can now state that the Lacanian notion of the anchoring point does not lend itself to the thesis that the metaphoric-metonymic padding of our language has its deepest roots in the unconscious.

Even in so far as it is possible to go back, in the synchrony of language, from metaphor to metaphor, from signifier to signifier, one does not, if one follows Lacan, arrive at the elementary signifiers of the *unconscious* or at any other functional psychoanalytic term. At best, one arrives at the source of 'learned' language.

It seems that for Lacan the double inscription principle works at every level, in every layer of learned language superimposed upon the unconscious, right back to the initial inscription of language. This principle must therefore be at work in primal repression, which must, then, include in its workings the distinction between the unconscious and everyday language.

Let us see what quotations from Lacan (cf. the summary of our conversation of December 1969 in the appendix) can be used as a basis for a critique of Laplanche.

My statement that the unconscious has the structure of a language positively cannot be understood other than in accordance with what I was saying a moment ago, namely that language is the condition of the unconscious.

The unconscious is purely and simply a discourse and it is as such that it necessitates the theory of the double inscription. This is proved by the fact that there may be two completely different inscriptions, although they operate on and are supported by the *same signifiers*, which simply turn their battery, their apparatus, in order to occupy topographically different places. For, in any case, these inscriptions are strictly dependent upon the site of their support. That a certain significant formation be at one level or the other is exactly what will ensure it of a different import in the chain as a whole.

If, then, we wish to conform to Lacan's directions, we must retain the hypothesis of the double inscription at every level and stress conditioning by language as regards the unconscious.

This being so, there can, as far as I am concerned, be only one way of conceiving of primal repression. Even so, I advance this hypothesis with many reservations.

According to the thesis proper to Leclaire (48, p. 162, n. 3) – and which seems more acceptable to Lacan – the psychical representative of the (imaginary) instinct sinks into the unconscious under the effect of the countercathexis of some elementary phoneme – the O and A, for example, relate to a traumatic lived experience in the imaginary. But at the same time and quite apart from their private unconscious meaning, these phonemes seem to me to be able to designate the concept 'gone' for the word *Fort* and the concept 'here' for the word *Da* in the child's conscious and verbal interrelational system.

The latter signifiers are intercalated into the midst of others, into the midst of the first stammerings of everyday learned language, and it is precisely the presence of this conventional unconscious context which thrusts the traumatic signification back into the unconscious and keeps it there.

My hypothesis concerns the level of the mythical join between the signifier and the imaginary, between conscious language and the unconscious.

The metaphoric process which subsequently comes into action with the first secondary repressions, installs the first truly linguistic signifiers in the unconscious. With every secondary repression, the repressed signifier is reduplicated in accordance with the double inscription principle. Every repressed presentation, that is, may be conscious and unconscious at the same time; conscious in that it is a term in the language of everyday life, and unconscious in that it is a conflictual element which goes to rejoin the interrelational network of the unconscious elements.

The reader must forgive the extremely mythical nature of this formulation. But in order to do justice to the precisions on Laplanche granted by Lacan, it is necessary to venture into the obscure labyrinth of the installation of the unconscious.

Lacan does not in fact attempt a detailed explanation of the process of primal repression and the interconnected establishment of the unconscious and of language. He limits himself to summary indications and statements of a general order, such as:

> The reduplication which discourse provokes is what Freud calls *Urverdrängung*.
> For a minimal composition of the battery of signifiers suffices to install in the signifying chain a duplicity which overlaps with its reduplication of the subject, and it is this reduplication of the subject of speech that the unconscious as such finds the means to articulate itself. (*Écrits*, 26)

But if these statements are related to others, such as:

> Language is the logical implication of the unconscious, the second inscription being verified by the simultaneous presence of the same signifier in different contexts,

they do sometimes allow the construction of an explanatory hypothesis – which cannot of course itself be attributed to Lacan.

On the whole, and perhaps he is right to do so, Lacan systematically drops any question which cannot be referred back to experience. The problem of the join between the imaginary and language, of the division to be made between conscious and unconscious language, are themes which he leaves in suspense and open to any hypothesis.

To return to my personal conception of the problem. The establishment of learned language is effected through a process comparable to that of primal repression in psychoanalysis as described by Laplanche and Leclaire. The process cannot, however, be said to be the same, at least in its function, as it establishes a different language.

As linguistics shows, learned language, the language which is a vehicle for our thoughts, is built upon metaphor and metonymy.

Everything in it holds together by connexions of contiguity and similarity. What is at the same time betrayed and neglected by it is, first, the Real and, second, the exact nature of the lived or thought experience. Our language merely represents things and it does so imperfectly and incompletely.

At the source of conventional language, which can be observed in the child who is learning to talk, it is possible for certain signs to take on a personal signification and a psychoanalytic context. At this moment, as I see it, these signs of the language are about to undergo repression, but still persist in everyday language without the burden of their traumatic charge. As the Freudian description of repression appears to indicate, the instinctual cathexis which the subject withdraws from one idea is transposed by countercathexis to another (this is the symptom) and the initial traumatic idea is decathected. This means that it can remain an integral part of conscious language, as its emotional charge has been transposed elsewhere. The idea in question is, however, at the same time cast into the unconscious in so far as it still carries the eternal mark of the traumatic lived experience, despite the countercathexis which displaces its emotional charge.

The example given in the preceding chapter of the repression of 'father' by little Hans seems to be a good illustration of this point of view. But we could also take the example suggested by Laplanche to illustrate his theses in the article which is the object of this discussion.

Thus, for me, the fixation in a child's unconscious of an elementary signifier like *Lili*, *corne* or *corps* [Lily, horn or body], to take the examples given by Laplanche, is simultaneous with the inscription of the 'same' signifiers in consciousness. The latter, however, have a completely different function, which is quite devoid of psychoanalytic resonances; they are inscribed in a succession of terms belonging to everyday language: the body of a subject, a woman's body, my body, etc. . . . The cow's horn, the horny skin on the foot, etc.

Certain words have at first a personal meaning for the child and the normal meaning of these terms, allied with other signifiers, is grafted on to this.

It therefore seems impossible to me to connect the fixity of signification in the secondary process of thought with the elementary signifiers of the unconscious as Laplanche does, even if these same signifiers are inscribed both in consciousness and in the unconscious.

I would be more inclined to say that the 'stability' of the terms of language, 'especially' in so far as they can refer back through psychoanalytic association to lived experiences relating to complexes in childhood, is due to the maintenance of the unconscious as a radically separate and censored domain.

In schizophrenia, for example, one can see that the lifting of the bar of censorship separating consciousness from the unconscious occasions a total confusion between conscious and unconscious language, between primary process and secondary process. Here it is a question of an invasion of life by the private sphere.

That there is a certain adequation of signifiers to the conceptual signifieds they designate is also, I think, due to a learned and conventional montage of terms: the superimposition of an inter-personal traditional and universal lived experience on to the personal lived experience.

Here we find a conception dear to Lacan: the signifier and the symbolic impose themselves on man from the outside, fashion him and direct him in an intersubjective social world in conformity with the laws and norms of that world.

In direct opposition to Laplanche's theory that the unconscious is the condition for language, Lacan says moreover that language is the condition for the unconscious, that it creates and gives rise to the unconscious.

By superimposing laws and rules as a superstructure, language maintains the unconscious as a separate domain.

Lacan introduces his fundamental and radical principle of division at several levels. First, at the level of conscious language, he introduces a division between signifier and signified, between signifier and thought.

Psychoanalytically speaking, this level of division separates the designatory 'I' from the designated 'I', the qualities one gives oneself from the qualities one has.

Second, the separating line comes into play between conscious language and unconscious language. This line is extremely mobile in the sense that the subject can progressively go back to what he is as unconscious. This is the meaning given by Lacan to Freud's 'Wo Es war, soll Ich werden', which he interprets as follows:

> There where it was just now, there where it was for a while,
> between an extinction that is still glowing and a birth that is
> retarded 'I' can come into being and disappear from what I say.
> An enunciation that denounces itself, a statement that renounces
> itself. . . .
>   Being of non-being, that is how 'I' as subject comes on to the
> scene, conjugated with the double aporia of a true survival that
> is abolished by knowledge of itself and by a discourse in which it
> is death that sustains existence.   (*Écrits*, 27)

Lacan places the third separating line between the elementary signifiers of the unconscious and the subject's imaginary, which precedes his entry into language.

One could even say that a fourth separating line exists for the subject: that which divides the physiological subject from the subject captive to the imaginary.

That margin beyond life that language gives to the human being by virtue of the fact that he speaks, and which is precisely that in which such a being places in the position of a signifier, not only those parts of his body that are exchangeable, but this body itself. . . .

This apologia hardly exaggerates the little physiology that is of interest to the unconscious. (*Écrits*, 27)

To go on with the critique of Laplanche's statements in 'The unconscious: a psychoanalytic study' (48).

In his concern to resolve Frege's paradox, Laplanche tries to establish the existence of a 'ballast', something which definitively fixes the signifier to the signified, rather like the weight in the hold which stops the ship pitching too much on the waves, to adopt a metaphor used by Lacan himself (41).

According to Laplanche, this ballast is the unconscious signifying chain.

In so far as it is a figurative representation of primal repression, the formula for metaphor does in fact allow the existence of an elementary signifying chain to be inferred. But Laplanche makes this inference – and this is the source of his error – by applying the procedure of mathematical substitution to the formula for metaphor given in 'On a question preliminary to any possible treatment of psychosis' (23).

In his personal communication of December 1969, Lacan makes it clear that he uses his metaphoric formula to didactic ends alone, as a symbol. One therefore cannot bring out all its mathematical consequences.

We should repeat here how unreasonable it seems from the outset to use the play of fractions and simplifications in a formula dealing with something human.

Beginning with the Lacanian formula for metaphor:

$$\frac{S'}{s} \cdot \frac{s}{x} \to S\left(\frac{1}{s}\right)$$

Laplanche ends up with

$$\frac{\dfrac{S'}{s}}{\dfrac{S}{S}}$$

Laplanche obtains this formulation, which Lacan calls 'quite unthinkable', by permitting himself the mathematical substitution:

$$\frac{A}{B} \times \frac{C}{D} = \frac{\dfrac{A}{D}}{\dfrac{B}{C}}$$

Lacan considers this mathematical transformation inadequate because it makes the mistake of turning the 'separating' line into mere lines in a fraction, and in doing so obviously arrives at the idea of a close inter-action between the unconscious and preconscious-conscious. Because of this short-circuit, Laplanche can advance the thesis that the un-conscious, i.e. $\frac{S}{S}$, is responsible for the connexion existing in the con-scious between S' and s.

This mathematical substitution also allows one to make a representation of the nature of the signifiers in the unconscious. They have, says Laplanche, the status of images: they are as much signifiers as they are signifieds and it is this merging of signifier and signified that is re-sponsible for the sliding of mental energy in the unconscious in accord-ance with the primary process.

Lacan, for his part, makes absolutely no pronouncements as to the nature of the signifiers in the unconscious or to the status acquired there by language. He contents himself with saying that an unconscious signifier is radically distinct from a conscious signifier even if it is formally identical and that the difference arises from the context into which the signifier is inserted.

It is impossible to know exactly how language functions at the level of the unconscious. We can know unconscious language only through its returns into consciousness. It reveals to analysis a looser organization which is, however, comparable on certain points (metaphoric and metonymic processes) to that of conscious language.

Another topical question is that of 'who' articulates unconscious langu-age. If, for Lacan, the unconscious is a discourse, the grammatical person in which it is elaborated remains to be determined.

By virtue of the principle of psychical unity, we are obliged to recognize that it is always the subject who speaks in the unconscious. But to what person?

In 'The agency of the letter in the unconscious' (22), Lacan denounces the philosophical prejudices which, in the 'cogito ergo sum', for example, have united being and conscious thought or even being and the reflection of consciousness upon itself: I think that I think, there-fore I am. To remain at this point is, of course, to deny oneself all access to the Freudian revolution. For Lacan, 'the question is whether I "am" as the subject of the signifier rather than of the unconscious' under the pretext that I dispose of a reflective power on this 'being'.

Freud's discovery, Lacan points out, obliges us to recognize that 'I think where I am not by thought, therefore I am where I do not think'. Furthermore, this formula leads us to see that I 'am' more surely there where 'I' do not 'think'. The contents of the unconscious form the very heart of our being.

It is clear, then, that knowing exactly in which person the unconscious subject thinks is a preoccupation of relative importance, as it is rather a question of recognizing a 'surplus being' in this unconscious.

One should still be suspicious of this 'being'. If it is simply a question of a mode of presence of human unity, then the problem is resolved, but what is to be understood by 'being'? A being of flesh and blood, of life, of thought? Or is 'being' simply a mode of presence?

To turn to the question of the person in which the subject speaks in the unconscious; in his Preface to the present book, Lacan suggests the image of 'the innumerable "I"' whose relation to unity is one of recurrence'.

The unconscious is what the 'I' was in the successive moments of the history of its division. The unconscious is the other of myself which sends my own message back to me in an inverted form.

The unconscious is the recurrent 'I' in Freud's 'Wo Es war, soll Ich werden'.

It is becoming clear that there is no place in Lacan's view of the problem of the nature of unconscious language for a philosophical search for a 'grammatical' articulation of language, for a privileged status for signifier or signified.

As Lacan acknowledges, there is, however, a certain final efficiency in one point in Laplanche's reasoning.

Despite the errors he has made, his follower does in Lacan's opinion arrive at one very valuable idea, namely the idea that there exists an unconscious chain of elementary signifiers of the phoneme or group of phonemes type.

> In this connexion, Lacan tells us that: If one omits the radical difference in aim which vitiates Laplanche's whole utterance, one cannot say that the idea of a minimum signifying battery is bad simply because it makes use of my utterances concerning the linguistic apparatus as I inherit it from Saussure. This idea has in it something of a premonition of the way in which I will later expand this Saussurian reference. He simply short-circuits the expansion by hurrying it. The short-circuit can be seen in a certain puerility in the handling of the formula I give for repression in so far as it is connected with the structure of metaphor. (41)

To turn now to a further implication of Laplanche's article – one of the most difficult implications to deal with.

According to Laplanche's logic, the hypothesis of the ballast of an elementary signifying chain in the unconscious accounts for the passage from primary process to secondary process (as Laplanche intends it to do) only on condition that one also assumes a fixed and stable binding of the instinct to a representative.

But it is precisely on the 'fixing' of the instinct to 'a' representative that Lacan's criticism will now be concentrated.

In accordance with the above logical demand (the binding of the instinct to a representative), Laplanche finds himself obliged to re-duplicate the process of primal repression.

In a first movement, he says, significant oppositions are cast over the subjective universe without any one signifier being bound in a stable manner to a particular signified. The signifying system introduced is simply parallel to the subjective lived experience of difference.

The second movement, however – and it is this which really creates the unconscious in accordance with the process of metaphor – is the movement of countercathexis or the substitution of S' for the earlier S.

This has the effect of definitively fixing this S to the lived experience, to the instinct (or even to the subjective, to the imaginary).

With this fixation, still according to Laplanche, the previous fluctuation of the first dichotomous signifiers comes to an end, as does their overlapping of one another, and the external world is ordered into stable dichotomies in the mind.

With reference to the above, we should in passing point out the note on p. 162 [of the article under discussion (48)] in which Leclaire and Laplanche, its two authors, indicate their differences.

Unlike Laplanche, Leclaire recognizes primal repression itself as early as the first movement of the constitution of the unconscious.

Leclaire's reservations are, as it happens, important, as they put him out of reach of Lacan's criticisms.

If, as Leclaire thinks, primal repression itself is not in fact effected in accordance with the mechanism of metaphor, if it consists simply of the establishment of a parallelism between oppositional signifiers and differentiated lived experiences, then strictly speaking there is no 'fixing' of the signifier to the signified, of the signifier to the instinct. Nor is there any possible limit, at this level, to the primary process. And the reasons for the interlocking of the secondary process and conscious language must be sought elsewhere.

According to Leclaire's views, when secondary repression proceeds for its part to a metaphoric substitution of S' for S, it is merely actualizing the possible paths of the return of the repressed, without these paths being traced in a definitive fashion.

Let us clarify Leclaire's position by means of an example. If O and A are the first opposed signifiers to fill in the instinctual *béance* (gap), and if *Fort* and *Da* are the S' substituted for the previous S by secondary repression, then the instinctual appeal for renewed maternal presence could make its way into consciousness by way of the *Fort* as easily as by the *Da*, since, in Leclaire's view, O is not strictly bound to the instinct of lack and A is not strictly bound to the appeal for presence.

Lacan himself has no conception of a fixed binding together of one signifier and one signifier at any level of language, be it conscious or unconscious.

In his own words:

> The drawing (the formula for metaphor as transformed by Laplanche) certainly gives one the feeling of attaining something, the feeling that the unconscious might be the condition of language. The function of the ballast, which is in the hold of the boat in order to prevent it pitching too much, would devolve upon the signifier at the level of the unconscious. This metaphor may provide an image, it may give a reflection of what experience confronts us with, but surely it is quite incapable of accounting for the dissociative, if not explosive, effect of the return of the repressed. (41)

And,

> Once the structure of language has been recognized in the unconscious, what sort of subject can we conceive for it? We can try to set out from the strictly linguistic definition of the 'I' as signifier, in which there is nothing but the 'shifter' or indicative, which, in the subject of the statement, designates the subject in the sense that he is now speaking.
>
> That is to say, it designates the subject of the enunciation, but it does not signify it. (*Écrits*, 27)

In other passages of his *Écrits*, Lacan goes even further. Not only is the unconscious signifier incapable of signifying the subject of truth exactly; what lies before the unconscious is not, strictly speaking, the 'instinct', nor is it the physiological or the biological. What lies before the unconscious as a language is the subjective, the imaginary, and what lies before the imaginary is unthinkable. Everything one could say about what lies before the imaginary belongs to myth. The field of psychoanalysis begins with the psychical, with language, and, what is more difficult, with the imaginary. As Lacan told me, in psychoanalysis, the wish to constantly push back the barriers of the unknown arises from 'anxiety at leaving things in suspense' and runs a great risk of making mistakes. For truth is incommensurable with the order of thought and language.

The frequent use of the term 'instinct', for example, is, according to Lacan, to be explained precisely by the difficulty of grasping what lies before the unconscious discourse and what lies before the imaginary. We therefore content ourselves with a general term: instinct.

The best way to get some idea of what, according to Lacan, it is in the human subject that enters into a relationship with language in primal repression and to see what he imagines as lying before the elementary signifiers of the unconscious is to describe his *myth* of human genesis from birth onwards.

In his intervention at the Bonneval conference (38), Lacan suggests an illuminating and attractive image of the beginnings of human life and the way in which what we normally call instinct takes shape.

The new-born child, he says, makes one think of the androgynes described by Aristophanes in Plato's *Symposium*, or at least the state in which they were left after the division imposed on them by Zeus.

With the cutting of the umbilical cord, the new-born child, like the androgynes, finds itself separated from a part of itself, torn from the mother's internal membranes. Birth causes it to lose its anatomical complement.

The *infans*, Lacan goes on, is like a broken egg which spreads out in the form of an *hommelette* [a portmanteau word meaning both 'little man' and 'omelette' (trans.)]. Allusion is made here to the instinct as it can be represented in its origins.

To prevent the *hommelette* invading everything and destroying everything in its path, it must be enclosed, it must be assigned limits.

The libido, the instinct, will be maintained within corporea llimits and will henceforth be unable to flow completely other than by way of 'erotogenic zones', which are rather like valves opening towards and by the outside.

As Lacan makes it clear (27), the delimitation of the erotogenic zone has the effect of canalizing the libido (or functional metabolism) and transforming it into a 'partial instinct'. The erotogenic zone is a cut or aperture inscribed in a suitable anatomical site: for example, the lips, the gap between the teeth, the edges of the anus, the tip of the penis, the vagina, the palpebral slit.

Limited and canalized in this way, the libido never appears in its entirety in the subjective world and a good part of it is lost. The permanent human feeling of dissatisfaction and incompleteness is therefore to be 'mythically' explained by the separation the child undergoes at birth.

Lacan stresses that the idea of unlimited libido is of the order of myth, but that the instinct, on the other hand, can be known to us by its site in an erotogenic zone or in a letter (we will see the meaning of this more clearly later) and by its being bound up with an imaginary object.

Unlimited libido may be that which precedes the psychical; it does not belong within the domain of psychoanalysis. It is part of the unknown dimension of truth and cannot be the object of any knowledge.

It is that part of the living which is lost by virtue of accession to that beyond of life – the imaginary and the symbolic.

On the other hand, this original loss will be represented in the psyche, in the imaginary – and here we leave the plane of myth – by an image of the anatomical cut or aperture, or by the imaginary presentation of the erotogenic zone, by what Leclaire calls the 'letter'.

From this time onwards, instinctual dynamism will give weight to various external objects capable of closing the *béance* of being. But these objects are themselves imaginary, because, primitively, they merge with the subjective lived experience.

At this stage the child is in the state of what Freud calls primary narcissism and his possible instinctual satisfaction is auto-erotic.

Furthermore, once a sufficient objective criterion – which dissociates pleasant and unpleasant objects – allows the child a certain recognition of the inside and the outside, the object is immediately 'introjected' or 'projected' into the outside, depending upon whether it is pleasant or unpleasant to the child.

We are still, therefore, in the realm of the imaginary, as perception of a pleasant object is immediately followed by introjection of that object.

Parallel to this first look at the genesis of the imaginary object of the instinct, we will for a while follow the transformations of the instinct itself.

The sexual instincts are at first supported by the instincts of preservation and only gradually detach themselves from them. In their transformations, the instincts follow the destiny of the instinctual object. The object is brought in from the outside to satisfy the instincts of preservation, and it is only gradually that such objects take on an erotic quality.

Freud also says that the sexual instincts are numerous, arise from different organic sources and have as their common aim the obtaining of organ pleasure.

Let us now go back to the objects of the instinct. In the same commentary at the Bonneval conference (38), Lacan tells us that these propose themselves from the outside as substitutes for the lost anatomical complement, as images capable of filling in the lack and re-establishing the lost connexion.

As a part object (relating to the mother) bound to the oral erotogenic zone, the breast is the first object of the instinct.

Lacan insists that a feature common to all such objects is that they have no otherness. 'They are the lining, the stuff or the imaginary thickness of the subject himself who identifies with them' (41).

Before the 'subject-object' there is nothing but a *béance*, a void, the −1 of total libido. Before these objects, there can be nothing consistent, as what they replace is the 'myth' of placentary unity.

At this point, Lacan articulates what we can call the first break, the first division between signifier and signified. This break is the most radical, as it is impossible, unless we resort to the power of myth, to pin down what lies before the imaginary, before the identificatory relation with the object.

With his entry into the imaginary, the child sanctions his death as a totality and as a truth. The subject is cut off from himself, represented and alienated in his representation: the image of the ego-object.

The phenomenon of this initial cut is constantly revived in the course of subjective experience, firstly by weaning and later by castration. Hence the 'metonymic course' of the instinct as it constantly tries to make up for the original loss by means of some substitute.

Each instinctual object is from its origin placed under the symbolic sign of the Phallus, the irreplaceable signifier of the hyphen of possible union with completeness.

At a stage of greater maturity in the ensuing development, the play of introjection and projection relative to the instinctual object will be replaced by the process of identification. But this is still a phenomenon connected with the imaginary.

Everything we have so far explained in the evolution of the object relation is synthesized by Lacan in the definition he gives of object (a). What is this object, where is it situated? It is as much object of lack as introjected part object; it is at once the mythical object of lack, which is out of reach, and its imaginary psychical substitute. It is not distinct from the ego which introjects it or identifies with it.

As an image, it endures in the psyche and is favourable to the development of thought. It is always present in that fundamental moment in which the child articulates himself with language.

When, in the subsequent development of the child, aural and visual perception become more refined, object (a) gradually becomes attached to the outside world. Finally, it becomes linked in the mind with phonemes; this is primal repression. The representative of the presentation (*Vorstellungsrepräsentanz*), in Lacan's translation (*représentant de la représentation*), can then undergo secondary repression.

At this stage, there is actualized what we can see as the second cut, which Lacan calls *Spaltung*. Then comes the Splitting, the process of the alienation of the subject in a signifier incapable of signifying him.

And the circle of human development is drawn as we recognize in Splitting the third signifying division to be observed in Lacan, that which disjoins the signifier and the signified in conscious language and renders the former more and more unsuitable for signifying the unconscious subject in any way.

Perhaps the three significant breaks which we have distinguished in the course of the subject's development quite simply correspond to the great moments of a permanent division in man. These great turning points of life correspond to the three essential phases of castration: (i) birth, (ii) the true castration complex in the Oedipus, (iii) the alienation of the subject in the word.

In each of these divisions, the determinant intervention of a typically human mode of organization manifests itself, be it the imaginary, language or constraining social organization. Man's alienating division is, then, simply a fact of human nature, as that which divides him is also that which makes him man.

It remains for our Lacanian critique of the article 'The unconscious: a psychoanalytic study' (48) to envisage – very briefly – the problem of the double inscription as Lacan sees it. We will do so succinctly, as the preceding development has adequately shown that, for Lacan, the problem is resolved by topography, by division. We have in any case given a fair indication as to the Lacanian solution in the preceding chapter.

In one of the interviews he granted me (41), Lacan resolved the problem with a statement which may be reconstituted as follows: the unconscious is a discourse, a language which is different from conscious language. It is gradually fashioned by metaphoric repressions. Metaphor substitutes another signifier S' for the repressed signifier S. The signifier S, on the other hand, can, although repressed in the unconscious, still remain conscious, but it will in that case be totally different from the signifier S of the unconscious; simply because it is integrated into a different context, the import of this signifier changes completely. Thus, to use the example developed in chapter 8, in his phobia little Hans substitutes the signifier 'horse' for his father. The signifier 'father' is, because of repression, present in both the unconscious and in consciousness. But it has a completely different function in conscious language. Lacan puts it more precisely:

> There may be a totally different inscription of the same signifier in consciousness and in the unconscious. These inscriptions are the same on the plane of the signifier, but they are, on the other hand, different in that they turn their battery to occupy topographically different places. That a certain significant formation be at one level or another is precisely what will ensure it a different import in the chain as a whole.

Lacan then suggests a metaphor of a number of hieroglyphs on the face of an obelisk; the fact that they are displaced from one side to another completely changes the meaning of the text.

This metaphor is closely related to that given by Lacan in his article 'La science et la vérité' (33):

> The question [of the double inscription] is not posed in theory alone, for all that it provoked the perplexity wherein my pupils Laplanche and Leclaire could have read its solution in their schism as they approached the problem. In any case, it is not of the gestaltist type, nor is it to be sought in the plate where Napoleon's head is inscribed in the tree. It lies, quite simply, in the fact that the inscription does not bite into the same side of the parchment when it comes from the plate that prints truth and the plate that prints knowledge. That these inscriptions mingle was simply to be resolved by topography: a surface in which right and wrong side are in a state to be joined everywhere was within hand's reach.

We have come to the end of what might well be called theoretical rectifications.

The remainder of the text studies in greater depth the unconscious and what lies before it. Essentially, it will be concerned with the inscription of a 'letter' in the imaginary and with the inscription of the elementary signifiers of the unconscious.

PART FIVE

The elementary signifiers constituting the unconscious

TEN

The unconscious as second structure

In their article, 'The unconscious: a psychoanalytic study' (48), mentioned in Chapter 9, Laplanche and Leclaire point out that the concept of the unconscious has been modified since Freud. G. Politzer is at the origin of this 'denaturing' of the unconscious. Since the appearance of the *Critique des fondements de la psychologie* (104), it has been possible to distinguish two notions of the unconscious, the more popular notion – that of Politzer – being precisely the less Freudian.

The problematic could be posed in the terms: *Is the unconscious a meaning or a letter?* The whole problem of the realism of the unconscious is thus brought into question. As a letter, the unconscious is a distinct entity interpolated on the basis of the lacunae in conscious discourse and made up of another discourse which groups the complements of these lacunary points together in another site.

As a meaning, the unconscious is, on the contrary, the meaning of everything the subject says. In the dream, for example – and this is the originality of the Politzerian conception – there is only one 'content'. The manifest is a story in an unconventional language; the unconscious is its meaning, but this meaning has no existence in itself. *Translated into the manifest, the unconscious thoughts no longer exist in themselves and, conversely, the manifest does not exist in itself when it is returned to the unconscious.*

The relationship between manifest and latent in Politzer's thesis can be conceived as being like that between a play and its theme, or between a game of tennis and the rules of the game. Politzer provides an illustrative example taken from the *Traumdeutung*: in the dream of Irma's injection, the sore throat in the manifest may be translated as 'I hope for an error in diagnosis.' The translation explains the manifest formula, just as 'pater' explains the French word *père* and just as jealousy explains Othello's action.

Politzer adds the critique of 'abstraction' to this critique of what he calls 'the realism of the unconscious'. According to Politzer, Freud has failed in his attempt to relate psychical phenomena, such as the dream, to a first person drama. By invoking the instance of the 'id', Freud falls back to the level of an abstract entity whose play is identical to that of a mechanism.

The reply made to Politzer by Laplanche, and by Lacanians in general, is that latent dream-thoughts can be seen as a discourse 'in person', without necessarily being in the first person. It is characteristic of unconscious structures to include voices other than that of the first person: the unconscious discourse could, for example, take place in the alienated form of the second or third persons.

In this connexion C. Stein reveals a certain reluctance to admit that an unconscious discourse could take place in the form of grammatical persons (113).

We can see that the solution put forward by the Lacanians is no more than a simple hypothesis; were it to be invalidated one day, this would not, I think, necessarily imply going back to Politzer.

We are already acquainted with Lacan's own point of view, as this is expressed in his Preface.

The unconscious is a discourse which was pronounced in person and above all in the first person. It has very probably undergone modifications through repression and through the work of censorship during its return to consciousness, and undergoes further modifications at the hands of the only conceptual categories we possess. It is therefore difficult to know what its nature is. The unconscious is, however, integrated into the totality of the person and contains the acts and thoughts of the 'I' throughout its history. To reduce it to the status of an abstract mechanism is the result of the philosophical prejudice which forbids us to conceive our individual 'being' outside the verbal and grammatical articulation of the 'I'. And this prejudice indicates the extent to which we remain prisoners to the determinism of a conventional learned language which is in reality no more than an artificial superstructure of our total being, a means for its expression.

Politzer's theory has also had a serious impact upon analytic practice. It allows a suspicion of inexactness to weigh on the totality of the patient's discourse; every act and every word is capable of dissimulating a hidden meaning and is no more than material to be translated into terms of pathology. The Lacanian conception, according to which the unconscious consists of signifiers which are repressed and replaced by others at the level of consciousness, also flows over into analytic practice. But here psychoanalysis practises a planned and diffuse listening and stresses only certain points in the discourse, points known as 'nodal points' which are particularly dense or, on the contrary, essentially lacunary (forgetting of names, slips of the tongue, enigmatic signifiers). Free association around these particular elements allows the unconscious text which complements the nodal points to be recovered.

In Lacan's thought, then, *the unconscious is a second structure.*

It is interpolated on the basis of the nodal points in the patient's discourse, to which the analyst lends an evenly suspended global attention. It is composed of fragments of discourse which allow a coherent sequence to be established in conscious discourse.

Since Freud, the unconscious has been a chain of signifiers that somewhere (on another stage, in another scene, he wrote) is repeated, and insists on interfering in the breaks offered it by an affective discourse and the cogitation that informs it.

(*Écrits*, 27)

The unconscious is also a letter, another lettered system which insinuates itself into conscious discourse, propelling itself through the lacunae in that discourse. These lacunae are to be found in what Lacan designates the formations of the unconscious: dreams, mistakes, absentmindedness, jokes, etc.

The most exhaustive description of the unconscious given by Lacan is as follows:

The unconscious is that part of the concrete discourse, in so far as it is transindividual, that is not at the disposition of the subject to re-establish the continuity of his conscious discourse.
The unconscious is that chapter of my history that is marked by a blank or occupied by a falsehood: it is the censored chapter.

But, Lacan continues, the truth can be rediscovered:

. . . usually it has already been written down elsewhere. Namely:
– in monuments: this is my body, the hysterical symptom reveals the structure of a language and is deciphered like an inscription;
– in archival documents: childhood memories;
– in semantic evolution: my particular vocabulary;
– in traditions and legends which, in a heroicized form, bear my history;
– in the traces that are preserved by the distortions necessitated by the linking of the adulterated chapter to the chapters surrounding it. (*Écrits*, 16)

In his very rich article, 'La réalité du désir' (42), Leclaire suggests various comparisons which facilitate our representation of the unconscious as second structure. We will close this chapter by quoting Leclaire who so often, I am happy to acknowledge, has the last word when it comes to solving difficulties:

The unconscious is not the ground which has been prepared to give more sparkle and depth to the painted composition: it is the earlier sketch which has been covered over before the canvas is used for another picture. If we use a comparison of a musical order, the unconscious is not the counterpoint of a fugue or the harmonics of a melodic line: it is the jazz one hears despite oneself behind the Haydn quartet when the radio is badly tuned or not sufficiently selective. The unconscious is not the message, not even the strange or coded message one strives to read on an old parchment: *it is another text written underneath and which must be read by illuminating it from behind or with the help of a developer.*

ELEVEN

The elementary signifiers of the unconscious

I suggest that we begin this chapter with the detailed analysis of a dream: the 'unicorn dream' of an obsessional in his thirties – Philippe. Philippe was a patient of Leclaire's and the analysis of the dream is taken from various publications by that author, notably (48). Leclaire also talks about it in 'La réalité du désir' (42), and in his book, *Psych-analyser, essai sur l'ordre de l'inconscient et la pratique de la lettre* (55). Here is the manifest story of the unicorn dream:

> The deserted square of a small town. I am looking for something. Liliane – whom I do not know – appears barefoot and says to me, 'It's a long time since I saw such fine sand.'
>
> We are in a forest and the trees seem peculiarly coloured in bright simple shades. I think that there must be a lot of animals in this forest, and just as I am about to say so, a unicorn crosses our path. All three of us walk towards a clearing we can see below us.

We are acquainted with the Freudian theory that the dream is the fulfilment of a wish.

According to the patient, he woke up shortly afterwards, feeling very thirsty. It is probable that at the moment the dream vanished the three of them were going to drink in the clearing. The dream therefore satisfies a need to drink.

But we also know that analysis of a dream always unveils a more fundamental wish than that fulfilled in the dream. The dream uses indifferent elements from the previous day in order to allow an unconscious wish to manifest itself through various relations of association (their particular mechanisms – metaphor and metonymy – will be revealed in a later chapter). This unconscious wish may date from childhood or it may be contemporary. Besides, the dream most often fulfils a cascade of older and older wishes, and the apparently anodine wish satisfied by the dream is revealed to be a deviation from or a sublimation of deeper childhood wishes.

What indifferent elements from the previous day are to be found in the manifest text of the dream in our example? Philippe had been for a walk *in the forest* with his niece *Anne*. They had stalked game and, at the bottom of a valley with a stream running through it, they had noticed traces left by *deer* and *does*, indicating one of the places where the animals came to drink. Anne said, '*It's a long time since I saw such bright heather.*'

The analytic technique of free association around the manifest elements also allows three childhood memories to come to light:

(i)   *the square of a small provincial town* with '*unicorn*' fountain and the memory of a summer holiday Philippe spent there when he was about three: he was trying to drink the water that bubbled out of the fountain from the hollow of his cupped hands.

(ii)   a walk in the Swiss mountains which were covered in *bright* heather and *forests*. He tried to imitate an older friend who could make the noise of a siren by putting his hands together in the shape of a conch and blowing through them.

(iii)   a beach on the Atlantic with Lili, a cousin of his mother's, when he was three years old. Throughout this summer month, Philippe kept saying to her in a serious and insistent tone, 'I'm thirsty', to such a point that Lili ended up nicknaming him 'Philippe-I'm-thirsty' (*Philippe-j'ai-soif*), an expression which later became a kind of sign of recognition between them.

Analysis of the dream takes us back, then, to the fundamental declaration 'I'm thirsty' addressed to Lili. Over and above the satisfaction of the real wish to drink, the dream refers back to an unconscious wish to drink, to an oral instinct directed towards Lili.

The instinct introduces an erotic quality into the sphere of need. The instinct as such has no place in the psychical apparatus and only enters into it through the mediation of the *Vorstellungsrepräsentanz* (11, p. 148) or ideational representative. It is upon this representative that the primal repression which establishes the unconscious will work.

In the dream we are dealing with, the representatives of the instinct will be obtained by association. We will underline two examples: the gesture engraved in the unconscious as an image of hands joined together like a conch, an image that will be forever bound up with the oral instinct, and the verbal formula *j'ai soif*, or *j'ai choif*, as the three-year-old Philippe would say.

It is upon Lili, then, that the oral instinct is concentrated. Philippe's wish is to establish a bridge, a link, to hide a crack and at all cost to fill in anything which might evoke castration. The unicorn in the dream is therefore the very realization of this unification, since in the place of a third eye it has a horn (or phallus). In passing, let us recall the legend of the unicorn: it is a difficult animal to capture and only lets itself be caught by a virgin. Then it is easy to master, for, having placed its horn in her lap, it goes to sleep. In this sense, we can say that the unicorn (*licorne*) is the metonymy of Philippe's desire, condensing Lili and horn (*corne*), and realizing the unification of Lili with the horn.

Analysis of this dream shows the way in which unconscious memories of the past use a recent event (the walk in the bright forest with Anne and the allusion to does and deer) to make their way into consciousness and carry the subject's original wish – libidinous union with Lili – into consciousness.

It also reveals the existence of linguistic and other signifiers in the unconscious.

The formula *j'ai choif* and the image of cupped hands are obviously not the only elements in Philippe's unconscious. Leclaire brings out a succession of elements: Lili – beach – thirst – skin – foot – horn – sand – wound – trace – billhook – unicorn. Several of these are strangers to us, as they were deduced from a second dream: the 'billhook' dream, which has a castrating content and from a symptom of Philippe's: the 'grain of sand symptom'. For the patient, being on a beach means having sand everywhere; in his hair, in his teeth, in his ears. If there is only one grain left – in a shoe, for example – it is even more irritating. Hence Philippe's obsessional irritation at any crease, a badly pressed seam, crumbs in the bedclothes, etc. This symptom refers back to skin, foot, sand. And finally this unconscious text also refers back to an earlier phantasy of Philippe's: having invulnerable soles, having feet as hard as horn.

For the sake of detail, we should note in passing that the term 'trace' in the manifest dream refers back to 'of the billhook', and to the scar which Philippe bears in the middle of his forehead. The billhook dream completes and deepens the analysis of the unicorn dream because it shows that the patient is no longer anxious to preserve his position as his mother's chosen one, but, on the contrary, wishes to leave the stifling circle of his mother and, by castration, put an end to her encroachment upon him.

Paradoxically, the thirst therefore represents an appeal for ties to be released rather than an expectancy to be filled by the mother or a substitute for her. It bears witness to the first infantile engulfment, to Philippe's nostalgia, but also to his revolt, to his wish to be liberated.

Thus, the unconscious signifying chain is revealed by analysis of the formations of the unconscious. It consists of signifiers and elements of language which have the peculiarity of escaping from all logic in their combinations. This is shown clearly by the fact that they can associate with other, less unconscious elements (beach – *plage* – is associated with the square – *place* – of the small provincial town), and by the fact that these less unconscious elements will replace them in the manifest, in accordance with a metaphoric process – *place* is substituted for *plage* – or a metonymic process: the bright colours of the trees in the manifest recall the hands joined together to make a conch during the walk in the Swiss mountains by way of connexions of unconscious thoughts.

The unconscious elements therefore obey the primary processes of condensation and displacement which Freud attributes to the unconscious system as opposed to the rational secondary processes specific to the preconscious-consciousness system.

Unconscious language therefore cannot be assimilated to conscious language on a functional plane because *unconscious language* is a language with only one dimension; *it belongs to the imaginary* and the terms composing it can carry their energy over on to other terms by displacement (metonymy) or by condensation (metaphor). It is by these means that the unconscious wish is conveyed into consciousness, passing from one signifier to another along a complex and twisted thread of signifiers.

In passing, it should be recalled that Lacan himself does not make any pronouncements as to the nature of signifiers in the unconscious or as to their being bound or not bound to signifiers of the order of thought.

C. Stein (113) points out that the chain of words which, according to Leclaire, constitutes Philippe's unconscious is in fact at the patient's conscious or preconscious disposal, or at least at the meeting point between preconscious and unconscious. To put it in a different way, words do not seem to him to have any place in the unconscious at its most essential or at least at its most elementary. *The elementary unconscious is composed rather of phonemes* or groups of phonemes which later enter into the composition of words and then into the composition of *unconscious phantasies* whose overall construction constitutes those unconscious strata which are more accessible to analysis. The elementary unconscious is for its part radically inaccessible.

Stein adds that this does not exclude the possibility of there being associative relations between the various stratified layers of the unconscious.

It should be noted that Stein's intervention at this point of theory is in the same vein as the intervention referred to earlier during the discussion of primal repression, the paternal metaphor and the subject's accession to language (Part Three, chapter 7).

Stein expressed some reservations as to the formulation of the primal metaphor put forward by Lacan.

He considered that the terms used were over-elaborated, too general and too specific for a formula whose role is to represent the mechanism of the simultaneous formation of the unconscious and learned language. If, he said, language and the unconscious are elaborated simultaneously in primal repression (in accordance with the mechanism of metaphor), one cannot at the outset evoke the Oedipal problematic within the metaphoric process, as Lacan does, because the child can talk long before the question of the Oedipus arises.

In the event, his solution was simply to point out that the question of desire for the mother is, in one form or another, on the order of the day from the earliest age, as the anecdote of the little boy with the cotton-reel and the string shows (the *Fort–Da* game). For Stein, accession to the symbolic through primal repression and in accordance with the mechanism of metaphor concerns any pair of phonemes connoting the repletion or emptiness of the instinct directing the child towards its mother. In the mechanism as it is described by Stein, the instinctual representatives (the phonemes) are denied entry to consciousness and are, together with the instinct, fixed in the unconscious, which is itself constituted by the same process. These phonemes, Stein continues, will later find their place in a fragment of discourse and then in a phantasy.

As we shall see in a moment, Leclaire accepts Stein's hypothesis without any reservations. Accordingly, in the case of Philippe, he undertakes a minute analysis of the elements of the unconscious which lie beneath the phonemes.

Before following him in his reflections, we should note that there is a quite identical intuition in Lacan. His seminars on the formations of the unconscious, his article, 'Subversion of the subject' (27), which is essential to this point, and his statements in the interview (41) reveal a conformity of inspiration.

In an addition to his article (48), Leclaire proclaims his agreement with Stein.

It is indeed the phonemes which fix the instinctual commotion and become, *among others*, the first representatives of the instinct. I say 'among others' because the *language elements are reduplicated by visual*, coenaesthetic, tactile and olfactory impressions in the form of sensory experiences of difference. Thus, in the case of Philippe, we have the reassuring oneness of contact with skin and the pin-prick irritation of a grain of sand, or the visually perceived difference between the flat sternum of a man and the breasts of a woman.

Leclaire then proceeds to make a detailed analysis of what might, in the case of Philippe, be considered the inaccessible text of the elementary unconscious. It consists of a sort of secret ejaculation, a jubilatory formula, an onomatopeia which might be transcribed with a minimum of distortion as:

Poor (d) J'e –Li.

The articulation of this formula, either out loud or in a whisper, connotes a jubilatory movement of the body, such as curling up and then stretching, taking pleasure in the result obtained and then starting again.

It is rare, Leclaire continues, for an analyst to arrive at these secret formulae, as admitting to them is, as it were, a violation of modesty. In general they are obscene or grotesque.

This is also the reason for our author's silence as to their existence in his first exposé.

143

We will retain only certain elements of the analysis to which Leclaire devotes himself:

– The Por (from poor) belongs to the patient's two names: Ge*or*ges and *P*hilippe, to the word *peau* (skin), to the word *corps* (body), which, Leclaire tells us, greatly preoccupied his patient;
– J'e is the *je* of the *Moi-je* (me-I) which was pinned on Philippe at a very early age and of the *je t'ai* (I've got you) of too tender a mother;
– Li is an abbreviation for Lili and the middle syllable of Philippe.

This elementary unconscious phantasy supports the *li-corne* (unicorn) chain.

As to the criteria which oblige the analyst to retain some phonemes in the patient's associations rather than others and to judge them an integral part of the unconscious chain, Leclaire suggests the following: their repetitive insistence, the difficulty in admitting to them, their active and insistent presence, which recalls the basic irreducibility of the individual.

Leclaire places special emphasis upon the links between the unconscious phantasy and the subject's name, which in a very rudimentary way designates the incidence of the Name-of-the-Father.

Lacanian psychoanalytic theory has taken us a long way in the discovery of the unconscious, even further than its practice could take us, since, as Leclaire tells us, it is very rare for the analyst to arrive at the broken linguistic formulae which weave the innermost part of us.

Leclaire could easily have considered himself satisfied and put a stop to his investigation of the unconscious. On the contrary in 1968 he published a volume, the implications of which I find extremely far-reaching, and which sets the theory of the unconscious on hitherto unexpected paths.

While giving the reader a glimpse into this book, I should like to pay homage to S. Leclaire whose numerous works, with their great clarity and deep insight, have been of great help to me when my study came up against difficulties arising from Dr Lacan's style.

The book in question is entitled *Psychanalyser, essai sur l'ordre de l'inconscient et la pratique de la lettre* (55).

The question discussed in this volume is that of the essence of the elementary unconscious elements, and that of the process whereby they become fixed.

As early as 1966, Leclaire wrote an article in *Cahiers pour l'analyse* (51) which foreshadows this new contribution to the study of the unconscious:

I put it forward that a signifier (in the order of the unconscious) can be called a signifier only in so far as the letter which constitutes one face of it necessarily refers back to a movement of the body. It is this elective anchoring of a letter (gramma) in a movement of the body which constitutes the unconscious element, the signifier in the true sense of the word. The signifier is as much body as it is letter, it has a somatic and palpable aspect.

The contribution made to the study of the unconscious by Leclaire's book consists, therefore, in making a connexion between a movement of the body and a letter.

The anchoring of the letter in the 'lived' body will be effected around an ephemeral corporeal sensation of palpable difference, accompanied by pleasure or unpleasure.

Thus, in the case of Philippe, it could be the difference perceived between Lili's soft skin and the irritation of the sand or between the uniformity of a man's chest and the swelling of a woman's.

At a still more primitive stage, the difference perceived will always refer to the moment of birth which, as a break and a separation, gives castration its somatic anchoring; it will also always refer to the phallus, the signifier par excellence of difference and of the impossible identity.

> Any separation, any cut, even and especially that of parturition refers back to the Phallus. 'Phallus' is to be understood in the sense of that kingpin, that articulation which cannot be apprehended in either the anatomical figure of the male sex (penis) or that of the female sex, but at best as a copula. It is even, one might say, the hyphen in the evanescence of its erection; the Phallus is the signifier of the impossible identity. (51)

The experience of pleasure or unpleasure, that moment of almost imperceptible difference, can, Leclaire tells us, only be realized (and conceived) in a body, the whole of which is seen as an 'erotogenic zone', as Freud put it in 1938 in his *Outline of Psychoanalysis* (9). In Freud, the notion of the erotogenic zone designates a site in the body which is able to become the seat of excitement of a sexual type.

Having previously taken only the whole area of the skin, the mucous membranes and the orifices to be erotogenic, Freud, in the name of hypochondria, extends to all the internal organs, the possibility of becoming a site of excitement of a sexual type (11, p. 84). The whole body can thus be said to be erotogenic. To be more accurate, it is a set of possible erotogenic zones.

To give the notion of erotogenic zone its full meaning, the excitability of a sexual type which characterizes it must be correctly defined.

Pleasure is always defined by Freud as the sensation marking the end of a state of tension (11, p. 85).

For Freud as for Leclaire, the time of pleasure, of *jouissance*, is therefore the time of difference, the difference, as it happens, between more and less tension.

145

To sum up: the excitability of a sexual type which specifies the erotogenic zone is therefore to be defined as 'the property of the site of the body of being the seat of an immediately accessible, palpable difference between pleasure and unpleasure and of being in some way able to receive the mark of that difference' (54, p. 67).

And,

The erotogenic zone appears to be defined as a site in the body in which the syncope of a difference remains marked and in which the gap of pleasure opens, lips of a mouth, lids of an eye, exquisitely and sensibly different points of an epidermis on a secret shore.

If there is to be any possibility of pleasure, then some part of the body must be felt as a gap, an opening which can for the space of a moment offer an empty reflection of the absolute of *jouissance*, a time in which tension is annulled.

In order to get a better grasp of Leclaire's theory, it may be preferable to examine with him the particular destiny of an unconscious by posing the question: what is it in an individual that privileges one zone rather than another?

For a satisfaction to be inscribed in this decisive way as the seat of an appeal without a reply, soothing must already have been regarded as *jouissance* in the eyes of another, the person feeding the child as it happens. The inscription in the body is the fact of this sexual value projected by another on to the site of satisfaction.
(54, p. 71)

Leclaire proposes a fictional example to illustrate the manner in which an erotogenic zone is opened up:

Imagine the softness of a mother's finger as it 'innocently' plays with the exquisite dimple at the side of the neck, and the baby's face illuminated with a smile. One could say that, with its loving caress, the finger is imprinting a mark in this hollow, opening up a crater of *jouissance*, inscribing a letter which seems to fix the almost imperceptible immediacy of the illumination.   (54, p. 72)

The last quotation introduces the terms 'mark' and 'letter', and the letter, says Leclaire, is in fact inseparable from a sensory experience of difference. As an erotogenic zone opens up under the effect of some experience or other, a mark, a letter is at the same time inscribed in the unconscious as an abstract signifier designating the palpable gap which marks the limits of the erotogenic zone.

The level of analysis at which Leclaire places himself comes long before the establishment of language in any real sense. The affixing of a 'letter' goes right back to the very beginning of the child's life and is situated in the imaginary. In this phase of primary narcissism, the child's unconscious is not yet formed as such, as symbolism alone has the definitive power to establish conscious reflection and to engender the unconscious.

The inscription of a letter is, however, effected in a manner which conforms to the inscription of the first phonemes which separate the conscious and unconscious systems and actualize what we called the second cut. I think, moreover, that there must be a link between the two types of inscription.

In general terms, we can say that, for Leclaire, the letter (or the signifier) is a pair of opposed elements, which may be acoustic, visual or tactile.

The letter which imprints and fixes the *béance* (gap) is not, it will be noted, to be confused with the object that closes it.

The object is that which manifests itself from the outside and closes the open breach of the erotogenic zone. To begin with, it may be anything, but in a second period, the cycle of repetition of the sexual appeal will result in the election of a privileged object.

The object is therefore as different from the letter as it is from the erotogenic zone. Any part of the body may become a sexual object in so far as it is distinct from the erotogenic zone.

Freud's clinical experience puts a real example at our disposal: the wolf man who is, as it happens, a wonderful illustration of Leclaire's theory. In this case, one can see very clearly the way in which a letter becomes fixed and determines the impossibility of the wolf man's finding a normal sexual object. Should more complete information be desired, the detailed story of the wolf man is to be found in chapter 24 dealing with psychosis.

Freud discovered the primordial element of the wolf man's unconscious through an analysis of one of his patient's childhood symptoms: the butterfly phobia:

> He was chasing a beautiful big butterfly with yellow stripes and
> large wings which ended in pointed projection. . . . Suddenly,
> when the butterfly had settled on a flower, he was seized
> with a dreadful fear of the creature and ran away screaming.
>
> (5, p. 89)

The yellow-striped butterfly is linked by association with the memory of a pear known in Russia as a gruscha, which has yellow stripes on its skin. Gruscha is also the name of a young maid who looked after the child at a tender age and with whom he lived a decisive scene.

The maid in question was on her knees, washing the floor. As she worked, she was in a particular position; that adopted by the child's mother during a coitus a tergo which he had had the opportunity to observe when very young. The child unconsciously associated Gruscha with this memory of his mother and urinated in the room. This action assimilated him sexually to his father in an act which, at the time, he could see only as micturition. Young Gruscha replied to his action with a threat of castration.

We know of the attraction exercised over the wolf man from that day onwards by any woman kneeling and leaning on her hands with her buttocks in the air.

The example of the wolf man, instantly burning with irrepressible desire at the sight of a crouching woman, is a good illustration of Leclaire's theory.

There is in fact no doubt that on these two occasions (the scene of coitus and the event with Gruscha), a sort of impression, an indelible trace was inscribed in the unconscious in an unalterable way. This is the letter. But what exactly is the letter in the wolf man's case?

Leclaire suggests the Roman V. This abstract stroke in effect covers an enormous number of significations for Freud's patient. It reminds him of his mother's position, the time at which the parental coitus took place. This figure or letter also represents a movement of opening and closing: that of the butterfly's wings, that of his mother's legs, that of his own eyelids.

Turned upside down and reduplicated thus $\Lambda\text{-}\Lambda$, this stroke is also an excellent image of the attentive ears of the wolves in his dream, or even of his own ears listening for the variations in his parents' breathing at five o'clock that day.

As Leclaire says, the letter inscribed in the wolf man's unconscious fixes the limits of the erotogenic zone, just as it also determines the object capable of closing the *béance* of desire. We in fact know that as he observed intercourse between his parents, the wolf man alternated between two types of reaction: associating himself with his father in his movement to take the object, and associating himself with his mother in her reception of the paternal phallus. It is in this dual reaction that we can grasp the meaning of the sexual duality of the wolf man for whom the anus is strongly erogenized, but for whom the normal sexual act of possessing a woman seems equally attractive.

The example of the wolf man is a perfect demonstration of the value of Leclaire's theories.

No letter, then, can be abstracted from the libidinal movement of the body which underlies it. The letter is the positive index of an erotogenic difference, the trace in the ground of the gap of pleasure.

At this stage in his theorization of the unconscious as the order of the letter, Leclaire poses a new question which will take the connexion between the body and the letter even further, but which will also and above all allow the subject to be introduced directly into the heart of the phenomenon of the inscription of a letter.

Leclaire goes on:

If the destiny of the psychotic brings out more clearly the necessary function of the fixation or determination of some literal elements of an unconscious, an order founded upon the primacy of *jouissance*, is to be really founded, it still does not enlighten us as to the specific mechanism of that function.

The question is important: it concerns the way in which a connexion is established between the palpable and immediate experience of difference (pleasure, unpleasure) on the one hand, and the stroke, the mnemic trace on the other.

We can formulate the reply at once and then go on to substantiate it: '*The connexion established is on the pattern of the stressing of the weak beat in a syncope.*'

I am of the opinion that our explanation should be illustrated by using the fictional examples of the fixing of a letter given in Leclaire's text.

In the confusion caused by striking one's head against a stone, a confusion which comes close to being a faint, a single element keeps us conscious, a single element keeps us alive; it could, for example, be the scent of the honeysuckle climbing in the nearby bushes. This scent seems to us to mark the instant in which all coherence is annulled and, more important, this scent in some way maintains our internal coherence.

In the same way, one could say that the young boy who is surprised by a sudden orgasm as he is climbing up a rope will feel that the coil of hemp in his hand is the only purchase preserving him from a fall in the very moment of pleasure.

In each case, the letter is determined and fixed at the very moment when the difference between pleasure and pain is produced, and it is shown to be an indifferent element in a temporal and situational conjuncture which prevents the total disappearance of the instant. This term stresses in counterpoint the weak beat of the syncope.

As we said above, the deep insight provided in this way by Leclaire is precisely that it brings to light the major characteristics of what we call a subject. The author is in fact reformulating, but this time in a more lived manner, that constitution of the subject through accession to language which we expounded in previous chapters. 'The subject is the alternating function which is capable of engendering in turn its annulment and the effacement of that same annulment.'

The function of the subject is to support or to instigate that disappearance of self constituted by pleasure, but at the same time to conceal that annulment. And, as one might guess, it is the letter which allows the subject to overcome the subjective annulment of *jouissance*.

As Lacan would say, no one can in fact say 'I enjoy' (*je jouis*) [*jouir* also has the slang meaning of 'to come' (trans.)] unless he or she is referring to past pleasure or pleasure to come, because as soon as he or she begins to speak, the subject ceases to enjoy (*jouir*) in the true sense, or, what amounts to the same thing, ceases to be annulled as subject.

> The subject founds the possibility of the letter in the time of the effacement of the zero and is supported by the literality of the stroke in that other time where he vanishes in order to assert or realize the zero.

To sum up the function of the subject introduced here, we can again quote Leclaire:

> The function of the subject is to support the most perfect of antinomies: this antinomy may be described as being that between the assertion of a truth and its transgression, that between zero and one, between speech and *jouissance*.

We will bring this passage on Leclaire's contributions to a close here, but not without attempting to find some indication of similar conceptions of this question in the work of certain other Lacanians.

If, for example, one reads Piron's *La Psychanalyse, science d'homme* (116), certain passages seem to reveal intuitions similar to those found in Leclaire's latest work.

> All our intentions find their symbolic matrix in the body and no concept expresses cultural, ethical or religious values without slipping into metaphors of the lived body. . . . The lived body affectively bathes in language, and in return language has the power to model the body, to deploy or to repress its virtualities. . . . Exchanges of signification between the body and language bear witness to the fact that the most fundamental language is metaphorical language, which privileges modes of expression other than logical relations: resemblance, agreement, contact, 'the same as'. . . .
> The word itself is a symbol for the lived body.

In this connexion, H.-T. Piron quotes the famous slip of the tongue made by the wolf man:

> 'I had a dream of a man tearing the wings off an Espe. You know that insect with yellow stripes on its body, that stings. Espe, why that's myself.'

The wolf man's dream is, of course, about a Wespe (wasp in German) and S.P. are his initials.

As we know, the wolf man's basic problem is castration. In this slip of the tongue, he admits, through the suppression of the W, to his own castration, but he of course does so in a manner which escapes his consciousness.

Jacques Lacan himself asserts that there is a connexion between language and the body:

> Language is not immaterial. It is a subtle body, but body it is. Words are trapped in all the corporeal images that captivate the subject; they may make the hysteric pregnant, be identified with the object of *penis-neid* (penis-envy), represent the flood of urethral ambition. (*Écrits*, 16)

To close this chapter, I propose the following synthesis.

Whether it proceeds from secondary repression or from primal repression, the repressed has in the unconscious the status of a signifier.

When Lacanian psychoanalysts speak of repression, they are not only thinking of the repression of a need or a tendency, but of the repression of signifying elements.

When a truth in everyday life is barred in this way, it does not disappear, but persists and is expressed in the clandestine form of the formations of the unconscious.

The formations of the unconscious contain a truth, a discourse which has been spoken but which the subject no longer has at his disposal. This truth is the unconscious, which functions in accordance with definite laws regardless of any intervention on the part of the conscious subject. The unconscious, says Lacan, is the discourse of the Other: the subject's other.

The subject finds himself divided into two parts: the unconscious whence 'he receives in inverted form his own forgotten message', and conscious discourse.

It follows that the formations of the unconscious are to be taken as rebuses, i.e. literally and element by element. In the last analysis, free association leads to the elementary text of the unconscious, the linguistic status of which we have just determined.

To close the chapter with several quotations from Lacan:

> It is the signifier which is repressed; no other meaning can be given to the word: *Vorstellungsrepräsentanz*. (*Écrits*, 26)

> What the psychoanalytic experience discovers in the unconscious is the whole structure of language. The pretensions of the spirit would remain irreducible if the letter had not shown us that it produces all the effects of truth in man without involving the spirit at all. (*Écrits*, 22)

> Linguistics is certainly the science from which the unconscious derives. It is made like a language and unfolds in the effects of language. It happens that 'it' (*ça*) thinks there where it is impossible for the subject to articulate: therefore I am, because, there, it is structurally out of the question that the subject should accede to consciousness of self (naming oneself as being he who

speaks). I think where I cannot say that I am, where I must posit
the subject of the enunciation as being separated by a line from
the being. I articulate the status of the unconscious through the
function of the signifier. . . . I say that the letter (*la lettre*)
succeeds being (*l'être*).

(Interview with Lacan on Belgian Radio, 14 December 1966)

The Other is the locus from which the question of his existence
may be presented to him . . . concerning his sex and contingency.
This question is not presented in the unconscious as ineffable,
prior to all analysis it is articulated in discrete elements: those
which linguistic analysis forces us to isolate as signifiers.

(*Écrits*, 23)

As a sequel to this chapter on the nature of the content of the unconscious according to Lacan, we shall now make a short summary of
Freud's opinions on the subject. We shall thus be clearer as to the basis
on which Lacan has elaborated his original theory. We will also see
that it is strictly impossible to in any way invalidate Lacan's theses on
the unconscious on the basis of the Freudian data.

It will be left to a later part of this text to make a detailed exposition
of Lacan's assimilation of the Freudian mechanisms of condensation
and displacement in the return of the repressed to metaphor and
metonymy.

TWELVE

Structure, organization and functioning of the unconscious order in Freud

For Freud, the unconscious is a nucleus of ideational representatives of the instinct.

Its dynamic is defined by the tendency of these representatives to discharge their libidinal cathexis in a compromise-form, out of respect for censorship.

Clinical psychoanalysis led Freud to recognize the existence of certain 'contents' inaccessible to consciousness without the lifting of certain resistances. These unconscious thoughts are efficient in man and determine the symptomatic acts known as the formations of the unconscious. Freud therefore postulates the existence of an unconscious, a psychical site grouping together representatives separated by a cleavage.

He specifies that these instinctual representatives are of the order of representation, that they are a 'succession of inscriptions and signs' worked up into phantasies, and that the instinct fixes itself to them.

It should be noted that Freud speaks elsewhere of unconscious contents which have not been acquired through repression, through being cut off, but which form a kind of phylogenetic luggage.

These are the 'primal phantasies' which we will mention later. The notion of the unconscious worked out by Freud seems therefore to be directly related to that proposed by Lacan.

In effect Lacan insists upon the representational nature of the unconscious and upon the fact that the formation of the unconscious takes place 'by cleavage'. One could even see in Freud the beginnings of the Lacanian idea of the necessity of accession to language if there is to be an unconscious. For Freud, secondary repression, like primal repression, in fact works upon the instinctual representatives.

In seeking to define the mechanisms of the primal repression which constitutes the unconscious, Freud also refers to the notion of the 'fixing' of an instinct to a representative:

> We have reason to assume that there is a *primal repression*, a first
> phase of repression, which consists in the psychical (ideational)
> representative of the instinct being entry into the conscious. With
> this a fixation is established, the representative in question persists

unaltered from then onwards and the instinct remains attached to
it.   (11, p. 148)

Freud also says that it is the ideational representatives which fix the
instinct and provide the means by which it becomes inscribed in the
psychical apparatus. They form the contents of the unconscious and,
what is more, it is these ideational representatives which create the unconscious in the course of primal repression.

Freud's texts on the mechanism of primal repression are very limited.
Lacan's research on this question thus appears to be quite justified. He
does not distort Freud's thought in any way since he contents himself
with taking Freud's rare texts as they stand and extending them into an
original creation.

As far as the nature of the ideational representative is concerned, Freud
at times speaks of 'mnemic traces' – that part of the object which is
inscribed in the different mnemic systems – and at other times of thing-
presentations, as opposed to word-presentations. The thing-presentation is not, however, the presentation in thought of the thing itself, but
a mnemic trace derived from the thing.

Word-presentations on the other hand are restricted by Freud to the
conscious system, as, apart from the presentation in thought of the
thing, they also include verbalization of the content.

Freud will also add that it is by becoming speech that the mnemic
trace can gain access to consciousness.

For Freud, schizophrenia is the only illness in which the word-
presentation is treated in consciousness as a thing-presentation, in
accordance, that is, with the mechanisms proper to the unconscious.

The data provided in this way by Freud does then authorize the
Lacanian use of the linguistic term 'signifier' to designate the content
of the unconscious.

We will now look at the characteristics of the unconscious brought out
by Freud in his article, 'The Unconscious' (1915), which is also
included in *Papers on Metapsychology* (11). These characteristics are
completely taken over by the Lacanians. We are thus obliged to
acknowledge that Lacan is completely Freudian in his conception of
the unconscious.

(a) Although they are sometimes contradictory, the representatives
exist side by side without annulling one another. The principle of con-
tradiction does not exist in the unconscious. Unconscious elements
know neither negation, doubt, nor degrees of certainty. In the unconscious, there are only contents with a greater or a lesser cathexis.

Thus, for example, a doubt expressed by a patient as he narrates a
dream belongs to the secondary revision of that dream, as does the
negation (*Verneinung*) discussed above.

(b) The processes of the unconscious system are not ordered in time, they do not change with it and have no connexion with it. The re-establishment of temporality belongs to the conscious system.

(c) The processes of the unconscious system take no account of reality. They are subject to the pleasure principle. External reality is replaced by psychical reality.

The inhibition of the primary processes in their tendency to discharge, and the establishment of logical relations, are the work of the secondary process: conscious memory, the reality principle, negation and doubt.

(d) In the unconscious, there is a greater mobility of cathectic intensities. Thanks to the process of displacement, a representative can pass its whole cathectic charge to another and thanks to the process of condensation, it can take on the total cathexis of several other representatives. These are indices of the primary process.

In the preconscious system, on the other hand, the secondary process is dominant.

The Lacanians, for their part, distinguish two further characteristics of the elements of unconscious discourse, characteristics which are only apparently contradictory:

(i) the fixity and rigidity of their formulations and structure:

(ii) the interchangeability of the elements they are called upon to cover in the subject's existence.

For example: for the patient, all the people in a real situation come to occupy the place reserved for a single person in the structure of the complex.

As we have seen, the Lacanians also privilege the representational nature of the instinct. We know that there are two types of phenomena through which the instinct becomes palpable in the psychical apparatus:

– the ideational representative of the instinct (*psychische Vorstellungsrepräsentanz des Triebes*);

– the affect (*Affektrepräsentanz*).

What becomes of the affects during repression?

Following Freud, Lacan says that 'the affects are not repressed, but only displaced' (*Écrits*, 26).

To be more precise, the affects undergo a particular destiny as a result of the repression of the representatives whose charge they are:

– they are displaced on to other representatives and their import is misrecognized, or

– they are suppressed (but not repressed). In that case they can no longer be seen. Anxiety could be the whole body of affective charges without an object bursting into consciousness.

On the basis of this Freudian data, the Lacanians have provided a structural representation of the unconscious as a complex network of ideational representatives. Freud himself provides the basis for such a representation in the *Traumdeutung*. He speaks of a network of criss-cross threads zigzagging in all directions and of connecting knots which bind the divergent threads together.

For the Lacanians, then, the unconscious, from its original text to its 'formations', reveals itself to be structurally comparable to a language.

Through displacements and condensations, the original unconscious chain contracts associative links with representatives repressed *a posteriori*, the latter being themselves connected with other representatives, either by meaning (the signifying path) or by form (the literal path).

The psychoanalytic use of the Saussurian algorithm $\frac{S}{s}$ results in the image of a network of plurivalent relations between signifiers.

In his article (54), Leclaire draws a happy comparison which allows us to grasp the organization of this network:

A road which crosses the river by means of a bridge annuls the flow of the water and, as a road system, it constitutes a new limit which the railway can in its turn cross by way of a level crossing.

He goes on:

In the unconscious order, therefore, the sequence of terms constituted by these crossings can rightly be called a chain, in the sense that, considered in both its closure and its openness, each element can best be represented as the ring of a link.

H.-T. Piron (116) describes the structural organization of the unconscious as being the drawing together of memories into themes which are then organized into *concentric layers around the pathogenic kernel*, offering increased resistance to analysis as it comes closer to the centre. Linguistic relations unite thoughts amongst each other and themes amongst each other, giving rise to a network of interlocking, ramified lines zig-zagging in all directions around the connecting knots. Several threads may thus run through a single symptom.

This way of seeing things 'reproduces in terms of structures what analytic procedure reproduces in time. . . . The unconscious refers back to a system of connexions which may be compared to a linguistic model' (116).

The notion of the overdetermination of symptoms and, indeed, of all the formations of the unconscious refers to the conception of just such a network of signifiers:

The overdetermination of symptomatic acts is a fact of syntax. It is none other than a symbolic determination, the most radical form of which is given by combinatory logic.   (*Écrits*, 20)

Appendix

Certain expressions typical of Lacan refer to different concepts, depending upon the context in which they are inscribed.

It is thus with the terms 'object (a)' and 'Other'. Object (a) will be discussed in the following section. To facilitate the reader's understanding of the texts quoted from Lacan, I should like here to bring together the various concepts covered by the term 'Other'.

The Other is:

(i)   language, the site of the signifier, the symbolic. 'The Other, by which name we designate a place essential to the structure of the symbolic' (*Écrits*, 21).

(ii)   the site of the intersubjectivity of patient and analyst, and hence the analytic dialogue. 'The Other is the locus in which is constituted the I who speaks with him who hears' (*Écrits*, 19).

(iii)   the unconscious in that it is constituted by signifying elements and that it is the subject's other. 'A conceptual junction must be established between this Elsewhere and the place where *it* (*ça*) thinks: another scene . . . this Other of the subjects' (*Écrits*, 23).

If *it* (*ça*) speaks in the Other it is because it is there that the subject, by means of a logic anterior to any awakening of the signified, finds its signifying place. The discovery of what it articulates in that place, that is to say, enables us to grasp at the price of what split (*Spaltung*) it has been constituted.   (*Écrits*, 24)

(iv)   the third party witness invoked in analysis as soon as it is a question of formulating a truth. 'The Other is the guarantor of the good faith one evokes in the pact of speech' (*Écrits*, 21).

(v)   it is the Father or the Mother.

Desire whose signifier is the phallus of which the giving and receiving are equally impossible for the neurotic, whether he knows that the Other does not have it, or knows that he does have it, because in either case his desire is elsewhere: it belongs to being.

(*Écrits*, 28)

PART SIX

The transition from lack to desire and to demand

THIRTEEN

From need (or lived lack) to the instinct and desire: accession to language

The three-point dialectic we are about to discuss is, at bottom, identical to the movement whereby the subject constitutes himself in discourse by splitting into two parts: subject of the utterance and unconscious subject; and whereby he subsequently alienates himself in language by constructing his ego.

In moving from lack to desire, the subject in effect accedes to language, and in moving from desire to demand he alienates himself in language, creates himself and fashions himself at will. This section, then, repeats in different terms the Lacanian themes of Spaltung and Splitting expounded in Part Three.

Lacan seems to have provided two different perspectives on these themes and I hope to plot them both. The first perspective is more general, whereas the second, which we will be dealing with here, is more closely concerned with man's subjective life.

Like Freud, Lacan makes a distinction between *need*, a purely organic energy, instinct and *desire*, the active principle of the psychical processes.

Before going on to expound Lacan's conception, it might be useful to include Freud's own views.

Between need and desire, Freud introduces the term instinct.

The instinct differs from the simple organic need in that it introduces an erotic quality and is thus from the outset inscribed in the domain specific to psychoanalysis.

The instinct is a constant force of a biological, organic (and not psychical) nature which tends towards the suppression of any state of tension.

It belongs to the psychical apparatus, be it conscious or unconscious, only through the intermediary of an ideational representative (*Vorstellungsrepräsentanz*).

Desire is the directing force of the psychical apparatus, which is orientated in accordance with its perception of the pleasant or the unpleasant. It alone can set the psychical apparatus in motion. It transpires from the distinctions made by Freud that desire comes into force as the tension of the psychical apparatus only in so far as a representative of the instinct appears. It then moves the psychical apparatus in function of that representative.

For Lacan, whose point of view was dealt with in Part Four, the instinct takes as its support organic need and metabolic function, and introduces an erotic quality.

Being canalized by the erotogenic zones, instinct is always partial if one compares it to the young child's vital and radical lack at birth.

The eroticized partial instinct refers back to the organic need which founds it, but it also refers back beyond this to a lived experience of radical lack resulting from separation from the maternal body.

For Lacan, lack is the void, the zero, that which lies before the instinct. It refers to the absence of an anatomical complement and induces organic need.

Lacan often uses the term lack (*manque*) or gap (*béance*) in his *Écrits*, and he always does so in a context which indicates what it is that lies before any form of instinctual expression or canalized desire.

Thus, lack is that which precedes the instinct 'expressed' by the erotogenic zone and the letter. It also precedes the desire expressed in a signifier. Lack implies the idea of the lived drama of an irreversible incompleteness rather than that of some erotic appeal. In a sense, it subsumes all the radical anxiety in man; the anxiety which results from his human condition.

To adopt the new terminology recently introduced by Leclaire in his book, *Psychanalyser . . .* (55), the instinct is the appeal for a return to the pleasure principle made by the crack inscribed in the body (the erotogenic zone) during some primal experience of pleasure or unpleasure. The instinct is the reactivation of an old commotion, the effect of external stimulation.

As for the concept of desire, it is difficult to see how it can be presented on the basis of Lacan's texts. We will therefore turn to 'La réalité du désir' (42), an article by Lacan's follower Leclaire.

Leclaire calls desire 'the force of cohesion which holds the elements of pure singularity together in a coherent set'.

By 'elements of pure singularity', he is designating the elementary signifying elements of the unconscious: the letter which marks the limits of the erotogenic zone.

Thus, Philippe's unconscious desire is to establish a link with Lili, to fill in the crack of castration, of separation from his mother. In the psyche, desire is the successor to the essential lack lived by the child separated from its mother, the successor to the organic need and the instinct, for desire is what instinct becomes when it is alienated in a signifier.

162

The above-mentioned desire will, in the case of young Philippe, be alienated in the desire to drink which is substituted for the instinct directed towards Lili.

We now understand more clearly why Lacan assimilates the transition from lack to desire to the subject's advent to language. In the movement whereby the child in one form or another translates his need he alienates it in the signifier and betrays its primary truth. The real object of lack, of need and of the instinct is lost for ever, cast into the unconscious. The subject is divided into two parts: *his unconscious truth and the conscious language which partially reflects that truth.* This is also the reason for man's radical inability to find anything to satisfy him.

Let us follow in detail Leclaire's reasoning in (42).

The elements of pure singularity are, he tells us, characterized by a total absence of logical connexions. As an example, the author suggests five elementary signifiers of the unconscious:
- the smell of a woman's neck on the way back from a walk;
- the acidulated edge of something sweet;
- the modulation of a voice;
- a beauty spot or mole;
- the fullness of the hand as the ball is caught.

One can imagine, says the author, what might characterize the unconscious desire of such a subject: to find once more the site of the beauty spot (noticed on the mother's neck as the child came back from a walk). The gradual imaginary alienation of the unconscious desire will be occasioned by the absence of logical or significant links between these pointillist impressions, which will contract various associative links with one another. On this basis, one could imagine the subject becoming obsessional, spending hours looking for the place for the bolt he found in the bottom of his car. A further displacement could, for example, be an obsession with exact references in texts. Subjected to free association around these symptoms, such a patient might come up with the signifying succession: bolt (*boulon*) – spot (*bouton*) – neck (*cou*) – beauty spot (*grain de beauté*). Thus, the formations of the unconscious (in this case the symptom) reveal the truth of the unconscious discourse *alienated in the signifier.*

We know how these elementary signifiers are inscribed in the unconscious. They arise in the very instant of lived pleasure, fix and delimit the erotogenic zone and the sexual agitation in the unconscious.

The elementary signifiers of the unconscious are witnesses to the subject's accession to language. But as no logical connexion holds them together, it is impossible for the subject to formulate the desire they enclose, except in a more elaborate linguistic form, such as the phantasy.

This, as I see it, is what Lacan means when he says repeatedly in his *Écrits* that: desire always lies both beyond and before demand. To say

163

that desire is beyond demand means that it transcends it, that it is eternal because it is impossible to satisfy it. By articulating desire with its own conditions as a linguistic form, demand necessarily betrays its true import.

But desire is also dug out of the area below demand. In this case, a reversal of roles seems to take place. Miming the frenzy of desire, the unconditional absolute demand recalls the radical lack of being which underlies desire.

Desire is then invaded, as it were, or overtaken by the demand from which, moreover, it will be reborn, as no demand is capable of fully satisfying it.

> Desire is produced in an area beyond demand, in that, in articulating the life of the subject according to its conditions, demand cuts off the need from that life. But desire is also dug out of the area below demand, in that, as an unconditional demand of presence and absence, demand evokes lack of being under the three figures of the nothing that constitutes the basis of the demand for love, of the hate that even denies the other's being, and of the unspeakable element in that which is ignored in its request. (*Écrits*, 28)

All the objects of the subject's desire will always be a reminder of some primal experience of pleasure, of a scene which was lived passively and will always refer back through associative links, which become more complex and more subtle with the passage of time, to that lived experience.

Connected with any phantasy-scenario there is a choice imposed by the ineffability of certain marks inscribed in the unconscious signifiers of desire. An object is required to unite these scattered points. Hence the metonymic course of desire, forever insatiable since it refers back to the ineffable, to the unconscious desire and the absolute lack it conceals. Sexual desire is a sort of held note in the crescendo of the alienation of desire. We have in fact seen that the father's speech forbidding the child its mother in the Oedipus put the child in a position to divert its desire on to something else by accepting the law.

> Freud reveals to us that it is thanks to the Name-of-the-Father that man does not remain in the sexual service of the mother, that aggression towards the father is at the principle of the Law, and that the Law is at the service of desire, which it institutes through the prohibition of incest.
>
> It is, therefore, the assumption of castration which creates the lack through which desire is instituted. Desire is the desire for desire, the desire of the Other and it is subject to the Law.
>
> It is the default of the phallus which mounts up the symbolic debt. Desire reproduces the subject's relation to the lost object.
>
> (*Écrits*, 31)

As Laplanche and Pontalis have said (46), phantasies are a form of the activity of thought separated off by a sort of cleavage (by access to conscious language). They are of the order of the symbol and in their themes they pretend, like myths, to provide a solution to the subject's basic problems.

What is more, through the mediation of a scenario, they account for the subject's insertion into the symbolic.

Phantasies are one of the modes of the hallucinatory satisfaction of desire.

The most basic are those which tend to recover those objects connected with the first experience of the rise and resolution of desire. They pin down the moment of separation of the lived experience and the hallucinatory reliving of it, the moment of the separation of the gratifying object from the sign which inscribes both the object and the absence of the object.

We should note that in alluding to phantasies and to the metonymy of desire, we are already speaking of the 'defile of the signifier', or what Lacan calls: demand. In Lacan, demand appears to be a generic term designating the symbolic, significant site in which the primordial desire is gradually alienated.

The elementary signifiers of the unconscious in fact contract multiple associative connexions with one another and with those signifiers which join them as a result of successive repressions. They organize the phantasies, become condensed in metaphors and associate metonymically, so that when they rise into consciousness, where they determine the avatars of our human quest, they are indecipherable. We can see that the definition of demand that we can draw from *Écrits* may be assimilated to the notion of splitting:

> The fading of the subject (splitting) comes about in the suspension
> of desire, because the subject is eclipsed in the signifier of demand
> and in the fixation of the phantasy.   (*Écrits*, 29)

To sum up: the primal division of the subject (Spaltung) into conscious discourse and unconscious discourse is, for Lacan, identical to the transition from lack to desire. Both these movements are precociously realized in the subjection of the subject to imaginary representations. They are definitively established during the Oedipus in accordance with the schema of the paternal metaphor.

The future 'subject' wishes to be the phallus for his mother, to be, that is, everything to her. The father intervenes as the author of the Law, the representative of the symbolic order, and forbids the dual union of child and mother. The instinct is repressed into the position of something misrecognized and is replaced by a symbol.

The subject then enlists in the order of symbolism and of language, and his primitive instinct (to be everything to his mother) becomes a desire to know, to have, to possess. Through endless sublimations, through multiple displacements from one signifier to another, the primal unconscious desire becomes alienated in demand: this is Splitting.

> In the quest for the phallus the subject moves from being it to having it. It is here that is inscribed that last Spaltung by which the subject articulates himself to the Logos. (*Écrits*, 28)

> The phallus symbolizes privation or lack of being, and the latter derivatively settles in the lack of having engendered by any frustration of the particular or global demand.
> (J. Lacan: *Pour un Congrès sur la sexualité féminine*)

The summary we have just made is a theoretical and general look at a process whose articulating links are not in fact of a macroscopic but of a microscopic order.

In short, we should establish a connexion between the microscopy of Leclaire's theories and the macroscopy of those of Lacan.

How in fact are we to find the meeting place between, on the one hand, Leclaire with his detailed description of the transition from instinct to desire through the intervention into the unconscious of a letter which will determine the desire's object choice, and, on the other hand, Lacan with his panoramic view of the transition through the Oedipus from lack of being the phallus to having the phallus?

We could make a personal attempt to establish this 'new' bridge by interpolating on the basis of Stein's contribution, which was discussed above. If we assume – and it seems more and more necessary to do so – the fact that accession to language is not, strictly speaking, effected at the time of the Oedipus (limited to the age of three or four years), or, again, if we consider the Oedipus in a broader perspective, as a global and gradual phenomenon integrating the origins of the formation of the subject through accession to language, we can then begin to see the connexion between Leclaire and Lacan. On the basis of a few experiences of pleasure lived by the child in direct and permanent contact with its mother, a desire is born and is subtended in the innermost part of the unconscious by one or more signifiers. The unconscious position of these signifiers, the sole witnesses to the lived experience, will direct the desire towards certain objects connected by some law of association with the primitive object of pleasure whose letter will appear as the negation inscribed and dug out in the unconscious. The particular and personal object of the subject's desire will be determined step by step in this way.

The period assigned to the Oedipus will *reactivate the desire* to receive erotic pleasure from the mother and in this period the desire will take on a more specific character related to the sexual maturation of the child.

From need (or lived lack) to the instinct and desire: accession to language

One could say that at this stage the child wishes to be everything to its mother, to be the phallus, the symbol of the complement of its own lack. The child wants to possess its mother completely and without sharing anything. We now come back to Lacan's own articulation.

Having said that, I think it judicious at this point in our study to include some remarks on the notion of the death instinct in the Lacanians.

The Lacanians have given an original signification to the death instinct, a signification directly connected with the organic incoherence they consider specific to the child before its entry into language. Following Leclaire in his well-known article, 'The unconscious: a psycho-analytic study' (48):

The death instinct is the specific energy which allows the counter-cathexis necessary to the primal repression that creates the unconscious. In that sense, it is also the matrix of desire, as the latter arises together with language.

It is an 'active void', whose only connexion with the libidinal instincts is that it founds them.

Language – which also makes desire possible on the basis of lack – is linked with the surfacing of the death instinct.

The death instinct is that radical force which surfaces in the catastrophic or ecstatic instant when the organic coherence of the body appears as though unnamed and unnameable, a swoon or ecstasy, screaming out its appeal for a word to veil and sustain it. It constitutes the basis of the castration complex and allows the development of language, together with the possibility of desire and the development of the sexual instincts.   (48, p. 144)

One could say that the original text of the unconscious fixes the death instinct by founding desire and the libidinal instincts. The primordial signifiers do in fact conceal the surfacing of the void of the death instinct, establish desire and give the subject his organic and psychical coherence.

If we now turn to Leclaire's book, *Psychanalyser . . .* (55), we see that the death instinct is the *ecstatic void* met with by the subject in pleasure or in pain, and from which the subject is preserved only by the letter (not merely a linguistic term but a mnemic trace whose form may vary), which appears in order to support his organic and psychical coherence. The death instinct is the *attractive 'zero'* around which the subject gravitates, the *antimony of the 'one'*, which is also the subject when he has been able to maintain himself in consciousness with the help of some letter.

It seems therefore that the death instinct intervenes in the constitu-tion of the 'subject' in two phases: *that which inscribes 'the letter' in the unconscious*, an olfactory, visual, audible or other element, and fills in the primitive void; and that which leads the subject to language in the true sense by way of the metaphoric function whereby *the letter is*, one might say, *replaced by an alienating symbol*.

This definition of Leclaire's seems to conform to that found in the following text from Lacan; it must be realized that this text is inscribed in the context of the death instinct.

> The game in which the child plays at making an object disappear from his sight in order to bring it back once more, and at the same time modulates the alternation of distinctive syllables, manifests the determinacy man receives from the symbolic order.
>
> Man devotes his time to deploying the structural alternative in which presence and absence take their call from one another.
>
> It is in the moment of their conjuncture, the zero point of desire, that the object comes under the seizure which, annulling its natural properties, subjects it to the conditions of the symbol. This game provides an illuminating insight into the individual's entry into language, which superimposes the determination of the signifier on that of the signified.
>
> (*Écrits: Le Séminaire sur la lettre volée*, pp. 46–7)

The moment in which desire becomes human is also that in which the child is born into language.

> The subject is not simply mastering his privation by assuming it, but . . . is raising his desire to a second power, for his action destroys the subject that it causes to appear and disappear in the anticipating provocation of its absence and presence. His action thus negatives the field of force of desire in order to become its own object to itself . . . the desire of the child has become the desire of another, of an *alter ego* . . . whose object of desire is henceforth his own affliction.
>
> So when we wish to attain in the subject what was before the serial articulations of speech, and what is primordial to the birth of symbols, we find it in death. (*Écrits*, 16)

FOURTEEN

From desire to demand

The repressed instinct does not stop straining after complete satisfaction, which would consist of the repetition of a primal satisfaction:
union with the mother.

Nothing can put an end to this state of tension.

It is the difference between the satisfaction obtained and the
satisfaction sought which maintains this motive force.

Pleasure is linked to the satisfaction given by an object whose
only value is its imperceptible difference from a lost model.

(S. Leclaire, 52)

One could say that it is the incidence of the signifier as an autonomous
chain which diverts man's desire into demand through displacements
and condensations of cathexis on to certain signifiers or, to be more
precise, through metaphor and metonymy.

In the section which follows we will see the justification for Lacan's
assimilation of linguistic metonymy to Freudian displacement and
metaphor to condensation.

Thus, demand will always be supported by the unconscious desire
and will not in fact be really concerned with the satisfactions it appears
to call for. This is why demand, again according to Lacan, is intransitive
and eternal and is not concerned with any specific object in a stable
manner, no object being capable of replacing the lost object.

In cases where the object of demand is knowing (*connaissance*) or knowledge (*savoir*), the subject will always have to transgress the known in
search of the unknown and will do so in memory of that omnipotence
of his desire which man has given up for lost. In the words of P.
Aulanier-Spairani (74): 'Whatever the object of the subject's interrogation: birth . . . the order of the world . . . the real object of the search is
knowledge of the desire of the Other (the mother).'

We are now perhaps in a better position to understand Lacan's words
(35): 'There is always a beyond to demand. In analysis desire presents
itself as an irreducible residue, the result of the gap between the
exigencies of need and the demand articulated.'

The Lacanian analytic cure then seeks to unfold in reverse order the
sequence of signifiers in which the subject's desire has gradually been
alienated. It interrogates the patient's signifiers, taking them literally
and in the order of their appearance, an order which is always regressive:

from the more recent to the older. It retraces their genesis or the order in which they arise.

> Desire can only be taken literally, since it is the nets of the letter that determine, overdetermine its place as a bird of paradise.
> (*Écrits*, 28)

> Through the mediation of demand, the whole past opens up right down to early infancy. It is in this way that analytic regression may take place and present itself. Regression shows nothing other than a return to the present of signifiers used in demands for which there is no prescription. (*Écrits*, 28)

This chapter will, I hope, cast some light upon the enigmatic sentence which Lacan repeats in various places in his *Écrits*: 'The desire of man is the desire of the Other.' Lacan himself justifies this statement as follows:

> If desire in the subject must pass through the defiles of the signifier . . . it must be posited that man's desire is the desire of the Other. (*Écrits*, 28)

> This is what I mean by my formula that the unconscious is the *discours de l'Autre* (discourse of the Other), in which the *de* is to be understood in the sense of the Latin *de* (objective determination): *de alio in oratione* (completed by: *tua res agitur*).
> But we must also add that man's desire is *désir de l'Autre* (desire of the Other), in which the *de* provides what grammarians call the 'subjective determination', namely that it is *qua* Other that he desires. (*Écrits*, 27)

Lacan's enigmatic phrase would therefore appear to mean that man's true desire is to be sought in his unconscious: the other scene, the Other where this desire is articulated in discrete (in the mathematical sense) signifiers. However, here is another quotation from Lacan which seems to have another meaning:

> In splitting, the second operation in which the causation of the subject is closed, the subject comes to find again in the Other's desire its equivalence to what he is as subject of the unconscious. By this means, the subject realizes himself in the loss from whence he sprang forth as an unconscious. (*Écrits*, 32)

I think that this sentence can be interpreted as follows: the subject, articulated with language, alienates his primary unconscious desire in the signifier. But this alienated desire does nevertheless reflect the truth of his unconscious desire and does in some way satisfy it with a substitute (the fetish for example). 'The desire of man is the desire of the Other' would thus also signify the wanderings of the true desire caught in the nets of the signifier, where it is no more than a shadow of its former self.

In short, understanding this quotation takes us back to the appendix on the Other at the end of Part Five.

Returning to the general line of this chapter, we will now recount an analysis of a dream made by Leclaire. It is one of Freud's own dreams: the dream of the botanical monograph. What is revealed by this dream could not be better summarized than by quoting H.-T. Piron (116):

> Man becomes conscious of his finite nature. This knowledge is
> given weight as a lived reality only by the impossibility of its
> obtaining the ardently desired appeasement. The sexual instincts
> try by every means, through metonymy and through metaphor, to
> fulfil the child's wish to possess its mother all to itself. Inhabited
> by death, this wish is destined to endless sublimations.

The text of the dream recounted by Freud in the *Traumdeutung* is as follows:

> I had written a monograph on a certain plant. The book lay before
> me and I was at the moment turning over a folded coloured plate.
> Bound up in each copy there was a dried specimen of the plant,
> as though it had been taken from a herbarium.   (2, p. 169)

In connexion with the analysis of Philippe's dream, we said that the dream fulfils a cascade of wishes linked together by connexions which become looser and looser as one moves from the deepest wish – the most primitive – to the most superficial – the most recent. As for the qualifications 'primitive' or 'recent' as applied to wishes, it should again be noted that, in the psychoanalytic domain, the terms do not have a merely temporal meaning. The wish which is described as being primitive may be active in the psyche of an adult, but it will be active in the veiled form of a metonymy or a sublimation. In the context of Lacanian thought, it would not be wrong to say that, in this sense, from primitive to recent, it is always the same wish striving to make its way into consciousness, but in different forms which are further and further removed from its original form.

The dream of the botanical monograph lends itself readily to the classical analysis of dreams.

A superficial examination leads us to find its origins in certain elements of the previous day which revived Freud's wish to make fertile discoveries.

The previous day, Freud had met a friend – Dr Königstein – who had reproached him with being too absorbed in his favourite hobbies. At this thorny moment in the conversation, the Gärtner (German for gardener) couple had arrived.

The conversation then took a more pleasant turn as they talked about 'Flora', one of Freud's patients, and Freud complimented Frau Gärtner on her 'blooming' looks.

The same day, Freud had noticed a monograph on cyclamens, his wife's favourite flower, in a bookshop window.

The dream finds its manifest elements in this context of flowers and herbs, and fulfils a first wish, which is simply a reply to Dr Königstein's criticisms: the wish to produce a useful and fertile work – the monograph on a plant.

Free association around the elements of the manifest taken individually will take analysis of the dream further.

By way of the recent memory of the previous day, the plant monograph reminds Freud of the reproach he often makes against himself: forgetting to give his wife cyclamens, whereas she for her part never fails to prepare him the artichokes of which he is so fond.

Thinking of the artichoke, which one pulls apart leaf by leaf in order to eat it, Freud recalls a distant scene from his fifth year, a scene which caused him an intense and uneasy joy: he and his sister were pulling to pieces, leaf by leaf, a richly coloured book about a journey through Persia. He remembers the infinite joy he felt in this act of slow destruction.

The manifest term 'coloured picture' should be linked with this screen memory.

Coming to the end of his spontaneous associations, Freud then turns to the 'herbarium' element in the manifest text of the dream.

A memory comes back to him from adolescence. The headmaster of his school had entrusted the pupils in the higher forms with the task of ridding a herbarium of the little worms (*Bücherwurm*: bookworm) which had found their way into it.

With the apparent disorder of associations, the memory of the memorable day when Freud's father gave him his Bible, the thing he held dearest to him in the world, 'except his spouse', comes to mind. Freud hurriedly devoured it, rather as a bookworm would do.

In this way, the deep meaning of the dream is decanted little by little, especially if one compares it to another of Freud's dreams in which the theme is incest: his mother being attacked in her sleep by strange figures with birds' beaks (*vögeln* is German for having sexual intercourse with a woman).

It becomes clear that in Freud's unconscious, his father's gift of the Bible was interpreted as being the gift of his wife. Freud assimilates his mother to the Book, and hence to all books. The Bücherwurm is Freud himself, with his passionate interest in books (since the scene of tearing up the book on Persia, as he himself says); as a fertile discoverer he devours them, tears them apart and violates them. It will be noted that the German *Bücherwurm* has the same double meaning as the English 'bookworm'.

The unconscious wish to commit incest (to be a passionate discoverer of his mother) is sublimated, thanks to the gift of the Bible and the scene of tearing up the book, into a passion for reading and scientific discovery. This is the wish satisfied by the dream, since the dream shows Freud to be the author of a monograph, but we have shown the unconscious detours through which a more primitive wish comes to light at the same time in this dream.

Leclaire adds that the element of 'pure singularity' which marked the advent of desire in Freud and alienated the incestuous instinct is 'a coloured picture in a book', but there must, I think, have been others, for it is impossible for the sublimation of the incestuous passion to have been effected in Freud at an age as late as five years. One would have to concentrate more on these dreams to find the other elements, but we know that certain memories played a role similar to that of the coloured picture: diverting the libidinal instinct. Notably, for those who have read the *Traumdeutung*, the memory of snatching yellow flowers away from his younger sister Paula when he was three, and the memory following that scene: seeing himself gleefully biting into a slice of whole-meal bread. Picking, snatching, biting and devouring are in fact so many variations on the act of rape.

Let us now for our part attempt to reconstruct by means of a diagram a part of the unconscious network of signifiers revealed to us by the free association (see Figure 14.1).

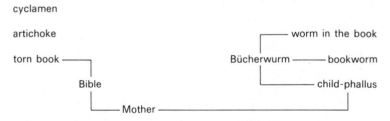

FIGURE 14.1

The child-phallus who wishes to reintegrate his mother's body might well be assimilated to the worm which finds its way into the book and devours it. Analysis of this dream has, I hope, allowed us a better understanding of the formation of the unconscious and a clearer idea as to its mode of organization: *a kind of complex network of signifiers through whose intermediary desire is alienated and diverted into eternal sublimations.*

The line which leads from truth to knowledge can be traced from the desire in which the object of the subject's instinct is crytallized in a signifier to the demand in which the objects pursued by the subject are modified and varied. This path, which is none other than the path of lures and of alienation, is sign-posted by a series of objects. Exhausted in its course, desire ultimately becomes its own object. By this I mean that it is the desire of another desire, that of the other.

Is this the oblativity which represents the perfection of morality? Every desire, even the apparently purest of desires, is a desire to have oneself recognized by the other, in this case the *belle âme*, and a desire to impose oneself in some way upon the other.

I would now like to show the point in desire's metonymic course in which what Lacan calls object (a) is situated.

> The division in which the subject verifies himself because an object passes through him without them penetrating one another in any way is at the origin of object (a). We call upon this object as being at once the cause of the desire in which the subject is eclipsed and as something supporting the subject between truth and knowledge. (Preface to *Écrits*, p. 10)

As I see it, this text by Lacan summarizes the two meanings he gives to object (a).

Whether one refers to Lacan's texts, to Leclaire's article (51) or to A. Green's, 'L'objet (a) de J. Lacan . . .' (81), the signification of object (a) always seems to be reduplicated.

In its first sense, it is the object lost in the subject's Spaltung, the unnamed, the phallus which the child wishes to be in order to complete its mother, the symbolic complement of its own lack.

Object (a) is, then, the cause of desire, its irreparable absence engenders the eternity of desire and its incessant flight from one signifier of demand to another. '(a) symbolizes that which, being lost in the sphere of the signifier, is lost to signification. That which resists this loss is the designated subject' (A. Green).

At a more primitive level still, (a) is, in mythical terms, the object of the radical lack lived by the child who is separated at birth from the mother. It is also the instinct's part object in its generality (the nipple, the breast), which is substituted for the object of lack and which merges with the subject himself. It is the first image to fill in the crack of separation. As such, it necessarily refers to the phallus, taken in the symbolic sense of the hyphen, *par excellence*, of the impossible unification.

In a second sense, (a) is the representative of the object of lack (the phallus), or the metonymic object of desire (the fetish for example). It is, to use another of Lacan's expressions, the fallen (*le caduque*), the remainder fallen from the signifying concatenation. In short, object (a) is the signifier of desire, whatever it may be, deprived of its symbolic reference to the unconscious signified (the object of lack of being: the phallus).

The position of object (a): this object receives a function from the symbolic: that same function which gives it its usage as a weapon against the disappearance of desire in the phobic outpost, as a fetish in the perverse structure, as the absolute condition for desire. a is the object of desire.

In so far as it is selected amongst the appendices of the body, as an index of desire it is already the exponent of a function, that of the index pointing towards an absence. It is reinstated in the place of the Other, functioning as an exponent of desire in the Other. This is why it is what will allow the thing before which the subject will see himself abolished by realizing himself in desire to take on its elective value at the end of analysis, to figure in phantasy. This point is reached beyond the reduction of the person's ideals. (*Écrits*, 29)

Every object of desire, every object of alienating identification will reveal itself to be necessarily ephemeral and destined to be supplanted because it is incapable of stopping up the lack inscribed in the subject from the start by the very fact of his being eclipsed in the signifier.

At the same time, however, every object of desire is a compromise in which the subject's truth breaks through, in which the unnamed object repressed by the Law is evoked: the Phallus. In 'Position de l'inconscient' (32), Lacan puts it in these terms:

Desire making its bed in the significant break in which metonymy is effected, the diachrony (called history) which is inscribed in the fading effects a return to that kind of fixity which Freud confers upon the unconscious wish.

FIFTEEN

The dialectic of identifications

The Lacanian themes of Spaltung and Splitting or transition from desire to demand are both intended to promote in an insistent manner a single discovery: that of man's subjection to the laws of the symbolic order.

The rupture of the circle going from the inside (the self) to the outside (the subject in the symbolic) is a drama of division and alienation. Above all, it is the doing of the symbolic.

We should, however, stress one very important point. The symbolic is the order which gives man his grandeur and his supremacy over the animal. If it is also the cause of human alienation, this is because a loss of the symbol's significant reference occurs in the subject, and a loss of collateral references occurs in the signifiers.

Alienation is the fact of giving up a part of oneself to another. The alienated man lives outside himself, a prisoner of the signifier, a prisoner of his ego's image or of the image of the ideal. He lives by the other's gaze upon him and he is unaware of this. Misrecognition is the parallel to the imaginary lived experience; the passion of the other and the obnubilation of an image of the self by the other. The imaginary lived experience does not allow a clear distinction between the image and its signification; the subject lives it in an immediate presence without keeping his distance.

The Lacanian theories of identification, with which we are particularly concerned here, completely account for this dispossession of the being by itself.

This chapter once more retraces human genesis, but with special emphasis on the phenomenon of identification, of man's exteriority to himself.

The mirror stage

In the course of human history, the child who is searching for self, life or meaning will invest with narcissistic libido everything which can in his eyes represent him.

Self-recognition in the mirror takes place between the ages of six and eight months and is accompanied by an intense jubilation. The child recuperates the totality of his body in an image and gradually becomes conscious of himself as an entity. Hence the importance of a phase whose various effects continue to have repercussions until the age of about one and a half years.

The mirror stage takes on a primordial importance in Lacan not so much because of its intrinsic value as because, by its structuring function, it prefigures the whole dialectic between alienation and subjectivity.

Self-recognition in the mirror is effected in three successive stages.

At first, the child who is together with an adult in front of a mirror confuses reflection and reality. He tries to seize hold of the image or tries to look behind the mirror, but, at the same time, he confuses his own reflection with that of his adult companion.

In the second phase, the child acquires the notion of the image and understands that the reflection is not a real being.

Finally, in the third stage, he realizes not only that the reflection is an image, but that the image is his own and is different from the image of the other. He manifests his intense joy in the classic game of the registration of the movements of his own body in the mirror.

Parallel to self-recognition in the mirror, a typical behaviour towards his homologue in age can be observed in the child. Confronted with another, the child observes him curiously, imitates his every action, tries to seduce him or impose upon him by play-acting, is, moreover, aggressive towards him, and then cries when he sees him fall.

It is no longer a question of a mere game; by behaving in this way, the child anticipates his motor co-ordination, which at this age is still imperfect, and seeks to situate himself socially by comparing himself with another. It is important to the child to recognize someone able to recognize him, and even more important to impose upon him and dominate him.

The behaviour of young children placed face to face with one another is marked by the most striking transitivism: the child who hits will say that he has been hit, the child who sees another fall will cry. We recognize here the instance of the imaginary, the dual relationship, the merging of self and other. It is in the other that the subject first lives and registers himself.

The mirror stage is therefore the first articulation of the 'I', it preforms the I through the entry into the imaginary which precedes the symbolic.

Its importance is twofold: both positive and negative. Positive in that it represents a first step towards the acquisition of a functional totality of self. The child does not in fact immediately have a unified representation of his body. On the contrary, he perceives it as being in pieces, as is shown by certain recurrent phantasies in dreams and in schizophrenia: phantasies of aggression or of the fragmentation of the body, the hallucination of a double, phantasies of mutilation, castration, being devoured, etc.

In this sense, then, the final balance of the mirror stage shows a profit: a total representation of one's own body.

On the other hand, this phase provides the key to the division between the imaginary and the symbolic, and its theoretical importance is that it shows the line of fiction in which the subject constructs himself.

Disguised as a deceptive access to the instance of the total corporeal 'I', as distinct from the background, this stage is in fact only the first step in human alienation. The constitutive role of the first identification with an image, that of one's own body, can be seen at work in it. In this sense, the mirror stage is already structuring the ego in the line of alienation before symbolism restores subjectivity to the child and before his relapse into the imaginary and the dialectic of identifications cause him to lose all the benefits of thought and speech.

The ego is the mirror image with its inverted structure, external to the subject and objectified. The entity of the body has been constituted, but it is external to the self and it is inverted. The subject merges with his own image and the same imaginary trapping by the double can be seen in his relationships with his fellows. It should be noted that the subject is ignorant of his own alienation and that this is how the chronic misrecognition of self and the causal chain determining human existence takes shape.

To sum up: we may say that the jubilatory assumption of the mirror image by the *infans* represents a mould for the symbolic, a prefiguration of his roles.

In it the I is precipitated in primordial form before becoming objectified in the dialectic of identification with the other through the intermediary of identification with its own image, and before language restores to it in the universal its function as subject. The mirror stage realizes the conquest of the totality of one's own body, but it does so by way of a narcissistic identification with the image of the self and with others.

Because of the image's characteristics of exteriority and inverted symmetry, the balance of this rough sketch of subjectivity is alienation in the imaginary.

The mirror stage shows the future importance of the Imago, whose role it is to establish the organism's relation to itself or to establish a relation between *Innenwelt* and *Umwelt*; a relationship which is every time effected by means of a mediate element, either the image or – later – the symbol or the ideal.

The presence of an imaginary mediation breaks the *Innenwelt–Umwelt* circle and begins the inexhaustible cycle of the 'setting' of the Ego. Whatever the dialectical syntheses by which the mind tries to rejoin its reality, its essence, the fusion of Ego and truth will never, at best, be any more than asymptotic.

With Lacan, we can therefore discern a veritable 'structural crossroads' in the mirror stage, since the stage commands (i) the formalism of the ego, that of an erotic relationship between an individual and an image which alienates him, and that of an identificatory transitivism directed towards the other; (ii) the formalism of the objects of desire, always chosen with reference to the object of the other's desire; (iii) the constitutional aggressivity of the human being who must always win his place at the expense of the other, and either impose himself on the other or be annihilated himself.

The Oedipal phenomenon

The essence of the Oedipus is that it is a transcending of the dual relationship of alienation effected through the internal assumption of the triadic symbolic order.

It is preceded by an imaginary relationship between child and mother, and is closed, according to Lacan, by a splitting and by the cycle of the subject's identifications with various ideals, a cycle which punctuates the formation of the ego.

The resolution of the Oedipus constitutes the sense of reality in that it is a liberation from the fascination of the image.

The symbol represents the term necessary first to the constitution of the Family, the triad of father, mother, offspring and, second, to the establishment of the relations between persons.

The subject's accession to the verb does, however, cause him to experience a sort of lack of being: speech is no more than a mediator; it relates to appearance alone and fails to reach the essence.

The signifier of desire, which is inadequate to the expression of that desire, will gradually be modified and will take on multiple forms in the demand; the object of desire, which has been radically lost, can now only be obtained in the form of equally variable substitutes, none of which is capable of reproducing the lost satisfaction.

Caught up in the symbolic, where he is simply represented, obliged to translate himself through the intermediary of a discourse, the subject will become lost, lured away from himself, and will shape himself in accordance with the other's look. Identification with various ideals and rationalizing discourse upon oneself are so many forms in which the subject becomes fixed and betrays himself.

Language and social laws determine the subject and form him in accordance with their own characteristics.

The Oedipus does have a function of sublimation, but this in fact comes down to a refashioning of the subject in his identifications. The child identifies with its rival of the same sex through introjection of his or her Imago. Here, the function of the ego-ideal is twofold, ensuring both libidinal normalization and cultural normalization.

For the young child whose ambition is to seduce its mother, to be for her the phallus, the unique object of her desire, to succeed in sublimating the Oedipus is in fact to accept reality: differences in age, time and generation. It means accepting that he has a real penis and a limited power. It means internalizing the Law of the Father (the super ego) and waiting for biological maturity in order to be able to fulfil his wish.

As we have said, the function of the Oedipus is also to ensure a cultural normalization. The child in effect comes to realize that he is a third member of the family and that he is still in the making. He thus directs himself into the struggle for recognition on the basis of work, sublimating his lack of being in an ever more perfect quest for accomplishment. In this search for himself, the child will make a series of identifications with different ideals, from the classic ideals of childhood (the champion, the hero, the aviator) to the ideals of the adult. The child who is conscious of his title 'member of society' will assume the norms of society, its laws, taboos and ideals.

Through the Oedipus, the subject also transcends the aggression inherent in the primary registration of self during the mirror stage. The Oedipus is thus the source of the recognition of the other and of the principle of equality.

The nature of the ego

Throughout his work Lacan strives to denounce the common illusion which identifies the ego with the self and attributes it with a reality of the order of being.

This belief arises from a failure to recognize the real nature of the ego as being completely derived from a dialectic of narcissistic identifications with external Imagos.

The first of these identifications is that made in the mirror stage, that which gives rise to the inexhaustible cycle of attempts at cirumscribing the self.

The Imago's power to capture has determined the subjection of the subject to the look of the other, to the form of the other.

Secondary identification with the parent of the same sex has in its turn caught the subject up in the quest for an ideal which conforms to the moral verdicts of society, to the desire which the subject senses in the other. At the same time, the necessity for social success has made itself felt and the child has taken the path of the norm, expecting the fruits of his labour in the social recognition which will circumscribe him as being one thing or another. Civil status, profession, titles, membership of social, political or cultural circles are so many forms assumed by the Ego and all demonstrate the symbolic's dominance over man.

It must be stressed that Lacan is not trying to denigrate the value of these various institutions, which are characteristic of man and which give him his grandeur. He simply wishes to make us aware of man's subjection to the other and by the other. Every human action, even the most altruistic, ultimately derives from a demand for recognition by the other, from a wish for self-recognition in some form or other.

We would allow the sharpness of our experience to become
blunted if we deluded ourselves, if not our patients, into believing
in some kind of pre-established harmony that would free of all
aggressive induction in the subject the social conformisms made
possible by the reduction of symptoms.　　　　　(*Écrits*, 13)

Thus, every genetic phase of the individual, every degree of human
achievement, reveals the constitutional narcissism in which the subject
assumes a frustration of being or becoming in a normative sublimation.

It follows that, like Lacan, we must define the ego as:

That nucleus given to consciousness, but opaque to reflection,
marked by all the ambiguities which, from self-satisfaction to 'bad
faith' (*mauvaise foi*) structure the experience of the passions in the
human subject; this 'I' who, in order to admit its facticity to
existential criticism, opposes its irreducible inertia of pretences and
misunderstanding to the concrete problematic of realization of the
subject.　　　　　　　　　　　　　　　　　(*Écrits*, 13)

In other words, the ego is the conscious data we have upon ourselves,
data which resists any critical analysis of its deep origins in the passions.
It shies away from all analysis or questioning under cover of complac-
ency, a clear conscience or the most obvious bad faith. Bad faith is reduplicated, in its discharge, by a profound failure to recognize the
conditioning which fashioned it and the instinct for preservation which
forces it to refuse all questioning.

The role of the symbolic is the social and cultural realization of man
and the normalization of his sexual and aggressive instincts; but it therefore also has the effect of alienating him. It is here that the origin of
human aggression is to be sought. Obliged to fashion himself with
reference to and in rivalry with the other, obliged to wait for recognition
from or judgment by the other, man is naturally inclined to a whole
range of aggressive behaviour, from envy, morbid jealousy and real
aggression to mortal negation of self or other.

We find here the particular meaning given by the Lacanians to the
death instinct.
　　Each stage in the process of becoming, in which man fashions his
world by assuming his original rent (*déchirement*), is marked by a
sacrifice bordering upon suicide. The narcissistic identification with the
mirror image already reveals this tendency on the part of man, as he
alienates himself in a double, just as the Narcissus of legend fell into
the water and drowned through trying to rejoin his image.

The alienation of the ego always has as its corollary a sacrifice: the sacrifice
of the truth of ourselves. The progressive discordance between the ego

181

and the being is accentuated throughout the course of psychical history, a history which is no more than a cycle of attempts at resolving this discordance by consummating it. Each stage of the subject's history will be marked by a transcendence, a normative sublimation of a desire, corollaries of a destruction. Man devotes himself to his own death and consummates it in the movement whereby he seeks to assert himself in the social and cultural world.

One could say that, as the ego proliferates in form, it becomes limited in being. The subject of the verb consummates his alienation by the very effort he makes to neutralize it and to rejoin what he believes to be his essence. Originally intended to circumscribe the individual, language ends up by being the means used by the subject to repress his insufficiencies, his failures and the repeated frustrations which mark his history.

It is certain that the social and cultural symbolic order imposes the path of sublimation on the child, but, on the other hand, man's natural tendency is to find an equilibrium, to reject what disturbs him, to deny his frustrations and his fall from grace. There is always a reciprocity in dependence and it seems to me accurate to say that man 'transcends himself' just as much as he 'is' transcended by being captured by the symbolic.

As we come to the end of this chapter, which closes Part Six, let us pause for a moment and bring together in a few sentences the principal themes of Lacanian thought.

Lacan denounces the abuse of the *cogito ergo sum*, the philosophy of the supremacy of mind and consciousness over the whole of the phenomena of human experience.

What Lacan, helped by long clinical experience, has for years been demonstrating, not only to patients, but to all men, is that even before his birth, the individual is caught up in and completely assimilated into a causal chain of which he can never be any more than an effect. From the mirror phase, when, through narcissism and structural necessity, the child lives himself in his external image, until his accession to the symbol which respresents him in the pre-existing symbolic world, the human being is subjected to the pressure of external symbolism and submits to it.

This submission is a limit on being, which may well be beneficial to humanity as a whole, but which is still a limit. The history of the subject, who is de-centred from himself, is an endless dialectic of the vain search for the self. The ego is its construction and each stone in the edifice sacrifices part of the truth of the essence.

Like the philosopher, the analyst should demystify this being by means of a radical subversion.

The origin or cause of the division between essence and manifestation of essence actualized in this way is the symbolic.

This order, which distinguishes man from the animal, makes him the subject of science and which bears witness to his grandeur, is also the cause of his fall from grace. For if man is an individual only on condition of being 'a member of society' and a 'speaking being', he at the same time bears the weight of all the human mediocrity and baseness accumulated by this order. Grandeur and the fall from grace go together in man. He must struggle against his fellow in his search for a position of strength and prestige, he must appear one thing or another under the right-minded gaze of the other, and he must therefore mask his truest and innermost tendencies in order to be answerable to a universal morality.

Let us now continue our investigations and see how the unconscious functions in its attempts at bringing its contents to the surface. We shall see what the Lacanian analytic cure consists of and, finally, give a detailed account of the nature of neurosis and psychosis in the light of these theories of human evolution.

PART SEVEN

The mechanisms of the formations of the unconscious: structure and organization of the unconscious signifying network

SIXTEEN

The revelatory formations of the unconscious

The progress made by the Lacanian school of psychoanalysis has allowed us to come to grips with the profound nature of the unconscious which had, until then, remained unknown.

The unconscious consists of elementary signifying elements.

What is more, from its original text to its formations (dreams – slips of the tongue – forgetfulness – symptoms), the unconscious shows itself to be comparable in structure to a language; it is organized into a network of multiple relations by displacement and condensation of cathexis from signifier to signifier.

Contemporary developments in linguistics were needed to make such a profound advance in the knowledge of man, and Freud did not have sufficiently advanced studies at his disposal for him to make these discoveries.

Lacan may therefore be considered as having taken up from where Freud left off. For all that, he does not appear to me to have revolutionized Freudian thought. Certainly, he expresses himself in a very esoteric language which may, at first sight, give the illusion of being a labyrinth that never opens out on the real. In fact Lacan is translating into the new terminology offered him by an epoch rich in recent discoveries the very conceptions of symptoms, mental illness and repression held by Freud himself. Lacan has rethought Freud in the wider framework provided by linguistics and structural anthropology.

From this point onwards in our study we will in fact come back more and more clearly to the letter of the Freudian text, as the theories so far expounded are related to analytic practice.

Lacan studies the 'formations of the unconscious' in a very Freudian spirit.

The formations of the unconscious are psychical phenomena in which the intervention of the unconscious is manifested in a veiled form. Taken as it stands, the dream, for example, is meaningless. A careful analysis, using the technique of free association around each detail, reveals, however, a whole network of signifiers united by various associative links. This is the unconscious network of which we have earlier read.

The Lacanian thesis which is the main object of Part Seven is: the assimilation of the processes of condensation and displacement proper to the unconscious to two linguistic mechanisms: metaphor and metonymy.

These two linguistic mechanisms are responsible for a major characteristic of language: that of saying something quite different from what is literally being said.

We can already foresee the content of the Lacanian thesis: like conscious discourse, *the formations of the unconscious* are saying something quite different from what they appear to say. These formations *are governed by the same mechanisms as language, namely metaphor and metonymy*.

For Lacan, then, the unconscious works in accordance with the principal mechanisms of language.

Before going on to describe their workings, let us briefly look at the nature of the formations of the unconscious.

Freud said that 'conscious discourse is lacunary'. What does he mean by this?

At certain privileged points, such as slips of the tongue and jokes, language seems to be torn apart, to burst with a kind of madness. It then allows the true speech – the unconscious – to break through, usually in a veiled and incomprehensible form.

Conscious discourse is rather like those manuscripts where a first text has been rubbed out and covered by a second. In such manuscripts, the first text can be glimpsed through the gaps in the second.

> The unconscious is the discourse of the Other. This appears in the coincidence of the subject's remarks with facts about which he cannot have information. A coincidence, moreover, most often constituted by an entirely verbal, even homonymic convergence.
>
> (*Écrits*, 16)

We have for a long time known that the dream has a meaning, that it is the fulfilment of an unconscious wish, but the dream is neither a vast metaphor nor the stage performance of an underlying theme. It is a rebus to be taken word by word. The associative chains unfolding from each of its details are organized into a network of signifiers, and this network leads to a coherent web of unconscious thoughts. The dream is, therefore, the indirect fulfilment of an unconscious wish.

Symptoms are metaphors. They symbolize, at the level of an organ or a function, an unconscious signifier. The relationships in which such symptoms stand to the repressed thoughts are always of a verbal order: one signifier is put in the place of another:

> The symptom is a return of truth. It is to be interpreted only in the order of the signifier, which is meaningful only in relation to another signifier.   (Lacan, *Du sujet enfin en question*, p. 234)

> The symptom is the signifier of a signified repressed, a symbol written in the sand, it participates in language.   (*Écrits*, 16)

Inside us, then, a subject is thinking in accordance with laws identical to those which organize the signifying chain. The unconscious is the signifier in action, refracting desire as it makes its way towards consciousness.

Screen memories themselves must be examined on a linguistic plane:

> The screen memory derives its possibilities for rememoration, not from its own content, but from its relation to some other repressed term.
> This relation is of a verbal type. Memory appears here as an instrument handed over to the tender mercies of human desire which uses to its own ends all the linguistic effects it is possible to derive from it. (H.-T. Piron *et al.*, 116)

The phantasy, with its mixed character, participating in both the pre-conscious-conscious system and the unconscious system, is also a formation of the unconscious in that it allows desire to arise. Since Laplanche and Pontalis (46) cast light on this point in Freud, we know that phantasmatic formations, divided between the most unconscious pole and the pole of the daydream, refer to a single unit of content – the unconscious wish – but do so in varying forms: the subject lives his daydream in the first person; in the unconscious, on the other hand, the subject is an integral part of the scene. The unconscious phantasy is usually impersonal in form: 'a child is being beaten', for example.

Although it is indeterminate as regards subject and complement and although it is the site of multiple substitutions and permutations, the unconscious form of phantasy does, however, always reveal the subject's place by means of an identifiable term.

In a conscious or preconscious daydream, the phantasy is to be analysed like a dream: it is a form of compromise. The daydream may be bound up with unconscious phantasies which are themselves re-fashionings of infantile memories.

It is in the dream that the profound link between unconscious phantasies and conscious or preconscious phantasies can best be seen. In the dream, phantasy is in fact present at both extremities of the process: it is bound up with the deepest unconscious wish and it is also present in the secondary revision of the dream, as well as in subliminal or conscious daydreaming.

The various levels of phantasies all refer to the same content, the unconscious wish, and are all, in varying degrees, a symbolization of the wish. To use Lacanian terms, they all recall desire's passage into demand or the alienation of desire.

The 'primal' phantasies, however, have the peculiarity of being found in every man, whatever his personal experiences may be. They all deal with seduction, castration, the primal scene or intra-uterine life. This is what leads Freud to say that they are a phylogenetic patrimony rather than the personal luggage of lived experiences. Freud puts forward the hypothesis that their contents were realized in the very early days of the primitive family. As Freud underlines, it is therefore difficult to know whether they correspond to some lived event in the subject's personal life or whether they are purely imaginary. Even supposing that there was a real event in the individual's personal life at the basis of the primal phantasies, the event will always have been refashioned in the psyche in an imaginary mode.

SEVENTEEN

The mechanisms of the formations of the unconscious. Displacement and condensation or metonymy and metaphor

All formations of the unconscious reveal the same formal structure to analysis. The true speech erupts into the subject's discourse and its attempts to outwit the censor bring about a rupture between the signifier and the signified: the unconscious. Through the play of condensation and displacement, the repressed word is transposed (this is the first meaning given by Freud to transference: *Entstellung* or transposition, distortion), and emerges into consciousness wearing a mask. This is why the formations of the unconscious always signify something different from what they are actually saying. The two main mechanisms defined by Freud as effecting this transposition are displacement and condensation.

Lacan has compared these two Freudian processes to the stylistic figures known as metonymy (displacement) and metaphor (condensation).

It will be recalled that Part Two of the present study designated metaphor and metonymy as the two linguistic phenomena responsible for the autonomy of the signifier, or for the supremacy of the signifier over the signified in language. This supremacy of the signifier was defined by language's peculiar aptitude for signifying something other than what it is literally saying.

For Lacan, then, metaphor and metonymy in linguistics and condensation and displacement in psychoanalysis account for the alienation of a thought or a signifier by the simple fact that it must be mediated in language.

It is therefore appropriate that Lacan should make a formal comparison between certain linguistic mechanisms and the essential modes of primary activity proper to the unconscious.

There is a homogeneous structure in symptoms, dreams, parapraxes and jokes. The same structural laws of condensation and displacement are at work in them: these are the laws of the unconscious. These laws are the same as those which create meaning in language. (*Écrits*, 35)

It is a question of rediscovering in the laws that govern that other scene . . . the effects that are discerned at the level of the chain of materially unstable elements that constitute language: effects determined by the double play of combination and substitution in the signifier, according to the two aspects that generate the signified: metonymy and metaphor. (*Écrits*, 24)

The essential article in which Lacan effects these comparisons is 'The agency of the letter in the unconscious or reason since Freud' (22). In this article, the author develops the preceding argument and justifies the comparisons in question as follows:

Verdichtung (condensation) is the structure of the superimposition of signifiers characteristic of metaphor.

Verschiebung (displacement) shows the same transfer of signification as is met with in metonymy.

In this chapter, I will try to shed some light upon the comparisons made by Lacan.

As a first step, I will give strictly linguistic definitions of metaphor and metonymy.

The second stage will be an examination of the use made of these two notions by Lacan in psychoanalysis. Finally, we will try to see more clearly the relationship between metaphor and metonymy and condensation and displacement respectively.

Linguistic definition of metaphor and metonymy

The term metaphor comes from *metaphora*: transport, and *metaphorein*: to carry.

The Larousse and Littré dictionaries define metaphor as follows: 'a figure in which the signification proper to a word is transported to another signification which only fits it because of an implied comparison.'

The alphabetic and analogical dictionary of the French language (Robert) will allow us to make the connexion between the literary definition of metaphor and the definition accepted by modern linguistics. It tells us that:

metaphor, from *metaphora*, transport or transposition, is a figure in rhetoric considered to be the transfer of an abstract notion into the concrete order: an object is designated by the name of another object which bears some relation of analogy with the first object.

Modern linguistics defines metaphor as the birth of a new meaning in a substitutive relation between signifiers connected by a link of similarity.

These definitions allow the part played by metaphor in the signifier's autonomy from the signified to be grasped immediately.

Metaphor is common in poetry. Let us analyse that used by Hugo in a line from his poem *Booz Endormi*:

Sa gerbe n'était point avare ni haineuse
(His sheaves were not miserly or spiteful).

The line is applied to Booz dozing by the side of the woman who will give him a son.

If sense arises from the non-sense, it is because of the general context of fertility in the poem, but mainly because of the immediate connexions of similarity uniting *gerbe* (sheaf) with phallus. The substitution of *gerbe* for Booz and for phallus is authorized and comprehensible because of the links of similarity uniting these terms.

Turning now to metonymy, let us once more use the dictionary.

In Littré, metonymy is defined as a rhetorical figure in which one word is put in the place of another word whose meaning is to be understood. In that sense, metonymy would be a name common to all the tropes. It is in fact restricted to the following usages:

1 the cause for the effect (or vice versa).
    E.g. He lives by his labour for he lives by the fruit of his labour.
2 the container for the contents.
    E.g. drink a cup.
3 the name of the place where something is made for the thing itself.
    E.g. the names of wines: Bordeaux, Champagne, etc.
4 the sign for the thing signified.
    E.g. the eagle for Germany.
5 an abstract noun for a concrete noun.
6 the parts of the body considered to be the seat of the feelings for the feelings themselves.
7 the name of the master of the house for the house itself.
8 the antecedent for the consequence.
9 the use for the thing.
10 the part for the whole.
    E.g. thirty sail.

For modern linguistics, metonymy is based upon the substitution of signifiers between which there is a relation of contiguity, of contextual connexion. Thus, in the example 'thirty sail', sail is put in the place of boat. The substitution is understood because of the significant connexion between the signifiers 'sail' and 'boat'.

193

Now that these definitions have been grasped, we come to the second stage of our research: what, in Lacanian theory, are the psychoanalytic applications of these two stylistic figures?

In his article, 'The agency of the letter in the unconscious' (22), Lacan proposes a symbolic formula for the process of metonymy:

$$f(S \ldots S')S \cong S(-)s$$

He comments on the formula in these terms:

> It is the connexion between S and S that permits the elision in which the signifier installs the lack of being in the object relation, using the value of the 'reference back' possessed by signification in order to invest it with desire aimed at the very lack it supports. The sign − placed between ( ) represents the maintenance of the bar — which, in the original formula $\dfrac{S}{s}$ marked the irreducibility in which, in the relations between signifier and signified, the resistance of signification is constituted. The sign $\cong$ designates congruence.

In his explanation of metonymy, Lacan combines the linguistic definition with the psychoanalytic use of it.

It seems preferable to make our interpretation of this formula in two stages. First, I will try to provide a linguistic justification and second a psychoanalytic justification.

Let us analyse an example of metonymy and try to show how Lacan's formula symbolizes the process at work in it.

Example: I drink a cup.

This expression is put in the place of 'I drink the tea contained in the cup'. 'Cup' is put in the place of 'tea': the container is substituted for the content, which is simultaneously elided. If the signification does arise from this expression, it is because there is an immediate connexion in thought between the two signifiers concerned. Could one not say that: the central signifier in the metonymy, the cup, is a function of the connexion between certain signifiers? This is the phrase symbolized in mathematical form by the left-hand side of Lacan's formula: $f(S \ldots S')S$.

The right-hand side symbolizes the maintenance in the algorithm $\dfrac{S}{s}$ of the line which is resistant to signification. And in fact metonymy is always apparently such non-sense (one does not drink cups) that one must mentally make the significant connexions indispensable to the understanding of the metonymic expression.

We can make the following comments on the formula as a whole, including Lacan's sign for congruence or convergence: $\cong$.

The relation between signifier and signified from which meaning is generated in language is, in metonymy, mediated through a chain of signifiers connected by meaning: this mediation is responsible for a resistance of signification.

Turning to the psychoanalytic justification for the Lacanian formula, we will translate Lacan's own explanation for it: 'the signifier installs the lack of being in the object relation. It finds itself invested with the desire which fills in the lack thanks to the signifier's significant "reference back" to the other.'

This part of the Lacanian explanation makes allusion to the author's theory of the transition from lack to desire and to demand.

We should note that Lacan frequently makes use of the term 'desire' to denote both the lived primal lack or need for union with the mother, and the desire to have which succeeds it after the entry of the subject into language.

Lacan uses the formula 'desire is a metonymy' to indicate the fundamental and progressive alienation of the need for union with the mother which results from the mediation of this need through language. In the demand, the primal need is no more than a shadow of its former self.

To quote a passage from the same article (22) in which the author explains in what way desire is a metonymy:

The enigmas that desire seems to pose for a 'natural philosophy' – its frenzy miming the abyss of the infinite, the secret collusion with which it envelops the pleasure of knowing and of joyful domination, these amount to nothing more than the derangement of the instinct that comes from being caught on the rails – eternally stretching forth towards the desire for something else – of metonymy. Hence its perverse fixation at the very suspension-point of the signifying chain where the screen memory is immobilized and the fascinating image of the fetish is petrified. There is no other way to conceive the indestructibility of unconscious desire.

I suggest that we use an analysis of a dream to show how desire can effectively be metonymic, how it can, that is, evoke by a sort of distant allusion, the subject's unconscious desire and the primal lack which this desire filled in. We will then see how the Lacanian formula for metonymy can also symbolize the notion of metonymic desire.

The dream chosen is Freud's dream of the botanical monograph.

This dream fulfils Freud's wish to make fertile discoveries. This is simply a reply to his friend Königstein who had, the previous day, reproached Freud with being too absorbed in his hobbies. If, however, analysis is taken further, it reveals the existence of a more primitive wish, which has also found satisfaction by way of metonymic pathways.

Besides, in chapter Five of the *Traumdeutung* ('The Interpretation of Dreams'), Freud tells us that:

Dreams frequently seem to have more than one meaning. Not only . . . may they include several wish-fulfilments one alongside the other; but a succession of meanings or wish-fulfilments may be superimposed one on another, the bottom one being the fulfilment of a wish dating from earliest childhood.

Freud's wish to make fertile discoveries, which is fulfilled in the dream, is immediately connected with his well-known passion for books. By Freud's own admission, this passion for books was born in the course of a scene which gave him an intense, if not voluptuous, pleasure when he was five. In this scene, he was gleefully tearing up a coloured picture book leaf by leaf. This memory refers back through metonymic association (connexion of ideas) and a transfer of signification to all later memory: cleaning out a herbarium infested with little worms (*Bücherwurm*). In his passion for books, Freud behaves towards them like the worm which devours them. Such an interpretation is justified by the double meaning of the German word *Bücherwurm*, which designates both the actual worm in the book and the passionate devotee of books. We have already studied this case.

In its turn, the memory of the herbarium refers by metonymic connexions to an insect dream. We know that in psychoanalysis, the *Wurm* symbolizes the child-Phallus. This time, again through a transfer of signification supported by the double meaning of a word, we find ourselves in the presence of the dreamer's profoundly unconscious wish: to devour his mother, just as he devours the book.

It should again be pointed out that the association of the mother with the book was facilitated by a particular event. One day, Freud's father gave him his Bible, the thing he held dearest to him. In Freud's unconscious, the gesture was interpreted as being the gift of his mother, made by his father for Freud's benefit.

The dream also shows quite well, I think, how desire can in effect be metonymic. By means of a series of significant connexions, the wish to make fertile discoveries and therefore to have written a book supports the profoundly unconscious wish to sleep with the mother.

Articulated with signifiers, expressed in words, the desire can never be satisfied since, beneath this significant articulation, there still remains the primal need which aims at fusion with the mother. Having been caught in the signifier by the paternal metaphor, this need can aim at satisfaction only by following the signifying 'concatenation'. It thus becomes metonymic, a reflection, that is, of itself and it is, therefore, always elsewhere, eternally straining after a more adequate substitute for the lost object.

We should, however, note that, in general, the Lacanian expression 'desire is a metonymy' simply justifies the alienation of desire in a signifier which is removed from the original signifier by a series of associative connexions. These associative connexions are not necessarily metonymic; they may be metaphorical. To my mind, the expressions 'desire is a metonymy' and 'symptom is a metaphor' simply try to give the general orientation of the associative connexions in one direction or the other. Lacan would distinguish between metaphor and metonymy only in quite specific cases of association.

Analysis of the dream of the botanical monograph now makes it easier to grasp the symbolic value of the Lacanian formula as a representation of desire-metonymy.

The signifier which rises into consciousness in the dream is a metonymy for the signifier supporting the unconscious desire: its signified. The significant relation between signifier and signified is not immediate; in other words, the dream resists signification. The reason for this resistance lies in the existence of a chain of connecting signifiers going from the signifier in the manifest dream to the unconscious signified: the need for union with the mother.

Lacan also considers the fetish-object and the screen memory to be metonymically connected with the reality of desire.

Because of the dimensions being reached by the present study, we must content ourselves with simply pointing this out.

Turning to the psychoanalytic use of *metaphor* found in Lacan, we can state the definitions given in two other articles:

> Metaphor must be defined as the implantation, in a signifying chain, of another signifier whereby the supplanted signifier falls to the level of a signified and, as a latent signifier, perpetuates there the interval in which another signifying chain may be grafted.
> (*Écrits*, 26)

> Metaphor occurs at the precise point at which sense emerges from non-sense. (*Écrits*, 22)

I now suggest analysing the metaphoric line already quoted from Victor Hugo and showing how these definitions can express the process inherent in metaphor in the linguistic sense.

> Sa gerbe n'était point avare ni haineuse.

In this line, the metaphor is contained in the word *gerbe*. We have already indicated the signifier replaced by *gerbe*: Booz himself. *Gerbe* has been put in place of Booz, which has fallen to the rank of signified. But, as a latent signifier, Booz perpetuates the interval introduced into the signifying chain by the play of substitution; an interval into which another associative chain of signifiers may be introduced, the chain which links Booz with father, then with phallus and with fertility.

197

In its substitution of one signifier for another, metaphor is, moreover, creative of meaning.

Lacan does not, however, accentuate the relation of similarity which exists between the elements substituted for one another in metaphor. It is this which distinguishes his point of view from that of the linguist. This is understandable, given that unconscious relations are not so dependent upon relations of analogy as those established in the conscious secondary process.

Lacan also adds a notion which is absent in linguistics: that of sense in non-sense. This addition, however, is well justified. In the example of the line from Victor Hugo it is clear that a signification of paternity and fertility is derived from an assemblage of words which is apparently inadequate to the theme. Similarly, in the domain of unconscious formations, a repressed truth will be expressed through apparent nonsense.

To turn now to the symbolic formula given by Lacan in 'The agency of the letter . . .' (22) and the explanation he simultaneously provides for it:

$$ f\left(\frac{S'}{S}\right) \cong S(+)s $$

It is in the substitution of signifier for signifier that an effect of
signification is produced that is creative or poetic . . . The sign +
between ( ) represents here the crossing of the bar − and
the constitutive value of this crossing for the emergence
of signification.

I suggest another explanation: the emergence of signification is immediate, being effected by a sort of spark in the mind which, from the start, establishes the relationship between the signifiers substituted for one another.

Metonymy, on the other hand, necessitates a longer mental trajectory in search of the links uniting the signifiers.

Lacan assigns the value of unconscious metaphor to the symptom. Its meaning remains a mystery to the patient until analysis throws light upon the substitutive relationship between the manifest and latent terms. The symptom disappears as quickly as it arose once association has allowed the forgotten relationship to be re-established. Here is an example of a metaphoric symptom given by H.-T. Piron (116):

The patient was suffering from pains at the bottom of her back.
During free association she stops at the word *Kreuz* (cross) and
says that the cross signifies her pain. In fact, in German *Kreuz*
also means the sacrum. Freud points out to her that the word
Kreuz is also used to designate moral suffering. This interpretation
causes the symptom to disappear.

This symptom arises out of the mechanism of metaphor in the sense that the physical pain in the sacrum (S') has been substituted for the moral pain (S the cross) thanks to the double meaning of the German term *Kreuz*. This symptom therefore takes as its support the symbolic relationships which unite signifiers of the order of spiritual existence.

The mechanism which provoked the symptom in the patient in question is exactly that of metaphor. What is crystallized in the patient is the physical pain in the sacrum. That is how the symptom presents itself in its conscious, physical and natural aspect.

In the course of her free associations, the patient recognizes that the cross which obsesses her is bound up with her physical pain. Yes, replies Freud, since, in German, *Kreuz* means sacrum, but the word is also a symbol for moral suffering.

One can imagine the patient making, for an ephemeral moment, the following reflection: my suffering is a cross, I bear my cross, thus rejoining a well-known traditional symbolism.

But as soon as the connexion between cross and sacrum is established for her, the moral suffering she wanted to forget is transformed into a pain at the base of the spine through the intermediary of a pun. There remains some misty connexion between the sacrum and the cross, whereas the moral suffering falls definitively back into the unconscious.

The mechanism of this symptom is indeed the substitution, in a signifier-signified relationship (moral suffering is a cross), of another signifier (the sacrum), whereby the first signifier S 'falls below'.

'The hysterical symptom', said Freud, 'is a mnemic symbol.'

The connexion has been made between the Lacanian psychoanalytic definition of metaphor and metonymy and the linguistic definition.

I now suggest to the reader that we make a personal attempt at justifying the comparisons drawn by Lacan between, on the one hand, metaphor and condensation and, on the other, between metonymy and displacement.

The comparisons in question are asserted by Lacan in numerous passages in his *Écrits*, they are applied to analytic examples, but there is no text which justifies their theoretical basis.

In this third part of our study, we shall therefore try to provide some justification for the positions adopted.

Metaphor and condensation; metonymy and displacement

We can begin by citing one of Lacan's most exhaustive texts on the metaphor-condensation, metonymy-displacement comparisons:

> The mechanisms described by Freud as those of the primary
> process in which the unconscious assumes its rule, correspond
> exactly to the functions that this school believes determine the
> most radical effects of language, namely metaphor and metonymy,

in other words, the signifier's effects of substitution and combination on the respectively synchronic and diachronic dimensions in which they appear in discourse.   (*Écrits*, 27)

In short, Lacan assimilates:

I.	1 condensation	II.	1 displacement
	2 metaphor		2 metonymy
	3 substitution		3 combination
	4 synchrony		4 diachrony

The terms numbered 3 and 4 refer the reader back to Part One, chapter 2, 'The two great axes of language'. Let us briefly recall the content of that chapter.

In the construction of the discourse, the selection of linguistic units is made from within groups of words which are associated in the code on the basis of some similarity or other. These groupings authorize a series of *substitutions* of signifiers. Within these groups, signifiers are associated by similarity in sound or similarity in meaning.

In Lacan, *synchrony* refers to the terms implicitly inscribed on the vertical axis of the elementary signifying elements of the sentence. The terms implicitly associated with the units of the discourse are also united through some similarity in sound or meaning. It will be recalled that similarity also characterizes the signifiers substituted in metaphor.

Combination, on the other hand, refers to the idea of context, to the links of contiguity which unite the units of discourse. The spoken chain is the (horizontal) site of *diachrony* (the notion of temporal evolution).

In metonymy, the substituted terms are contiguous, being united by links looser than those found in metaphor. The terms are, however, neighbours, as far as meaning is concerned.

For example, the evolution in thought which leads from the knife to its use 'to cut' shows a transfer of signification, but the terms are still contiguous, they belong, that is, to a single register of thought.

How can the comparison between the notions of *condensation* and *metaphor* be justified?

The notion of condensation is not homogeneous in Freud's various writings.

Chapter Six of the *Traumdeutung* and the *Introductory Lectures on Psychoanalysis* (7) give two different notions of condensation and we will analyse them in turn.

The notion of condensation in the joke deserves an analysis to itself, and will form the object of a third paragraph.

In the *Introductory Lectures* . . . (7) we read that *condensation operates through the omission* of certain latent thoughts and therefore through the lacunary restitution of these thoughts. It acts through a selective choice of latent elements.

This definition is implicitly stated in the following text from Freud: 'It is far from being the case that one manifest element always takes the place of one latent element . . . one manifest element can replace several latent ones. These ideas are not necessarily linked to each other' (7, p. 125).

The elements of the manifest are, therefore, 'overdetermined', referring back through a series of associations to various latent thoughts.

If we limit ourselves to the linguistic definitions of selection and metaphor, then condensation does not permit the comparison drawn by Lacan, or at least does not allow it completely.

Linguistic selection retains one signifier from amongst other signifiers united by links of similarity which are therefore capable of being substituted for the first signifier.

Metaphor is the substitution of one signifier for another, the first being caught in a chain of synchronic terms which are similar in meaning or in sound. But Freud specifically states that the latent thoughts which overdetermine a detail in the manifest are not necessarily connected to one another.

It seems to me that the notion of metaphor in Lacan is wider and looser because it applies to the human and above all to the unconscious, in which logic does not exist. Lacan takes the notions of selection and substitution from linguistics, as well as the notion of the synchronic chain of signifying terms, but shows little interest in similarity.

The elements which are associated in the unconscious with a signifier in the manifest do not belong to the code of the language, with its fixed laws, but to the patient's personal code, which is enriched by his or her lived experiences and phantasies. As we will see, despite everything the links uniting the unconscious signifiers do follow laws of assonance and relations of signification. But, on the other hand, certain associations are facilitated by some lived concomitance, by individually felt analogies. They do not, therefore, enter into language's catalogue of associations. A comparison between metaphor and condensation may, then, be valid, on condition that the rigour of linguistics be relaxed.

We now come to the second form of condensation proposed by Freud in the *Traumdeutung*.

Freud says that *condensation* can also result in a composition formation: latent elements with *features in common* fuse together into a single manifest element which represents all of them.

A composite figure may be formed in three different ways:
- the features of different people are fused together in a single face;
- the single face may bring together only common features;
- the single person may evoke others by the diversity of the situations in which he is found or by a sum of heteroclite qualities.

Still in chapter six of the *Traumdeutung*, Freud also assimilates the use of words with multiple meanings to condensation. This particular form of condensation seems to me to have its place in this division.

We shall now illustrate the notion of collective figures and of the multiple meanings of a word. And we shall try to show how these forms of condensation resemble metaphor.

In the dream of the botanical monograph, *Bücherwurm* is a word with multiple meanings.

Through *Bücher*, it refers back to the Bible Freud received from his father as though he were receiving his mother as a gift.

Through *Wurm*, it refers back to the child-phallus who discovers his mother through incest.

On its vertical axis, *Bücherwurm* holds appended Bible and mother on the one hand and bookworm and child-phallus on the other hand. Book, Bible and mother stand in a metaphoric relation to one another, as do the terms: worm, child-phallus.

In the dream of Irma's injection, Irma appears in a situational complex and performs actions each of which refers back to a different person. All these people show a certain similarity at the level of the latent thoughts.

This second form of condensation does indeed appear to lend itself more readily to Lacan's deductions, because of the similarity between latent thoughts evoked by Freud. In conclusion, we can say that the comparisons made by Lacan are justified on condition that the linguistic domain is adapted to the human domain, which is in essence original and extraordinary.

To turn to the third stage of our analysis of the notion of condensation: what is its status in the joke?

In the joke, condensation consists of the important ellipsis of latent thoughts which are nevertheless represented in the substitute formation resulting from the condensation.

Lacan himself (35) has analysed the 'famillionaire' joke quoted by Freud in accordance with the technique of metaphor.

In the play *The Baths of Lucca*, an extract from the German poet Heine's *Reisebilder*, the main character boasts to his doctor about his relations with Baron Rothschild:

> 'And as true as God shall grant me his favours, Doctor, I sat
> beside Solomon Rothschild and he treated me quite as his equal –
> quite famillionairely.'

The joke can be decanted as follows:

Fami	lli	on	aire
Fami	li		ar
mi	lli	on	aire

[In French it is even more direct: Fami-li-onn-aire, Fami-li-ère, mi-li-onn-aire: trans.] The substitute formation condenses within it two ideas: familiar and millionaire.

The author of the joke meant to say familiar, but, as Lacan says, the intentional chain interfered with the signifying chain. The word millionaire, which is latent because the smell of the millions was spoiling the atmosphere, adds the complementary syllable (on) to familiar.

In the composite formation 'famillionaire', the elements of the intentional and signifying chains are imbricated in a substitution, thanks to their partial homophony.

Here, meaning is produced from within non-sense.

Freud also points out that the poet Heine had an uncle Solomon, who was very rich and who always treated him as a poor relation. He may even have refused Heine his daughter's hand. Famillionaire therefore refers back through the intermediary of millionaire to Uncle Solomon, who sanctioned the poet's timidity. No doubt it also refers back to all the bourgeois imbued with the fallacious prerogatives of the rich who haunted the poet's youth.

It now remains for us to establish the connexions between *metonymy* and *displacement*. We will proceed in the same manner as we did for metaphor and condensation, dividing our text into three paragraphs: the first two being reserved for the two forms of displacement given by Freud in Chapter 5 of the *Traumdeutung*, and the third dealing with displacement in jokes.

We begin by looking at the first notion of displacement given by Freud (*Traumdeutung*, Ch. 5):

> In the manifest content of the dream, only the *indifferent*
> impression was alluded to. . . . All the strands of the *interpretation*,
> on the other hand, led to the *important* impression. . . . What takes
> place would seem to be something in the nature of a 'displacement'
> . . . in this way, ideas which originally had only a *weak* charge of
> intensity take over the charge from ideas which were originally
> intensely cathected and at last attain enough strength to enable
> them to force an entry into consciousness.

Again, we can take the dream of the botanical monograph as an example.

The important event of the previous day is Freud's conversation with his friend Königstein and the latter's reproach: 'You are too pre-occupied with your hobbies', or, in other words, 'You are not making fertile discoveries.'

The manifest content of the dream refers back by way of the signifier 'plant' to another event of the previous day: the intervention of the Gärtner (gardener) couple and the ensuing conversation. They talked about Freud's patient Flora (flower), and Freud said to himself that Frau Gärtner was 'blooming'.

In this dream, it is clearly a matter of displacement.

Perhaps we can also recognize in it the metonymic pathways of thought along which one theme leads to another in accordance with a relation of context, of contiguity. Thus, the heated conversation with Königstein about Freud's analytic performances was followed by the Gärtner's anodine allusion to his patient Flora.

In the dream, the signifiers of the range of plants will replace the signifiers of the important event by means of displacement . . . or metonymy, and will allow the latter to accede to consciousness.

The second notion of displacement given by Freud in chapter five of the *Traumdeutung* (V, p. 182):

> The displacement which replaces psychically important by
> indifferent material . . . (may have) taken place at the early period
> of life and since then become fixed in the memory.

This notion comes back to the problem of the screen memory.

The dream of the botanical monograph once more provides us with an example with which to illustrate these notions.

The coloured picture which figures in the manifest refers back to the important memory of the coloured book torn up by Freud when he was five. The picture has become fixed in the memory alongside a memory whose importance derives from the sensual impression which accompanied the act of tearing.

The memory of a coloured picture in a book is metonymically connected by contiguity with the act of tearing. There is also a transfer of the psychical accent from the primordial to the indifferent.

For Lacan, the coloured picture in the book in the manifest is the signifier which both supports and masks the desire for incest through its value as a 'reference back' to the torn book, to the Bible and to the mother, the term which closes the signifying concatenation.

Finally, *in the joke*, displacement is characterized, according to Freud, by the *pivotal function* attributed to an anodine term spoken by someone. This term allows the author of the joke to come back with a reply which has a completely different meaning.

Like metonymy, displacement shows a transfer of signification allowed by the confusion as to the meaning to be accorded to the pivotal word. Nevertheless, it is the pivot-word which maintains the relations of contiguity between the two trains of thought.

Freud suggests various different examples of jokes whose construction is based upon metonymy. We will take up only one of them here.

The poet Heine, whom we have already mentioned, is conversing in a Parisian salon with one Souillé. One of the financial kings of the nineteenth century arrives and is immediately surrounded. 'Look,' says

Souillé, 'the nineteenth century is worshipping the golden calf.' 'Oh, he must be older than that by now!' replies Heine.

In this joke, the term calf is used by Souillé in a metaphorical sense and is taken in its literal sense by Heine. The second usage allows a witty comeback in the domain of age, together with a transfer of signification. Heine's reply could be translated as 'Oh, he's not a calf but a full-grown ox'.

This example does indeed belong to the metonymic process of thought, proceeding through connexions of contiguity of thoughts and of the transfer of meaning.

EIGHTEEN

Analysis of unconscious formations following metaphoric and metonymic processes

We will analyse only three examples of the formations of the unconscious, but we will analyse them as completely as possible: one somatic symptom, whose localization and form stand in a metaphoric relation to the unconscious signifier they represent; and two classic examples of the forgetting of names and false recollection.

In the second and third examples, we will see how the elements composing the unconscious signifying chain are knit together and the nature of the links which bind them together.

The new teaching to which Lacan invites us is both theoretical and practical. A classic play of language should be seen in symptoms of mental illness and the relations between unconscious signifiers and conscious signifiers should be brought to light.

Let us take the metaphor-symptom as our first example of a formation of the unconscious.

> The symptom resolves itself entirely in an analysis of language,
> because the symptom is itself structured like a language,
> because it is from language that speech must be delivered.
>
> (*Écrits*, 16)

> The double-triggered mechanism of metaphor is the very
> mechanism by which the symptom, in the analytic sense, is
> determined. Between the enigmatic signifier of a sexual trauma and
> its substitute term in the actual signifying chain there passes the
> spark that fixes in a symptom the signification inaccessible to the
> conscious subject – a symptom being a metaphor in which flesh
> or function is taken as a signifying element.   (*Écrits*, 22)

These two quotations tell us that the symptom is a formation of the unconscious in the sense that, in it, the true speech of the unconscious is translated into an enigmatic signifier. But they also tell us that the process whereby the symptom becomes fixed is that of metaphor: the substitution in a signifier-signified relation of signifier S' for another signifier S, which falls to the rank of signified in accordance with the familiar formula:

$$\frac{S}{s} \times \frac{S'}{S} \to S'\left(\frac{1}{s}\right) \text{ or } \frac{\dfrac{S'}{s}}{\dfrac{S}{S}}$$

The symptom is, in effect, a substitutive sign for a traumatic experience.

A. Vergote (115) specifies that the link uniting the mnemic symbol and the traumatic experience may be individual or may on the other hand be of the order of symbolization. In the latter case, the symptoms express the traumatic experience in their very configuration and present an immediate relationship of analogy to that experience.

In the first case, analysis can only be based upon free association, since the patient alone holds the truth of his symptom. In the second case, analysis may be based upon universal symbolism.

Could not this duality in form in symbolization account for the gap between the linguistic and the Lacanian notions of metaphor, with the linguist limiting himself to universal symbolization, whilst the analyst is also interested in strictly individual symbolizations?

We will now take up Vergote's example: Dora's hysterical vomiting.

Here it is a question of a symbol-symptom of the order of universal symbolization.

It expresses the patient's moral repugnance at any sexual relation, oral (kissing) or otherwise, with Mr K.

This type of symbolization is inscribed in tradition: not being able to tolerate something is translated as 'it makes me sick'. The metaphor links corporeal registers with spiritual registers.

The vomiting is substituted for the impression of moral disgust she felt when she was kissed by Mr K, an impression which was repressed along with the memory of the scene.

The vomiting could also signify the pregnancy resulting from imaginary sexual relations with Mr K.

Freud's *Psychopathology of Everyday Life* (3) provides Lacanian analysis of the formations of the unconscious with a series of examples of psychical phenomena determined by the unconscious.

The forgetting of a name, for example, which is accompanied by the production of erroneous substitute names reveals to analysis a net of verbal associations showing the existence of complex processes of unconscious thoughts.

In the phenomena we think of as being anodine, the unconscious, like language, works autonomously without the subject being aware of it, and through the paths of association, a word contrives to be spoken despite the barrier of censorship.

Here, we will take the example of the forgetting of the name Signorelli (an Italian Renaissance painter).

The example shows that the false recollection of substitute names is determined by a play of purely phonetic associations between the latent signifiers and the recollected signifiers.

The technique for analysis of the forgetting of names is association around the substitute names.

Freud was travelling by train in the Bosnia and Herzegovina region in the company of a stranger, and they were talking about Italian art.

'Have you seen the frescoes at Orvieto by . . . (Signorelli)?'

Freud tries in vain to remember the name of the painter. He can only recall the names of two other painters: Botticelli and Boltraffio.

Freud and his companion had just been talking of the customs of the Turks in Bosnia and Herzegovina. Freud recalled how they had full confidence in the doctor and a complete resignation to fate. They say 'Signor (Herr), I know that if he could be saved, you would save him.'

Freud had, at this point, kept quiet about another detail which crossed his mind: the Turks attach such importance to sexual pleasures that they reach the depths of despair when 'that' ceases.

As he was thinking of this detail, Freud remembered the news which had just reached him from Trafoï: one of his patients had committed suicide because he was suffering from an incurable sexual disturbance.

Between these two repressed elements (the Turks' despair when faced with sexual disturbances, and the patient's suicide for the same reasons) and Signorelli, there have been established associative connexions which have drawn the name into the unconscious and made it impossible to remember it. On the other hand, the substitute names announce, by way of other associative connexions, both the forgotten name and the repressed elements. Figure 18.1 shows the associations, and is accompanied by a commentary.

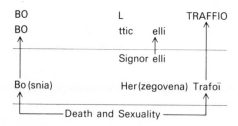

FIGURE 18.1

The associations are realized either by sound or by meaning, and are in both cases made through the intermediary of the signifier.

The substitute names are the terminal points of a chain of signifiers, they are the metonymic ruins of the repressed (the idea of death). (35)

– *Signor* is attracted into the unconscious by the relation of similarity between the *Her* in *Her*zogovina and the word *Herr*, which is the German equivalent of the Italian Signor.

The *Herr* is also the absolute master, Death.

– The anodine *elli*, on the other hand, comes to the surface in Bottic*elli*.

– The two repressed anecdotes about the Turks in *Bosnia* and Herzegovina and the suicide at Trafoï still manage to be spoken, first through the *Bo* because it is neutral and not very revealing – this gives *B*otticelli and *B*oltraffio – and second through Traffio, which reveals the town where the suicide occurred, but masks it by reduplicating the *f*.

Most of the associations are of a metaphoric nature, although in referring to the substitute names Lacan does speak of 'metonymic ruins'. *Bo* and *Traffio* are 'metonymic ruins' in that they are only phonemes, parts of the complete repressed signifiers.

Therefore one can say that, in one sense, Botticelli is a metonym for Bosnia on the one hand and for Signorelli on the other, as it only partially reproduces them. But in another sense, the links connecting *Bo* (in Botticelli) and *Bo* (in Bosnia) are metaphoric, as is the link between Traffio and Trafoï (see Figure 18.1).

It should be specified that none of this work of association entered into Freud's consciousness. The signifier acted autonomously. We are in the presence of the activity proper to the unconscious. Freud will add later that there is, despite everything, a meaningful connexion between Signorelli, which is attracted into the unconscious, and the latent thoughts. In fact the painter's frescoes at Orvieto have as their themes death and sexuality.

Here is another example of a word being forgotten, given by Freud. Although the analysis is not so clear here, it does again account for the associative play of the signifiers.

In the course of a journey, Freud makes the acquaintance of a young Jew who has read his work. Their conversation is about the unfortunate social situation of the Jews. Carried away by a thirst for vengeance, the young man wants to quote the famous line from Virgil in which Dido leaves to posterity the task of avenging her of the outrage Aeneas has inflicted upon her. He says:

Exoriare ex nostris ossibus ultor.

But he immediately realizes that another word is needed to give the rhythm of the text. Freud completes the line for him:

Exoriare *aliquis* nostris ex ossibus ultor.

Freud and his companion then begin to analyse why the word was forgotten. The young man's associations are:
- a – liquis;
- relics, liquidation, liquid;
- Simon of Trent (sacrificed as a child), whose relics he has seen;
- Jews accused of murder and their so-called victims being compared to new incarnations of the Saviour;
- St Augustine and his unfavourable opinion of women;
- St Janarius and the miracle of his blood which miraculously liquifies on a set date in a church in Naples;
- Garibaldi, who hoped that the miracle would take place in front of his troops, otherwise the soldiers would have been resourceless. He obtained the miracle;
- an Italian lady with whom he visited Naples, and who is, he fears, going to tell him that she has missed her period.

In general, we can say that two opposed unconscious wishes have given rise to a network of associations in which the word *aliquis* is caught up.
1 If there is *a-liquis*, then there will be a posterity to avenge the tribulations he suffers as a Jew. It also means that he will be a father, just as St Simon and St Augustine are Fathers of the Church, and that something will survive his death like a relic.
2 But *aliquis* also means that there is a reminder of his relations with the lady, since, unlike the miracle of St Janarius' blood, there has been no liquification on a set date.

Henceforth, it is a matter of vengeance. He wants none of this child. He will be obliged to sacrifice it like St Simon of Trent, to liquidate it.

Through a metaphor – the miracle of the blood – an associative relation of a metaphoric type is established between *aliquis* and the repressed thoughts about the lady. The signifier *iquis* is assimilated by sound to liquid, liquidation.

Simon of Trent becomes the signifier by which the repressed thought of abortion is forced into the unconscious, again in metaphorical form. And the two signifiers are linked together thanks to the assimilation of the child to a relic (like St Simon's relics), since it is a relic of his relationship with the lady and will, after his death, be a relic of him.

Psychical reality, therefore, is this language-matter and what happens in it: it is the set of unconscious processes whose law is that of over-determination.

A single signifier will have several layers of resonance, several possible levels of signification.

All formations of the unconscious derive from this regular play of substitution and combination in the signifier.

This is also the reason which leads the Lacanians to restore all the associations in detail during analysis, so that the act of becoming aware is not the sudden lifting of a veil which is immediately lowered again by the censor, but a complete refashioning of the preconscious–conscious systems from which these processes have escaped.

PART EIGHT

The general conception of the cure in Lacan

NINETEEN

Language: the primordial indicator of truth in the analytic cure

The application to psychoanalysis of the implications of the Saussurian algorithm $\left(\dfrac{S}{s}\right)$ has allowed Lacan a structural understanding of the subject as being divided into two parts by his accession to language: the unconscious and the conscious discourse in which the subject constitutes himself as an Ego. The unconscious, a second structure, cannot be apprehended in its truth by the logical analysis the patient makes of his being, his Ego or his past. The 'I' of discourse is radically separated from the Other of the subject, the unconscious. As a mediator, language distances the 'I' which speaks and believes itself to be telling the truth about its essence from the unconscious reality which founds it in its truth.

Listen to Lacan himself in 'The function and field of speech and language in psychoanalysis' (16), the article which inaugurated the schism between the Lacanian school and the original French stock:

> One does not have to know whether the subject has remembered anything whatever from the past. He has simply recounted the event. . . . He has verbalized it. He has made it pass into the *verbe*, or, more precisely, into the epos by which he brings back into present time the origins of his own person.

The Lacanian analyst is not greatly concerned with reconstructing the exact historical succession of the events recounted by the patient. Their historical reality is of little importance to him: the patient's discourse develops at the level of the imaginary. He transposes or invents his biography; in his discourse, he represents himself as another, as he wishes to see himself, or as he wishes to be seen.

> The jubilatory assumption of the image in the mirror shows the truly imaginary nature of the Ego. In the different modes of relation, the subject always imposes upon the other an imaginary form which bears the superimposed seals of the experiences of impotence in which this form was modelled in the subject, and this form is none other than the Ego. Discourse is situated at this level of the imaginary. (*Écrits*, 15)

The new orientation of psychoanalysis inaugurated by Lacan and instituted in 1953 consists nevertheless in having elected the patient's
speech and discourse as the essential, if not the only indication of the
truth: the unconscious.

> However empty this discourse may appear, it is only so if taken at
> its face value. . . . Speech, even when almost completely worn out,
> retains its value as a tessera. Even if it communicates nothing,
> even if it denies the evidence, it affirms that speech constitutes
> truth.
>   It is the psychoanalyst who knows better than anyone that the
> question is to understand which part of this discourse carries the
> significative terms. . . . It is therefore a fortunate kind of
> punctuation which confers its meaning on the subject's discourse.
>   (*Écrits*, 16)

The Lacanian analyst therefore operates upon the sole intermediary of
the truth: *the discourse of the patient in analysis*. He examines him in his
locutory, fabular behaviour. But, and it is this which justifies the
process, the analyst does not attend to the content of this discourse
itself, but to the rents in it, the 'formations of the unconscious' which
establish a new content: that of the motivations of the unconscious.

By means of this fortunate scansion of the discourse, the analyst
introduces himself to a new language: that of the unconscious, which
has its own rules.

We have just defined the evenly suspended attention proper to the
Lacanians, and recalled the existence of nodal points in the discourse
in which the truth breaks through.

> Psychoanalysis puts forward the whole set of phenomena which
> deserve the title of psychoanalytic semantics: dreams, slips of the
> tongue, absentmindedness, disorders of recollection, the caprices
> of free association.   (15)

Analysis thus bases its action completely upon communication and
dialogue, and interpretation will consist of an analysis of language.

TWENTY

The role of the analyst

H.-T. Piron defines the analyst's role for us as follows (116):

> The psychoanalyst is nothing by himself. His function resides in the fact of his representing something that transcends him infinitely. His true place is that of the listener. He is the one through whom the analysand addresses himself to the other in order to have the truth of his message recognized and to have it translated there where it hides in the cipher-language of discourse. His powers as a translator are conferred upon him by the linguistic structure inherent in the unconscious. It is by virtue of his participation in the world and in culture that the analyst has a role.
>
> The psychoanalyst loses his role as a model for the analysand. Analysis cannot pretend to the identification of the analysand with his analyst. The Oedipus complex introduces a triadic relationship between analyst and analysand, with Society as its third term. Interpretation derives from this third term. The therapeutic power is of the order of speech.

This text gives the Lacanian analyst the place of the Other: the third party witness to truth, the guarantor of good faith whom we always invoke when we address ourselves to someone in an effort at coinciding with what is absolutely true.

But, parallel to this, the text also indicates that the analyst represents the *symbolic*: Society, Culture and Language, and that it is from this third term that interpretation derives, since the unconscious is a language. It also indicates that analysis unfolds in language and has its sources in language alone.

In the third place, the analyst also represents the other, or, rather, *all the interlocutors* of the past life of the subject to whom he addresses himself in order to have his message recognized. The analyst is invested with this role through transference, which will be dealt with in the next chapter.

Lacan, however, seems to add a further role to these three roles of the analyst: that of the dummy (*le mort*). Let us try to come to grips with this idea.

A lot has been said about the analyst's neutrality, his non-intervention. This reaches its most radical form with the Lacanians, and is translated as the frustration of all response to the analysand: the analyst plays dummy, he plays dead. Why?

Everybody agrees that I frustrate the patient. Why? Because he asks me for something. To answer him, in fact. But he knows very well that it would be mere words. And he can get those from whom he likes. His demand is intransitive, it carries no object with it. His present demand has nothing to do with being cured, with revealing him to himself, with introducing him to psychoanalysis.

Through the mediation of demand, the whole past opens up, right down to early infancy.

It is in this way that analytic regression may take place.

Regression shows nothing other than a return to the present of signifiers used in demands for which there is prescription.

There is no need to seek further for the source of the identification with the analyst. It will always be an identification with signifiers. (*Écrits*, 28)

This text recalls that it is through the intermediary of demand that the subject's metonymic desire is conveyed and becomes fixed to the successive signifiers that refract it. The reality of the desire is, then, to be sought at the starting-point of this endless dialectic. And, consequently, a movement must be provoked which articulates in reverse order the scansion of the demand. It is to this end that the analyst frustrates the patient of any response to his demand.

Frustration of demand is the only means at the analyst's disposal to provoke the subject's regression from one signifier of his demand to another, and to reach, through this regression, the first unconscious signifier of the desire.

In this same movement, the analysand is progressively dispossessed of all the forms of his ego in which he has constructed himself in the imaginary through successive identifications with mirror images of his being. The analysand's aggressivity results from this growing dispossession of self.

With his attitude of non-intervention, the Lacanian analyst therefore plays the part of the dummy.

One should not be deceived by the metaphor of the mirror, appropriate as it may be to the smooth surface that the analyst presents to the patient. An impassive face and sealed lips do not have the same purpose here as in a game of bridge. Here the analyst is rather bringing to his aid what is in bridge called the dummy (*le mort*), but he is doing so in order to introduce the fourth player who is to be the partner of the analysand here and whose hand, the analyst, by his tactics, will try to expose. (*Écrits*, 28)

To put it in very simple terms, non-intervention may be assimilated to the 'don't touch' airs affected by certain people in society. Silence, the barely ironic glance, the look into which one seems to fall as though into a void, the glasses which throw an impenetrable veil over the gaze, are so many easy and profitable techniques used by human beings to attract attention or confidences. Who, in fact, unless he is very well-balanced, has not felt a wish to move this wall, to startle it, to shake this inertia with a flow of words rivalling it in charm, audacity or arguments? The need to prove, to justify oneself, to intimidate is inherent in man, and he will commit himself further and further, releasing the brakes and rapidly losing control over the *verb* which preserved his innermost being. This is what the analyst is counting upon when he remains silent. And no one can get out of this game.

TWENTY-ONE

Transference

Considered superficially, says J. Schotte (111), transference is a positive or negative 'fact', an event which can be localized, a sentimental manifestation of the patient's love or hatred for his or her analyst.

As a fact, transference designates the carrying over of an earlier lived experience, which has become inaccessible, on to the person of the analyst and the actual situation of analysis.

> The patient sees in the analyst the return, the reincarnation, of some important figure out of his childhood or past, and consequently transfers on to him feelings and reactions undoubtedly applied to this prototype.   (9, p. 174)

We can, however, Schotte continues, be introduced to the abysmal dimension of transference only by grasping the positive and negative oppositions of its manifestations and the dialectic established by these oppositions.

We can then see that if transference is a limited fact which can be localized, it is also and above all 'the process which produces the whole analysis, in the sense that it englobes its products in time, each time transcending them in its movement'.

As the author points out, taking a phrase from Lévi-Strauss, transference is somewhat akin to Mana, that mysterious power which grips man with a passion for someone, that strange thing, grammatically both substantive, adjective and verb, which is at once omnipresent and localized.

As a 'process', transference designates the path of analysis, which is ultimately identical to the 'process' of the cure itself.

This englobing dimension of transference may be interpolated into a text by Freud, where it is applied to the dream. Transference is the dream process itself, in that 'an unconscious idea enters the preconscious by establishing a connexion with an idea that already belongs to the preconscious, by transferring its intensity on to it and by getting itself "covered" by it'.

By applying this definition to the cure as a whole, we can say that the analyst is rather like the day's residue on to which the desire is transferred.

If we now look at transference in the light of Lacanian theory, we will find a similar conception.

As a premise to any discussion of transference, Lacan posits its inadequacy to the sum of the patient's positive and negative feelings towards the analyst.

Transference does not arise out of some mysterious property of affectivity, and even if it does betray itself in the form of agitation, the latter is only meaningful as a function of the dialectical movement within which it occurs. (*Écrits*, 14)

Lacan is opposing a psychologizing of transference as deriving from affectivity, and is restoring it to its true dimension as a movement in the analytic cure.

For Lacan, transference as a 'fact' is the identification of the analyst with the images which captivated the subject and sanctioned the alienation of his ego. But above all Lacan insists upon the 'process' aspect of transference: 'The concept of the exposé is identical to the progress of the subject, that is, to the reality of the cure' (*Écrits*, 14). Lacan has previously defined this as being a dialectical experience.

As a 'process', transference will mark the subject's regression from one stage in the formation of his ego to another, from one signifier of the demand, in which his desire, a prisoner in the nets of the signifier, is conveyed, to another signifier.

Transference is therefore identical to the evolution of the cure itself. What does this evolution consist of?

Characteristically, Lacan articulates it in terms of the intransitive demand of the subject which underlies what he says and in which his desire is alienated. In the text, Lacan says:

All the demands that have been articulated in analysis, and more than any other the original demand to become an analyst are merely transferences intended to maintain in place a desire that was unstable or dubious in its problematic. (*Écrits*, 28)

This again means that the patient's demand is expressive of a metonymic desire. And the aim of analysis will be to provoke the subject's regression through the frustration of all response to his demand. The regression is twofold: it is the passage from one signifier to another, and the dispossession by the subject of the narcissistic images in which his ego was constituted through multiple identifications. This dialectic is pursued until object (a), the object of the lack of being, is revealed: the phallus, and until, on the other hand, 'subjectification of the subject in death' is obtained, the recognition, that is, that the ego has never been anything more than the subject's work in the imaginary.

It is as a dummy that the analyst will provoke this regression by his silence and his frustration of any response or gratification. Analytic neutrality alone can maintain the framework of transference.

In conclusion, we can say with Lacan that the movement of *analysis unfolds 'according to the paths of a specific gravitation, which is truth'* (14): *the truth of the patient's desire.*

TWENTY-TWO

Interpretation

Interpretation in Lacanian psychoanalysis follows from the general conceptions so far expounded and from the methods which direct the cure itself.

Beginning with the premise that the analysand, a victim of repression, pronounces a fallacious discourse upon himself and upon incidents in his existence, the analyst will only listen to the historical narration in a distracted way. Ultimately, the exact chronology of the facts recounted and even the reality or non-reality of the events is of little importance.

The analyst should give a 'fortunate scansion', as Lacan puts it, to the patient's discourse, locating the capital elements in the flow of the discourse.

These present themselves in the most varied of forms: a very personal meaning given to some anodine vocable, an involuntary slip of the tongue, obsessional repetitions, verbal inability. Here, the anodine takes on the value of the essential. More sensitivized than normal to the effects of an open dialogue, paralysed by the attentive listening and the sustained silence, alarmed by the imminence of being unveiled, the patient will in his panic give language the means to betray him. The patient does not know the meaning of the symbols in which his desire is alienated, he has lost their symbolic reference. All the more so because every symbol in analysis is overdetermined, referring back to several signifiers, which are themselves inter-connected by complex and multiple associations. If a patient believes in his symptoms, it is because he does not know the status of the symbols representing an unconscious given.

The analytic interpretation will then be based upon free association around the part-elements of the formations of the unconscious.

In the course of time, the secret network of unconscious significations will be completed, and by restoring to each signifier which comes into play in a privileged manner during analysis the associative chain from which it has fallen, one will arrive, step by step, at a coherent web of more or less organized unconscious thoughts.

Translating, undoing the secret knots, verbally pronouncing significations are acts indispensable to the cure. For verbal expression is the opposite of repression.

By naming that which did not have a name, interpretation establishes a new relationship between the subject and the words

which rule his existence. It opens up the path of accession to
symbolic.   (H.-T. Piron, 116)

In short, the process of interpretation and of the cure is the transition
from the non-symbolized imaginary to a symbolized imaginary which is
restored to its symbolic dimension. And the play of interpretation, or,
to be more accurate, its methods are based upon the fact that '*the unconscious is structured like a language, that a material operates in it according to certain laws, which are the same laws as those discovered in the study
of actual languages*' (*Écrits*, 28).

PART NINE

The Lacanian conception of neurosis and psychosis

TWENTY-THREE

Neurosis

The linguistic distinction between signifier and signified, the notion of value and the stylistic processes in language account for the autonomy of the symbolic order in relation to the real, but also in relation to thought and concepts.

The signifier is neither the real thing, nor a unique concept of that thing. Turning the contribution of linguistics to his own advantage, Lacan articulates the problem of human existence by distinguishing three registers: the Real, the Imaginary and the Symbolic.

The normal man will be characterized by an economy balanced around these three poles, the neurotic by a disturbance of internal metabolism between them, and the psychotic by a radical and original alteration in the use of the linguistic sign. The psychotic's experience of reality will forever be deformed by this.

The imaginary relationship which has, throughout the present study, been assimilated to a dual relationship is specified by the absence of mediation between the self and the thing, the self and the object of desire, or the self and the idea. The genesis of a third term by which the subject distances himself from his surroundings and from the real corresponds to the birth of the triadic symbolic order. By naming the thing and, with this name, giving it the value of a concept which may be used without direct reference to the thing, the order of the symbol has the effect of giving the subject his individuality by delivering him from the alienating trapping of the imaginary. By naming a thing, man in effect distances himself from it, posits it as no more being him than the thing is the sign he substitutes for it or the isolated concept of the thing. The signifier and the symbol effect distinctions which are indispensable to the constitution of the subject.

The neurotic has effected the transition to the symbolic order, whereas the psychotic, as we shall see in Chapter 24, never effected it completely.

The neurotic's problem lies in a loss of the symbolic reference of the signifiers constituting the central points of the structure of his complex. For example, the neurotic represses his symptom's signified.

This loss of the signifier's referential value causes him to relapse to the level of the imaginary, to the absence of mediation between the self and the idea. This is what is realized by repression. 'The subject does not have access to the symbolic dimension of his symptoms. He believes in them, and establishes his imaginary lived experience in the real' (H.-T. Piron, 116).

The important point is that, for the neurotic, the experience which is the object of repression is already structured, it has, that is, entered into the circuit of discourse and has already been spoken, or has at least been brought into existence, before being rejected. As the neurotic has passed a judgment of existence on the repressed signification, that signification will always be capable of being re-evoked by analysis and of being re-integrated into the flow of discourse.

We shall see that things are quite different with the psychotic.

A further characteristic of neurosis is a certain disturbance in the universal usage of significant relations, the relations, that is, between signs whose nature it is to evoke one another. The patient's lived experience makes him associate one signifier with another in a metonymic relation, or makes him substitute one signifier for another in a metaphor. These privileged relations result in the constitution of a personal code which can only be translated by the technique of free association. The symptom and the dream thus cause symbols which do not always belong to the traditional symbolic storehouse to intervene. As Piron puts it (116), they are alienated discourses and desires.

The transition from the non-symbolized imaginary to the symbolized imaginary is the process of the cure of the neurotic. 'Every symptom and every oniric symbol is a compromise: a wish fulfilled and mutilated, a discourse addressed to the other but codified, a speech pronounced but deformed' (116).

The cure operates by reinstating the associative chains which support the symbols until access is gained to the truth of the unconscious, to the elementary signifiers which forced themselves into consciousness through metaphor and metonymy. The cure is the re-integration into the normal thread of discourse of a speech – full speech – which could not previously be spoken without being deformed.

Nevertheless, something more is necessary if neurosis is to be triggered off. Did not Freud in fact discover an unconscious structured like a linguistic network in normal subjects too?

Luce Irigaray attributes this supplementary crack to the primitive lived experience of the mother–child relationship. Either the child has been loved too much or it has not been sufficiently loved; this will produce, in that order, the drama of the obsessional or that of the hysteric.

Let us look in turn at hysterical and obsessional neuroses in order to bring out the general problem from a Lacanian point of view.

The *hysteric*, says Luce Irigaray (86), has not had enough love. He feels himself to be the signifier of his mother's desire, marked with the sign of incompleteness, or even rejection, ridiculous because he does not bear comparison with the phallic signifier. The hysteric's self-identity, to which he has acceded through language, will be feared and rendered precarious by this fact. He only accepts it as a fragment, a facet of a unity still to come. He wears himself out in trying to be an ideal object which he will at last be able to accept because it conforms to what he senses in the site of the desire of the Other (the mother). As nothing can fill the *béance* of his being, as no object is the whole to which the hysteric aspires, his desire is condemned to be raised incessantly. And, ultimately, the only way to maintain this desire, and not to let it suffocate, is to dedicate it to dissatisfaction in order that it may be endlessly reborn. Ultimately, it is 'being circumscribed' that the hysteric fears, being fixed within limits, determined as being one thing or another.

Unlike the hysteric, the *obsessional* has felt himself to be loved too much. He was judged by his mother to be too adequate a signifier of her desire. The denomination realized by entry into the symbolic order merely had the effect of confirming him in his singularity as the privileged being of his mother's desire. His name will be an emblem, an insignia of his phallic status.

The obsessional becomes encysted in his too great self-adequacy, unable to liberate himself for a perpetual process of becoming.

A hero in possession of his mother, the obsessional feels himself to be irremediably guilty. Fear of castration requires the necessity of the death of the father if he is to avoid feeling guilty. Castration is avoided by assiduous, obnubilant work.

For the obsessional, therefore, the important thing is to fill in a crack, that of castration, in order that he may be the unfailing phallus.

It will be noted that the *pervert* has reacted differently to castration. He denied it and became bogged down in the primary illusion. Castration is a lie, there *is* a coincidence between the object of desire (the phallus) and the object destined for sexual pleasure. The fetish, for example, will be the metaphor for the maternal phallus; as the object of desire, on the other hand, the phallus is metonymic in relation to the mother, to the body which possesses it.

TWENTY-FOUR

Psychosis

The current state of knowledge in the field of psychosis is scanty, and therapeutic methods are consequently vague and very diverse. This is why Lacan's contribution in this domain seems to me to be particularly timely.

Lacan has proposed a principle for distinguishing between neurosis and psychosis which differs, at the level of terminology, from that suggested by Freud himself. Freud in effect considers that, if the neurotic represses the psychical content which is destined to become unconscious, the psychotic represses the real. Such a conception would seem to mean that all repression is pathogenic. This is certainly not the case for the Lacanians, since, according to them, it is precisely the so-called 'primal' repression that is the precondition for the transcendence of the Oedipus, and it is precisely this that the psychotic has been unable to realize.

Lacan suggests that the term 'repression' be kept for neurosis and that the failure of primal repression which is co-responsible for psychosis be called 'foreclosure'.

The term 'foreclosure' (or repudiation) corresponds to the German *Verwerfung* used by Freud himself in the wolf-man case, where he opposes it to the term *Verdrängung* (repression).

The notion of foreclosure has been made remarkably explicit by A. de Waelhens in his Preface (78) to Dr Demoulin's work, *Notions de psychiatrie phénoménologique*.

The substance of this chapter will therefore be taken from A. de Waelhens's text, and will be filled out with the help of the following: Leclaire's articles, 'A propos de l'épisode psychotique que présenta l'homme aux loups' (43) and 'A la recherche des principes d'une psychothérapie des psychoses' (45); Lacan's articles, 'Réponse au commentaire de J. Hyppolite sur la *Verneinung* de Freud' (18) and 'On a question preliminary to any possible treatment of psychosis' (23); Freud's *From the History of an Infantile Neurosis* (5); and Ruth Mack Brunswick's 'A supplement to Freud's *From the History of an Infantile Neurosis*' (93).

The notion of foreclosure is essential to the understanding of psychosis in the framework of Lacanian thought.

In order to grasp the notion properly, let us oppose it to the idea of repression which, in the theory of Jacques Lacan, is, on the contrary, specific to neurosis.

Repression is:

> The interdiction made to a certain content to appear in
> consciousness. This interdiction does not destroy it, so that if its
> cathexis is too strong or the interdiction is too weak, it will
> manifest itself in a disguise or a camouflage which constitutes the
> symptom. (78)

This possibility of a return of the repressed results from the fact that

the neurotic has acquired the use of linguistic signs $\left(\dfrac{S}{s} \right)$. It results from

the fact that the element to be repressed was at some point recognized
as existing, that its signifier was symbolized, situated and registered in
a network of knowledge and inserted into the web of a personal
discourse.

> Repression can be conceived as the putting into parentheses, the
> sly occultation of an experience which has already been virtually
> structured. It is easy to conceive that whatever has been veiled in
> this way may, thanks to favourable circumstances, be once more
> unveiled and reintegrated into the dialectical current of experience.
> (43)

'*Foreclosure*, on the other hand, never conserves what it rejects: it
purely and simply crosses it out or bars it' (78).

S. Leclaire suggests an image to account for the difference between
repression in the neurotic and foreclosure in the psychotic:

> If we imagine experience to be a piece of material made up of
> criss-crossing threads, we could say that repression would figure
> in it as a rent or a tear which can still be repaired, whereas
> foreclosure would figure in it as a *béance* due to the weaving itself,
> in short a primal hole which will never again be able to find its
> substance, since it has never been anything other than the
> substance of a hole and can only be filled, and even then
> imperfectly, by a patch. (43)

It follows that a lived element which has been foreclosed can never
reappear. The impossibility of re-evoking the foreclosed experience
arises from the fact that the psychotic never really had access to the
principle of symbolization: one signifier is put in the place of another
which it is not. This also means that the psychotic never effected a
judgment of existence concerning this experience, a judgment which
would symbolize it and register it in the network of the constituted
discourse. Foreclosure takes place before there is any possibility of repression, since some preliminary recognition of the element which is
to be repressed is necessary if repression is to take place.

Let us take a very illuminating example of foreclosure, an example imagined by Leclaire in his article (43), and admirably exploited by A. de Waelhens.

Two drunken friends have been apprehended and taken home by policemen who swoop through the area on bicycles, and who are metaphorically known as 'swallows'.

The following day, neither of the drunks remembers the event, now lost in the mists of alcohol. A few bruises and the fact of being at home are all that bear witness to the event, which has been radically excluded from the web of memory.

Some months later, however, one of the friends suddenly develops an ornithological delirium in which he has the impression of being attacked by lots of birds, particularly swallows, as soon as he leaves the house.

The two drunks have, therefore, completely expunged, excluded from their memories and foreclosed their tumultuous encounter with the police cyclists.

Meanwhile, something has occupied the place left empty by the foreclosed element: the ornithological delirium.

The invalid is not aware of the connexion between the delirium and the foreclosed event. For him, the attack by the swallows is real. In this way, the pair of birds which constituted the centre of the non-integrated experience emerge into reality (phantasmatic and hallucinatory, evidently). All that remains is the signifier 'swallow', but it is devoid of all correlation with its signified: the police cyclists.

> It is what was rejected from the symbolic order, namely the signifier 'swallow', which reappears in the real in the course of the delirium, or at least in a delirious mode of the experience of reality, of a reality marked with the seal of the imaginary and devoid of any truly symbolic dimension. (43)

What has happened?

A. de Waelhens explains:

> I understand that a police cyclist is called a swallow, because I know that police cyclists swoop through the area, just as swallows swoop across the sky. But I cannot understand the relationship between the two and I therefore cannot use the word and the image of the swallow as a signifier of the police cyclist (its signified), unless, at the same time, I *deny* that a swallow is simply a policeman on a bicycle. It is this negation which co-constitutes the symbolic relation that the psychotic does not or cannot make. Once this relation is broken by the absence of the negation, then all the subject is left with is the visual and aural image – the word – of the swallow which, ceasing to be a signifier in the true sense, is transported as it stands into the real.

Apart from the absence of this negation, there is, however, in foreclosure an absence of any judgment of existence concerning the foreclosed element, unlike repression which presupposes the fact to be repressed has been recognized as existing, symbolized, registered and located in a network of knowledge.

> Foreclosure cuts short any manifestation of the symbolic order, that is, the *Bejahung* (affirmation) which Freud posits as being the primary process that gives the attributive judgment its value, and which is nothing other than the condition for something from the real to offer itself to the revelation of being.
>
> Judgment consists in speaking (*dire*) a property of a thing or going back on what one has said (*dédire*) and it must confess or attest to the existence of a presentation. (*Écrits*, 18)

There are, therefore, two aspects to any judgment: a judgment of existence and a judgment of attribution.

To go back to our example: 'police cyclists are swallows' asserts the existence of the signified (policemen) and, by a judgment of attribution, substitutes a symbol for it, but at the same time denies that a policeman is purely and simply a swallow.

Foreclosure effects neither the judgment of existence nor the negation; only the symbol remains, but, because of the absence of its relation to the signified, it loses its true value as a signifier, as a symbol. It is no longer any more than an image taken for reality. The imaginary has become the real.

We now see what differentiates foreclosure from repression. The latter has established the symbolic relationship and forgotten it. It will, then, be possible to re-establish the forgotten relationship.

The example we have just developed clearly shows the importance, in the constitution of a normal subject, of the primal repression which establishes language. We have also seen that the psychotic does not effect this repression and is therefore excluded from the truly symbolic dimension.

A. de Waelhens (78) defines primal repression in these terms:

> The act whereby he who will become a subject succeeds in removing himself from an experience or something lived and gives them a substitute, which is not them, a substitute which confers upon this subject a distance from and a respect for his own existence. Primal repression will, then, be the inaugural moment of all language, as well as of the constitution of the real as such. It is clear that the real achieves fullness of meaning only if it appears to me in itself and not merely for me and of me.

This repression therefore concerns reality in its immediacy. It effects the transition from the order of the real to that of designation. It is therefore the initiator of language. Primal repression has already been illustrated by the example of the game with the cotton-reel and the string, and we will not go back to it. We see that it is indeed the failure of this primal repression which leads to the psychotic's non-distinction between signifier and signified and hence to his inability to use language correctly. Primal repression in effect includes the judgment of attribution, the judgment of existence and the negation referred to above.

We also see that it is the failure of primal repression that is responsible for the psychotic's uncertainty as to his individuality: primal repression establishes the subject in his individuality by positing him as being neither the thing nor the name.

One question obviously arises at this point of development: what caused the failure of primal repression in the psychotic and placed the psyche under the rule of foreclosure?

In the act constituting primal repression, the subject distances and distinguishes himself from both the real and from the substitute he gives it.

This act therefore necessitates a symbolic support for the self, an 'original signifier of self'!

> There can be no possible substitute for any content, and hence no transition to the realm of the distinction between signifier and signified unless there is at the same time a substitute for the self. When the subject cannot posit a negative of his coenaesthesia in order to designate it, to signify it as being his body, the whole process becomes jammed or ceases to begin. (78)

The maternal attitude is determinant here. And we come back to what Lacan calls the paternal metaphor. If the mother treats her child as the complement of her own lack, as the phallus with which the child is in any case trying to identify, if, therefore, the child is everything to her and merges with her in a diffuse union, then the child cannot dispose of his own individuality.

If, on the contrary, the mother recognizes in the father the function of establishing the rule of the law of societies by respecting his speech, then the child can accept symbolic castration by the father, and by gaining access to the order of the symbol, he will find the original signifier of self: the name and the place he is destined to occupy in the family constellation.

He will then be able to operate upon things the act which names them and which situates them in themselves in their exteriority. The subject, the symbol and the real will be distinguished: this is the only way to escape from imaginary trapping by things.

It is an accident in the symbolic register and of what is accomplished in it, namely the foreclosure of the Name-of-the-Father in the place of the Other and in the failure of the paternal metaphor which I designate as the defect that gives psychosis its essential condition, with the structure that separates it from neurosis. (*Écrits*, 23)

It will be noted that it is, of course, possible for psychosis to be triggered off at a date later than that at which foreclosure of the Name-of-the-Father is effected. Lacan goes on:

For the psychosis to be triggered off, the Name-of-the-Father, *verworfen*, foreclosed, that is, never having attained the place of the Other, should be called into symbolic opposition to the subject. But how can the Name-of-the-Father be called by the subject to the only place in which it has never been? Simply by a real father, not necessarily the subject's father, but by A-father. It is enough that this A-father should be situated in a third position in some relation based on the imaginary o – o', that is to say, ego-object or reality–ideal that interests the subject.

Whether it occurs for a woman who has just given birth, in the person of her husband, for the penitent confessing her sins, in the person of her confessor, for the young girl in love with 'the young man's father', it will always be found (at the outset of psychosis). (*Écrits*, 28)

To sum up: when the mother denies the speech of the father its function as law, she prevents the child from acceding to the paternal metaphor, to the representation, that is, of a father who is the authority separating the child from its mother. Such an attitude leaves the child subjugated to the dual relationship, to identification with the mother, and takes from him any possibility of access to the order of symbolism and of language.

At this point, I think it judicious to recall that the formula given by Lacan for the paternal metaphor in the Oedipal stage is considered by some authors (C. Stein, for example) not to be the first draft of primal repression. According to these authors, primal repression takes place much earlier, the four-year-old child already having access to language. The substitution of some symbol for the lived experience of desire for the mother, a substitution whereby the subject renounces possession of the mother by distancing himself from the urgency of this lived experience, already constitutes a sort of elementary paternal metaphor.

What will become of this psychotic subject, deprived of the symbolic dimension of language, undecided as to his individuality and that of the other? What will the psychotic's mode of communication be, what will his vision of the world be?

Before going on to these questions, it might be useful to follow S. Leclaire (45) in distinguishing between the delirious subject (paranoiac) and the schizophrenic. In general, the psychotic is characterized by a radical alteration in the use of the linguistic sign $\frac{S}{s}$ but this alteration takes different forms depending upon whether it is a case of delirium or schizophrenia.

For the *schizophrenic*, all signifiers can be made to designate a single concept or signified. In other words, the signified or concept is not bound to any one signifier in a stable manner, and numerous permutations of signifiers designating that signified are possible.

The pattern for this disturbance is as shown in Figure 24.1.

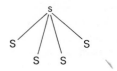

FIGURE 24.1

The schizophrenic lives, then, in a world of multiple symbols, and here it is the dimension of the imaginary, of concepts, that is altered.

For the *delirious* subject, on the contrary, a single signifier may designate any signified. The signifier is not bound to one definite concept.

The persecutor, for example, will be interchangeable. The alteration concerned in delirium could be represented as shown in Figure 24.2.

FIGURE 24.2

Here, it is the symbolic dimension which is missing. The subject will, therefore, live in an imaginary world.

Let us now turn to the problem of communication (the I–thou relationship) in delirium.

Our study of the psychotic's communication and his vision of the world will be essentially concerned with the characteristics of delirium, as this is the problem most frequently studied by our authors.

As a starting point, let us study the pattern of psychotic communication given by Leclaire (45) (see Figure 24.3). We will bring to it the wealth of A. de Waelhens's comments (78).

In this Z-shaped pattern, S and O represent the subject and the other, the two terms of communication. o is the subject's ego and o′ is the interlocutor's ego. It will be recalled that the ego is not the subject, that it is closer to the persona, the appearance and the role than it is to

FIGURE 24.3

subjectivity. The ego is situated on the side of the imaginary, whereas the subject is situated on the side of the symbolic. The ego is the site of the subject's alienating identifications. o – o′ is therefore the imaginary axis, whilst the diagonal joining S to O is the symbolic axis, since it virtually connects two irreducible subjectivities; S – O represents a sort of communication without an intermediary, without detours, as in mysticism.

We have shown that the psychotic is undecided as to his own subjectivity and as to that of the other.

The normal man makes his discourse the signifier of his own being, and if he speaks of things, he differentiates them from himself. Obviously, when the normal man speaks of himself, he is describing an ego, but he seeks to render this ego identical to his subjectivity, which is mediated through language.

The delirious subject, on the other hand, decentres the being of whom he is speaking (himself) from his subjectivity as much as from the I of discourse. He speaks of himself as though he were speaking of an other, of a thing amongst things. He sees himself as the other sees him, as an object. The delirious subject has, therefore, lost all transcendence in relation to objects, and his discourse does not express a subjectivity. The discourse of the delirious subject does not belong to his subjectivity, and the ego he describes does not coincide with it; it is other, an object. In short, the connexion between S and o.

Similarly, on the side of the interlocutor, there is a rupture between O and o′.

The only remaining path of communication is o – o′, the imaginary axis, the site of the dual opposition.

Having lost the symbolic indicator of his subjectivity, the delirious subject easily tends to merge with an other. There is a clear opposition between me and thou; the opposition between self and another self is much less clear. As A. de Waelhens says, confusion is easy in a world where there are only one's and they's. Hence, there is no exact distribution of roles in delirium, no 'I', no 'thou', but only 'they'.

It should be noted that the case of schizophrenia is different. Here, the privileged axis is the S – O axis.

The schizophrenic has no ego, identifies with no one and lives himself as a radical subjectivity, participating in the divine essence.

What, then, is the delirous subject's *relationship to the world*? We will briefly summarize A. de Waelhens's conceptions.

The delirious subject is constantly looking at photographs of a petrified real in which he himself figures. When he speaks of things, he is describing and producing these photographs.

The loss of the symbolic relationship rivets him to the imaginary, with no distance between himself and the things of this world.

We always have to apprehend the object perceived by multiplying its profiles in order to render it completely. For the delirious subject, the signifier is the thing and not its mediation, everything is an image, and the image is immediately all that it is, there is no sense in describing it.

Reality is the image, a painting. There is an absence of distinction between signifier and signified: the privileged axis is the imaginary.

We will, in the context of the present chapter, attempt to make a succinct analysis of the 'wolf-man' case related by Freud in *From the History of an Infantile Neurosis* (5).

The wolf man's case is not a definite case of psychosis, the analysis he underwent with Freud having delivered him, rather, from a neurosis taking various forms: hysterical, phobic, obsessional and hypochondriac.

Some years after the analytic treatment, he did, however, experience a psychotic episode which, according to Ruth Mack Brunswick, who was treating him at the time, showed signs of paranoia.

The case can therefore be illuminated by the Lacanian notion of fore-closure (or repudiation). Here, the element foreclosed is maternal castration, and his own symbolic castration in the Oedipus.

The case justifies Lacan's theories, as it shows clearly that, in the absence of transcendence of the Oedipus and castration, the subject cannot utilize the distinction between signifier and signified correctly, and puts himself under the rule of foreclosure, installing himself, that is, in a delirium in which castration will be lived, in hallucinatory fashion, as though it were real.

Without taking the analysis too far this is what I propose to show here.

To this end, I have reconstructed a chronological synthesis of the real or imaginary events in the wolf man's past. These elements will be presented in simplified manner, without details, and in a different order from that in which they were presented during the psychoanalyses.

Our aim is not to give an idea of the meanderings of the analytic cure, but to provide an example which can clarify and justify the notion of foreclosure in psychosis.

Age one-and-a-half years: The patient, who is suffering from malaria, is staying in his parents' room. At about five o'clock in the afternoon, he wakes up, opens his eyes and witnesses coitus a tergo between his parents, who are lightly dressed in white underwear. He is thus able to observe the sexual conformation of his parents. He sees his father's erect member and ascertains that his mother has been castrated. A *béance* or wound is all that remains in the place where the phallus should be. The child interrupts the copulation by defaecating: the meaning of this vegetative action is, as we will see, an identification with his mother in this scene of copulation, and hence of a sexual excitement due to imagined a tergo relations with the father.

Age two-and-a-half years: The patient lives the following scene: a young maid is kneeling down, scouring the floor. He recognizes this position as that adopted by his mother during coitus. He then assimilates the young maid to his mother and excitement takes hold of him. The child now identifies with his father in an action which he could only see as micturition, and urinates in the room. The young maid responds to his action with a threat of castration.

Age three years and three months: His elder sister takes hold of his member and plays with it, telling him that Nanya, his favourite old nurse, does the same thing with the gardener, first making him stand on his head with his legs forming a V shape.

At about this period, the child, who had been calm and gentle, becomes irritable and bad-tempered. At the same time, masochistic phantasies appear: the son who is heir to the throne is beaten on the penis.

Age three-and-a-half to four years: The child is confronted with a whole symbolic given: allusions by those around him to castration, children's stories in which wolves appear and unfortunately lose their tails. He finds himself confronted with phallic symbols: the cane, the serpent, the hat, etc.

This symbolic data, which could have provided the child with the true meaning of the copulation he observed and its conditions, will engender in him an internal duality: the simultaneous refusal and acceptance of the symbolic meaning of castration.

Age four years: The wolf dream occurs.

It was night and I was lying in my bed. There was an old walnut tree in front of the window. It was winter. Suddenly, the window opens of its own accord and, to my great terror, I see six or seven white wolves sitting in the walnut tree. They looked more like foxes or sheep dogs, as they had big tails like foxes and their ears were pricked up like dogs listening to something. In great terror of being eaten up, I screamed and called for my nurse.

The meaning of the dream is as follows:

– the long tails of the wolves compensate for the absence of a tail. The dream recalls the various stories in which the wolf's tail is cut off.

– the fear of being eaten up recalls the stories in which the wolf eats someone. The wolf is the substitute for the father, who used to scold him tenderly, saying 'I'm going to eat you up.'

– in his dream, the patient underlines the fixity of the wolves' gaze, their immobility and the impression of reality produced by the vision.

The feeling of reality in a dream often relates to a real event which was once lived and which has now been forgotten.

The dream refers to the copulation observed by the subject when he was one-and-a-half. 'The window opens of its own accord' means 'my eyes opened of their own accord' on to the primal scene. Looking attentively must, then, be displaced on to the dreamer himself and the wolves' immobility is an inverted representation of the violent movement of the primal scene. The white wolves allude to the whiteness of the underwear.

Interpretation of the dream allows us to sum up the psychical state the child was in at the age of four.

The dream took place on Christmas Eve, the day before the child's birthday. Thanks to the expectation of Christmas presents, the wish to receive sexual satisfaction from his father has made its way into the psyche. At the same time, this wish revives the memory of mode of sexual satisfaction by the father, and revives the vision of castration. The real meaning of the primal scene then comes to light, thanks to recollections of various stories in which wolves lose their tails, and thanks to the allusions to castration made by those around the child. The child was immediately seized with terror and fear, and the wish was repressed and replaced by the fear of castration and the wolf phobia. Assimilation of the father to the wolf was effected through the intermediary of the Little Red Riding Hood story, in which a picture showed the wolf standing up with one paw held out. The position of the paw brought back to the child the memory of the erection of the phallus in the primal scene. The succession of thoughts leading to the dream is therefore as follows. An unconscious wish to have relations with the father evoked the memory of the primal scene in all its violence, as well as the memory of the castration of his mother, which then appeared to him to be a condition *sine qua non* of such relations with the father. Panic and horror seized the child, who rejected both his wish and the reality of castration.

Following this dream, a terrible phobia about wolves, horses and butterflies is born in the child.

One day, he was chasing a beautiful big butterfly with striped yellow wings. Suddenly, as the butterfly settled on a flower, he was seized with a violent panic and ran away screaming.

What terrified him mainly was the opening–closing movement of the wings (the opening of the legs showing castration).

At the same age, he sometimes dirtied in his trousers. Copying his mother, he would say 'I can't go on living like this.' In saying this, he is identifying with his mother, who suffers from pains in the genital organs (intestines for the child). Besides, he believed this pain to be caused by his father's violent treatment of her. But, at the same time, the child is frightened of having dysentery, which would seem to indicate a refusal to identify with his mother for fear of the conditions of anal relations with the father.

The patient's duality towards castration is already manifesting itself here. By identifying with his mother and, on the other hand, by refusing to identify with her, he refuses castration, he refuses, that is, to be his father's partner in coitus.

Such phenomena give a particular meaning to stool; the meaning of a gift or of a child given in return for sexual commerce; and also the meaning of phallus, because of their similarity in form and the cutaneous impression they produce.

The rejection of faeces finally becomes a symbol for castration, since faeces also represents the phallus.

In short: according to Freud, faeces–child–penis formed a single concept for the child; that of something small which can be removed from the body.

Age five years: The child has the following hallucination:

> He was playing in the garden near Nanya, his nurse. He was cutting into the bark of a tree with a sharp pocket-knife. Suddenly, he saw that his finger was cut through and was only hanging on to his hand by the skin. It was not bleeding. He didn't dare say anything to Nanya and had to sit down to get over it. Having calmed down, he looked at his finger and saw that it was uninjured.

At puberty: The wolf man is attracted in a compulsive and fetishist way by women on all fours, kneeling down and leaning forward (in the wash-house for example). Such a predilection is a sign of the unconscious influence of the primal scene over the subject's whole life.

At the time of his analysis with Freud: The patient has enemas for constipation administered to him by a man servant, and the enemas are accompanied by a very significant phantasy which the patient resumes in the following words: 'The world is hidden in a veil, and the veil is torn only when, after an enema, the contents of the bowel pass through the anus. Then I feel well again for a very short time and I see the world clearly.'

During his analysis with Freud, the following two dreams occur; they are already a step towards his being cured.

'*A man is pulling the wings off an Espe.*' The dream obviously alludes to a wasp (*Wespe*). It should be noted that S.P. are his initials. The 'Espe' deprived of its W in his dream therefore shows him to be castrated. This is also borne out by the intervention of the signifier V, which has become fixed in his unconscious as a symbol for open legs showing a wound (cf. the butterfly, the Roman figure V in the primal scene at five o'clock, the inverted M of mother or Matriona – the washerwoman – the sign of the wolves' ears, the V of the gardener's position during Nanya's supposed acts).

The anonymous man pulling the wings off the wasp in the dream is Freud himself, from whom the patient is demanding castration. Freud is assimilated to his father, but at the same time the patient is thereby asking Freud to deliver him from his mother's domination.

In the second dream, 'the patient is in a room with his mother. *A wall is covered with ikons. His mother takes them down* and throws them to the floor where *they break.*'

This dream shows that the patient is on the way to being cured. He is escaping from his mother's hold over him. We know that she taught him Bible history between the ages of four and ten and, besides, provoked in him an obsessional neurosis with a religious content.

During the analysis pursued with Ruth Mack Brunswick, the patient alternates between a dental symptomatology and a cutaneous symptomatology localized in the nose (a phallic symbol). He goes from one dentist to another, two of them being called Wolf. He provokes their sadism through his demands and has a good number of teeth pulled out. One day he faints during treatment (a sort of ecstasy).

The same behaviour is reproduced towards dermatologists, in connexion with infections of the subcutaneous glands of the nose, or in connexion with spots and marks (often hallucinatory) on the nose.

He goes from dermatologist to dermatologist. One day, he faints in ecstasy because a doctor lances an infected spot. Finally, x treats him by electrolysis, leaves an indelible mark on him and brings the most savage hatred upon himself: x has castrated him, he is his mortal enemy.

– Dream of his father's castration: this is a question of vengeance for the castration he believes himself to have undergone at the hands of his father (x is identified with his father).

The wolf man's case shows strong tendencies towards delusional psychosis. The interpretation which may be given to it in the light of Lacan's theses follows.

When he was very young, the wolf man had heard it said that he was born with a caul, that is, privileged by fate. His mother did not attempt to rid him of his illusions in any way. On the contrary, he was at a very early age treated by her as the privileged object of her desire. One may even wonder, as Leclaire (51) does, whether the memory of being seduced by his sister at the age of two years and three months is not a screen memory hiding the memory of being seduced by his mother herself.

In any case, the child took himself for a demigod, an untouchable (he was born on Christmas Day).

During his observation of coitus when he was one-and-a-half, this status of being privileged by the mother leads to a real love drama.

If his mother can find pleasure with another in this way, his world collapses. His only defence is to say, 'It is not her', and to posit the body of a crouching woman as an object, denying her her real identity. This contestation is substituted for a true accession to castration. (S. Leclaire)

If we follow Leclaire, it would appear that the wolf man had denied his mother's identity in the primal scene in order to remain the unique and privileged object of her desire. Besides, his subsequent evolution shows that he has not had access to the symbolism of castration: that of his mother, which would have revealed to him the reality of the difference between the sexes.

Denying castration allows him to remain his mother's chosen one, identified with the phallus, but this negation at the same time deprives him of his individuality, of his singularity as an autonomous being.

Hence the basic duality towards castration which can be observed in the patient: he both wishes it and fears it.

He desires it in order to be cured, in order to find his autonomy again, but he fears it because it deprives him of dual union with the mother.

If Leclaire's interpretation is in many ways verified by the patient's life, it is still not sufficiently comprehensive. It transpires from Freud's analysis of the case that the observation of coitus had a more important effect on the patient than identification with the father in the sexual act.

The child's most violent reaction was to identify with his mother and to receive, in an imaginary mode, the father's phallus.

Freud tells us that the child interrupted his parents' copulation by defaecating. Anal excitement apparently prevailed in him.

At this stage of extreme youth, all the wolf man saw in his father's act was a micturition, received anally by his mother. Thus, he responded to the anal excitement he himself felt with a gift: that of a child, his stool.

One could say that the wolf man's primordial unconscious desire is for anal sexual commerce with his father. The child's masochistic phantasies and his frequent rages, which brought his father's wrath down upon him, are indirect fulfilments of this wish.

When the child observed the primal scene at the age of one-and-a-half, he did not see its true meaning: that of a relationship between two differently constituted sexes. He merely saw it as an anal relation.

It was only later, with the help of the unhealthy allusions made by those around him and with the help of certain children's stories, that the meaning of woman's castration came to light for him.

Unconscious elaboration of this data resulted in the wolf dream at the age of four. This dream shows that he had at last understood the real meaning of the primal scene, but had rejected it. Castration has been 'foreclosed'. But it seems to me that this is for a reason other than that invoked by Leclaire. The child rejected castration because it was the over-demanding condition for relations with his father. It should be noted that, henceforth, two trains of thought co-existed within him in this connexion.

> He rejected what was new . . . for motives connected with his fear
> of castration and clung fast to what was old. He decided in favour
> of the intestine and against the vagina. . . . His new insight
> became a motive for keeping the whole process of the dream under
> repression and for excluding it from being worked over later in
> consciousness.

> He rejected castration and held to his theory of intercourse by the
> anus. 'Rejected it' means that he would have nothing to do with
> it in the sense of having repressed it. This really involved no
> judgment upon the question of its existence. . . . We find good
> subsequent proof of his having recognized castration as a fact . . .
> but the second reaction did not do away with the first. . . . In the
> end there were to be found in him two contrary currents side by
> side, of which one abominated the idea of castration, while the
> other was prepared to accept it and console itself with femininity as
> a compensation.   (Freud, 5, vol. XVII, pp. 79, 84)

We can conclude from this duality of currents concerning the judgment as to the existence of castration that the wolf man had a clear predisposition to enter rapidly into psychosis. This is in fact what happened at the period when he was treated by Ruth Mack Brunswick. A first lapse into psychosis had already manifested itself when he was five in the hallucination of the cut finger. We will discuss this in a moment.

A sort of ephemeral recognition of castration did, however, keep him in various forms of neurosis for a good number of years.

On the plane of desire, on the other hand, we can say that the refusal of castration (witness his fear of dysentery, his animal phobia) must be situated in the line of interpretation proposed by Leclaire. The refusal arises from a protestation of virility issuing from a desire to possess his mother, to remain a demigod, an untouchable.

In another sense, his desire for castration (witness his love of tailors, his ecstasy when the infected spot was lanced) signifies both the wish to be free of his mother's domination and the wish to serve his father in coitus.

Let us now look more closely at the facts which may be considered demonstrations of the Lacanian notion of foreclosure.

The hallucination of the cut finger: This hallucination shows that castration, not having been registered and situated within a network of knowledge, and not having been integrated into the web of a personal discourse, has reappeared in the real, or, more accurately, in a mode of delirious experience of reality, a reality devoid of any truly symbolic dimension.

The finger, 'something small which can be separated from the body', is seen in a hallucination to be cut, and the experience enjoys an atmosphere of reality. This hallucination shows that the signifier 'castration' has never been applied to the signified 'absence of penis' through a judgment of existence and attribution. It follows that, in experience, this signifier can take on all possible signified forms. The classic symbolic and substitutive relationship is not stably fixed in the mind. Sometimes it will be the nose that is affected, sometimes the finger, and at other times the faeces coming out of the intestine will be assimilated to the lived experience of castration.

The absence of any symbolization of castration means that the child has not passed from the register of being (being the phallus) to that of having (having the phallus or not having it). The veil phantasy thus shows the patient's total identification with the phallus: he sees himself returned into the maternal body (in the form of the faecal 'stick'), assimilated in his totality to the phallus.

A further illustration of foreclosure is the symptomatology of the nose. In the mirror he constantly carries with him, the patient sees himself as being, and believes himself to be afflicted with an indelible mark, a hole, a crack on the nose. He throws the blame for it on various doctors.

Here again, it is a question of castration appearing in the imaginary real.

Finally, we can sum up the wolf man's duality of attitude towards castration with an analysis of the veil phantasy.

On the one hand, this phantasy shows the wolf man as having returned into the maternal body, as being identified with the phallus and satisfying a desire for incest. On the other hand, the expulsion of faecal matter causes him to be reborn into a new life, into a world of clarity in which he is liberated by castration from maternal domination; he recovers his autonomy; in another sense, castration opens up a happier life to him by realizing the conditions for coitus with the father.

This phantasy even condenses the fulfilment of castration and of anal intercourse, the faecal 'stick' being assimilated to the paternal phallus.

In short, castration is lived by the patient as a precondition for being cured because it delivers him from his mother and at the same time gives him the desired anal satisfaction.

This case shows clearly the value of the Lacanian theory of psychosis.

It shows that the absence of transcendence of the Oedipus places the subject under the regime of foreclosure or non-distinction between the symbol and the real.

The symbolic castration is lived as though it were real by this patient, who has not been able to detach himself from maternal domination and become an autonomous subject.

This case attests to the effects of this failure at the level of the use of language. The role of the persecutor, here the castrator, is successively filled by different men, from his teachers (often called Wolf) to his doctors. The object affected by castration is also interchangeable. In the case of the wolf man, it is indeed a question of an inability to distinguish signifier from signified.

Conclusion

Let us open these last pages with an essential question: what are we to think of Jacques Lacan and his work?

At the end of this study of the thought and work of Jacques Lacan, I find myself in a rather peculiar state of mind. With mixed feelings, shall we say?

What is generally called 'Lacanism' has, in the course of my repeated readings as I fumbled towards a clearer understanding of it, shown itself to be an exceptional edifice of thought. It is, in my eyes, a remarkable construction. It has a coherence and a solidity which can shake the person who applies himself to studying it.

To my mind, Lacan's genius consists in having turned to his advantage the elaborations of the most recent, and the most fashionable, thought.

Structuralism in general, linguistics, Freudian thought and structural anthropology are all so many elements in the framework that supports the Lacanian edifice and gives it its equilibrium.

But if Lacan is part of a general modern movement, he has been able to work alone. He has been able to propel the swift vehicle of his thought to the position of an audacious avant-garde which may be debatable, but which cannot be ignored or neglected by anyone who wishes to speak of the philosophy of man at the moment.

Profound reflection and a recasting of these bundles of theories have allowed Lacan to renew Freudian psychoanalysis. He treats the matter with a rare clarity of vision.

I do not follow D. Anzieu when he qualifies Lacanism as being dissident in relation to Freud.

Jacques Lacan does not seem to me to be an Adler or a Jung. It does not seem to me that he has simply deviated from the Freudian theme.

On the contrary, I think it can be claimed that Lacan has literally rejuvenated psychoanalysis by rethinking it within the framework of contemporary thought. For me, Lacan has indisputably enriched and deepened Freudian thought.

Thus, if one thinks particularly of the Lacanian theory of the relationship the subject has with spoken discourse, or even with that implicit discourse which is formed by the rules of society, non-thematic traditions and cultural data, one is led to recognize in it a radically new and astonishingly lucid philosophy of man.

Certainly, the determination of language – spoken or not – on the formation of the subject may seem to exist in Freud. It seems more accurate to say that we can deduce it from texts in which it is quite obvious without necessarily being stated as such.

Understanding consists in reading between the lines, establishing unexpected connexions between different branches of knowledge. This understanding permeates the whole of Lacan's work.

The characteristic genius of Lacan is also responsible for having proposed a remarkable explanation of some of the innermost aspects of the subject's unconscious.

Thanks to the efforts of the Lacanian school of psychoanalysis, we can today understand how the unconscious is formed at the beginnings of life, what it is composed of, and what its precise modes of arrangement and functioning are.

Or again, we can cite the Lacanian contribution in the field of psychosis. This field has become much more open to us since Lacan rethought the Freudian notion of *Verwerfung*, once more in the light of the data of linguistics.

Personally, I am convinced that psychoanalysis has taken a great step forward with the thought of Jacques Lacan. Its practice can now be enriched by a greater efficacity.

As far as I am concerned, I make no claims to have mastered all the difficulties to be met with in the study of a Jacques Lacan. I would be happy to be recognized as possessing the simple virtue of having proposed reasonable and clear explanations which will in future allow others to go further.

Appendix: general purport of a conversation with Lacan in December 1969

Solicited by my questions as to the value of the theoretical inferences of Laplanche's 'The unconscious: a psychoanalytic study' (48), Dr Lacan provided me with the basis of his criticisms, and also agreed to say a few words about it in his Preface.

He also gives his explanation of the profound causes of such a divergence of thought in the very heart of his school.

What follows is a synthesis of the essential content of our conversation in December 1969.

With his very first words, Lacan states his trenchant opposition to the fundamental proposition defended by his follower Laplanche. To state, as does Laplanche, that 'the unconscious is the condition of language' is, he says, to go directly against the very point on which his own statements leave absolutely no possible doubt, namely that, on the contrary, language is the condition of the unconscious.

Lacan declares himself to be perfectly aware of the problem which has led his follower to look for a principle limiting the primary process at the level of conscious language. But Lacan does not solve this problem in the same way; he does not solve it by resorting, as does Laplanche, to an interaction between the preconscious–conscious system and the unconscious system, and to a stable fixing of the unconscious signifier to the instinct.

The metaphor of the ballast in the bottom of the hold which stops the boat pitching too much is, he stresses, quite incapable of accounting for the extraordinarily dissociative effects of the return of the repressed; *a fortiori*, it is incapable of ensuring any limitation of the primary process at the level of conscious language.

Lacan places too much emphasis on the principle of the double inscription – the separation between the systems, the geometric and topographical distribution of the systems – to authorize any such conscious–unconscious interaction.

In this connexion, Dr Lacan recalls the import he gave to the notion of the anchoring point as the 'mythical' point at which discourse hooks itself on to signification.

There is no place in Dr Lacan's statements to me about the anchoring point for the interpretation worked up by his follower.

Discourse, remarks Lacan, leads, through stumblings and errors, towards a vain search for truth. It is inscribed in a dialectic in which the mistake, rather than the truth, is the object being run to ground. Through the play of references back from sentence to sentence and from word to word, 'it is possible' to arrive, not at the real, which is excluded from thought, but at a particularly successful signifying montage which is more effective than another and which proves itself in praxis.

There is no return to the elementary fixation of the unconscious in Lacan's views on the limits of the conscious primary process, and no recourse to the 'equivocality' of signifiers in his description of the anchoring point.

The notion of the anchoring point concerns conscious language, and, from the conversation as a whole, it transpires that Laplanche's interpretation of it – a sort of sudden metaphoric skidding towards the unconscious – cannot be reconciled with the importance given to the established principle of the double inscription.

Lacan in fact stresses that it is precisely because the unconscious is another discourse and is situated in another place that confirmation of the double inscription is necessary and cannot be denied, whatever level of analysis is examined.

Here again, the way in which Laplanche sees things does not meet with Lacan's approval. The gestaltist image proposed by Laplanche to explain the phenomenon of the double inscription derives from the overall aim of his text.

Lacan conceives the duality of inscriptions as being a reduplication of the same signifier in completely different – above all, topographically different – batteries. Each of the two inscriptions, supported, then, by the same signifier, has a different import because of the site of its support.

In support of this principal statement, Lacan gives the metaphor of a number of hieroglyphs inscribed simultaneously on both sides of an obelisk, and whose meaning changes completely from one side to the other.

Again, if one accords Lacan's position on the double inscription its full weight, it becomes impossible to follow Laplanche when he suggests the principle of an ordering of the conscious language system by the elementary discourse of the unconscious. The double inscription principle, based upon the topographical and functional separation of the conscious and unconscious systems, remains valid for every level of the fashioning of the unconscious and also for its origins. From the outset, it excludes any possibility of the two systems over-lapping.

Lacan considers that the compilation of a minimal signifying battery made in the article (48) fully conforms to his own intuition. He nevertheless objects to the logical process which leads his follower to this fortunate deduction.

The process in question is familiar to us: it is the algebraic transformation of the metaphoric formula for repression given by Lacan in 'On a question preliminary to any possible treatment of psychosis' (23). Lacan's Preface to the present text adequately denounces the error made by Laplanche, thus allowing us to take a short cut on this point.

The process of algebraic substitutions and simplifications leads to a whole collection of errors, the principal error certainly being the relation of reciprocity established between conscious and unconscious language to the detriment of the separating line, which is intended to split them irreversibly. A further error is that leading to the idea that a signifier can signify itself.

On the other hand, Lacan makes no pronouncements as to the problem of the nature of the signifiers in the unconscious or as to the status they acquire there.

The only precision he makes concerning the Freudian term *Vorstellungsrepräsentanz* is a remark about translation. The translation he proposes (*représentant de la représentation*) is certainly very different from that which prevails elsewhere. His own translation, 'representative of the presentation', includes an idea which is not contained in the alternative translation, 'representative' (*représentant-représentatif*), imposed until now by general usage.

According to Lacan, the use of the genitive – *Vorstellungs* with an *s* – followed by the term 'presentation' (*repräsentanz*) throws light upon Freud's intention. What Freud is indicating is the subject's status as representation, a status already brought out by the second Freudian topography which substitutes the triad id–ego–superego for that of conscious–preconscious–unconscious.

Lacan is also conscious of the fact that the present period is a historical turning point for him.

The incidence amongst the public of an article like that by Laplanche is a tell-tale sign.

For Lacan, the hour has come for 'discourse' to take hold of his work and retransmit it. His thought has become prey to partiality, something to be threshed, to be turned this way and that, to be distilled in the general consciousness; a thought refracted by multi-faceted intelligences motivated by many divergent currents of thought.

Within this classic phenomenon of distortion and dilution, it should be possible to make out the foreseeable lines of force as to the causes of the deformation and as to the forms it takes.

As far as Lacan's work is concerned, the movement of refraction will be marked by the convergence of three factors: the complexity of the text, the subject dealt with, and, finally, the intuitive, pointillist process of the thought.

His statements, he declares, have nothing in common with a theoretical exposé justified by a closure. To use his own metaphor, his *Écrits* are merely stones scattered along the way, the major part of his teaching having so far remained unpublished. The majority of the articles collected together in the 900 pages of the *Écrits* seek to pin down the essentials of the subject-matter of his seminars. What is more, they introduce this matter in the context of an epistemological critique of the current psychoanalytic view of the domain being studied.

The *Écrits* do not, then, form a didactic summa of his thought, nor the summa of a thought which has arrived at its full maturity.

As such, they leave certain points unsettled and trigger off multiple attempts at prospective exposés or premature explanatory inferences.

Lacan tells us that it is by way of this quest for something finite that error sometimes creeps in. He considers it as infiltrating itself all the more easily in that those who peddle his thought are constrained by their status as teachers to adopt a didactic position.

The academic discourse which conveys knowledge is therefore responsible for its slidings and its modifications in history.

The discourse of the university is closer to *doxa*, to opinion, whereas knowledge is closer to *epistemè*, to science.

This circular relationship in which knowledge and opinion engender one another attests once more to discourse's dominance over what it relates, and, above all, to the devitalizing power of discourse.

As far as the retransmission of psychoanalytic science by way of university teaching is concerned, other factors appear in addition to the simple play of meaning under the influence of language.

No proposition made by teaching psychoanalysts can be devoid of unconscious implications. And the search for social status could, without their being aware of it, provoke that wish to make innovations at all cost which can be seen in some of them.

Lacan's thought is becoming more and more widespread and is already undergoing basic modifications at the hands of this perpetual movement of oral republication. Based upon a de-centring of the statements from their context, these modifications reduce his thought to *doxa* by taking the edge off its authentic character.

In short, what emerge from this conversation are the points of theoretical clarification mentioned and, what is particularly important, the two lines of force in Lacan's mind. Namely, the sub-stratum of a behaviour founded upon a distrust of university teaching, its didactic character and its Cartesian research.

From this, there emerges a belief in the intuitive, 'impressionist' and essentially practical elaboration of scientific theses concerning psychoanalysis. A belief in this, and a certain pride in being able to discover rather than transmit.

Hence, instinctively and *a priori*, a distrust – once again – of any attempt on the part of his followers or pupils to prolong the roads he himself has left incomplete by throwing bridges over the unknown. A distrust which turns to open hostility when the bridges turn out to have been badly built.

Hence the Preface, which shows how little Lacan tolerates the denaturing of his thought.

Bibliography

Works by Freud

The following are all volumes in the Standard Edition of the *Complete Psychological Works*, Hogarth Press and Institute of Psychoanalysis, London, 1951.

(1) *Studies on Hysteria*, vol. II.
(2) *The Interpretation of Dreams*, vols. IV, V.
(3) *The Psychopathology of Everyday Life*, vol. VI.
(4) *Jokes and their Relation to the Unconscious*, vol. VII.
(5) Case Histories:
   Fragment of an Analysis of a Case of Hysteria, vol. VII.
   Analysis of a Phobia in a Five-year-old Boy, vol. X.
   Notes upon a Case of Obsessional Neurosis, vol. X.
   From the History of an Infantile Neurosis, vol. XVIII.
(6) *Five Lectures on Psychoanalysis*, vol. XI.
(7) *Introductory Lectures on Psychoanalysis*, vols. XV, XVI.
(8) *Beyond the Pleasure Principle*, vol. XVIII. *Group Psychology and the Analysis of the Ego*, vol. XVIII. *The Ego and the Id*, vol. XIX.
(9) *An Outline of Psychoanalysis*, vol. XXIII.
(10) *Three Essays on the Theory of Sexuality*, vol. VII.
(11) *Papers on Metapsychology*, vol. XIV.

Works by J. Lacan

A *Écrits*, Editions du Seuil, Paris, 1966
The titles of English translations by Alan Sheridan-Smith, published by Tavistock Publications, are given after the French titles.

(12) 'Le stade du miroir comme formateur de la fonction du Je' (1937).
   'The mirror-stage as formative of the function of the I as revealed in psychoanalytic experience.'
(13) 'L'agressivité en psychanalyse' (1948).
   'Aggressivity in psychoanalysis.'
(14) 'Intervention sur le transfert' (1952).

(15) 'Variantes de la cure-type' (1955).

(16) 'Fonction et champ de la parole et du langage en psychanalyse' (1956).
'The function and field of speech and language in psychoanalysis.'

(17) 'Introduction au commentaire de J. Hyppolite sur la *Verneinung* de Freud' (1956).

(18) 'Réponse au commentaire de J. Hyppolite sur la *Verneinung* de Freud.'

(19) 'La chose freudienne' (1956).
'The Freudian thing or the meaning of the return to Freud in psychoanalysis.'

(20) 'Situation de la psychanalyse et formation du psychanalyste en 1956' (1956).

(21) 'La psychanalyse et son enseignement' (1957).

(22) 'Instance de la lettre dans l'inconscient ou la raison depuis Freud' (1957).
'The agency of the letter in the unconscious or reason since Freud.'

(23) 'D'une question préliminaire à tout traitement possible de la psychose' (1957).
'On a question preliminary to any possible treatment of psychosis.'

(24) 'La signification du phallus' (1958).
'The signification of the phallus.'

(25) 'Jeunesse de Gide ou la lettre et le désir' (1958).

(26) 'A la mémoire d'Ernest Jones: sur la théorie du symbolisme' (1960).

(27) 'Subversion du sujet et dialectique du désir dans l'inconscient freudien' (1960).
'Subversion of the subject and the dialectic of desire in the Freudian unconscious.'

(28) 'La direction de la cure et les principes de son pouvoir' (1961).
'The direction of the analysis and the principles of its power.'

(29) 'Remarque sur le rapport de D. Lagache: psychanalyse et structure de la personnalité' (1961).

(30) 'Kant avec Sade' (1963).

(31) 'Du *Trieb* de Freud et du désir du psychanalyste' (1964).

(32) 'Position de l'inconscient' (1966).

(33) 'La science et la vérité' (1966).

B   Texts not included in *Écrits*

(34) 'Discours de J. Lacan dans les Actes du Congrès de Rome', *La Psychanalyse*, no. 1, 1953.

(35) 'Les formations de l'inconscient' (Seminars, 1956–7), *Bulletin de Psychologie*, 1956–7.

(36) 'Sur le désir et le transfert (discussion) dans les actes de la société', *La Psychanalyse*, no. 4, 1957.

(37) 'Réponse à des étudiants en philosophie sur l'objet de la psychanalyse' (interview), *Cahiers pour l'analyse*, no. 3, 1966.

(38) 'Discussion de l'article de S. Leclaire et J. Laplanche: l'inconscient: une étude psychanalytique', *L'Inconscient* (VIth Colloque de Bonneval), Desclée De Brouwer 1966.

(39) 'Scilicet', no. 1, *Le Champ freudien*, Éditions du Seuil, Paris, 1968.

(40) 'Scilicet', nos 2/3, *Le Champ freudien*, Éditions du Seuil, Paris, 1969.

(41) Private conversation with J. Lacan in December, 1969. Typed up on the basis of a complete tape-recording. A summary is given in the Appendix.

Articles by S. Leclaire, J. Laplanche and J.-B. Pontalis

(42) 'La réalité du désir' (Leclaire), Centre d'études Laennec, *Sur la Sexualité humaine*.

(43) 'A propos de l'épisode psychotique que présenta l'homme aux loups' (Leclaire), *La Psychanalyse*, no. 4, 1957.

(44) 'Les grands rythmes de la cure psychanalytique' (Leclaire), *Recherches et débats*, CCIF, no. 21, 1957.

(45) 'A la recherche des principes d'une psychothérapie des psychoses' (Leclaire), *Évolution psychiatrique*, 1958.

(46) 'Fantasme originaire –fantasmes des origines – origine de fantasme' (Laplanche and Pontalis), *Les Temps Modernes*, 1964. 'Fantasy and the origins of sexuality', *International Journal of Psychoanalysis*, 1968.

(47) 'Le point de vue économique en psychanalyse' (Leclaire), *Évolution psychiatrique*, 1965.

(48) 'L'inconscient, une étude psychanalytique' (Laplanche and Leclaire), *L'Inconscient* (VI Colloque de Bonneval), Desclée De Brouwer, 1966. 'The unconscious: a psychoanalytic study', trans. P. Coleman, *Yale French Studies*, no. 48, 1972.

(49) 'Discussion de S. Leclaire en réponse à Stein', *L'Inconscient* (VI Colloque de Bonneval), Desclée De Brouwer, 1966.

(50) *Vocabulaire de la psychanalyse* (Laplanche and Pontalis), PUF, Paris, 1967. *The Language of Psychoanalysis*, Hogarth Press and Institute of Psychoanalysis, London, 1973.

(51) 'Les éléments en jeu dans une psychanalyse' (Leclaire), *Cahiers pour l'Analyse*, no. 5, 1966.

(52) 'Notes sur l'objet de la psychanalyse' (Leclaire), *Cahiers pour l'Analyse*, no. 2, 1966.

(53) 'Compter avec la psychanalyse' (École Normale Supérieure, seminar 1966–7), *Cahiers pour l'Analyse*, no. 8.

(54) 'A propos d'un fantasme de Freud: note sur la transgression' (Leclaire), *L'Inconscient, Revue de psychanalyse*, PUF, Paris, 1967.

(55) *Psychanalyser, essai sur l'ordre de l'inconscient et la pratique de la lettre* (Leclaire), *Le Champ freudien*, Éditions du Seuil, Paris, 1968.

Linguistics

(56) R. Barthes, 'Eléments de sémiologie', *Communications*, no. 4, Éditions du Seuil, Paris, 1964.
Elements of Semiology (trans. A. Lavers and C. Smith), Jonathan Cape, London, 1967.

(57) R. Barthes, *Le Degré zéro de l'écriture*, with *Éléments de sémiologie*, Gonthier, Bibliothèque Médiations, Paris, 1970.

(58) F. De Saussure, *Cours de linguistique générale*, edited by Ch. Bally and A. Sechehaye, Payot, Paris, 1965.
Course in General Linguistics, McGraw-Hill, New York, 1966.

(59) R. Jakobson, *Essais de linguistique générale*, Éditions de Minuit, Paris, 1963.

(60) 'Quest for the essence of language', *Diogenes*, 51, 1965.

(61) A. Schaff, 'Language and reality', *Diogenes*, 51, 1965.

(62) A. Martinet, 'The word', *Diogenes*, 51, 1965.

(63) A. Martinet, *Éléments de linguistique générale*, A. Colin, Paris, 1967.
Elements of General Linguistics, Faber, London, 1969.

(64) É. Benveniste, 'Language and human experience', *Diogenes*, 51, 1965.

(65) É. Benveniste, *Problèmes de linguistique générale*, Gallimard, Paris, 1966.

(66) N. Chomsky, *Syntactic Structures*, Mouton, The Hague, 1957.

(67) N. Chomsky, 'Persistent topics in linguistic theory', *Diogenes*, 51, 1965.

(68) N. Chomsky, *Cartesian Linguistics*, Harper & Row, London, 1966.

(69) N. Chomsky, 'The formal nature of language', Appendix to E. H. Lenneberg, *Biological Foundations of Language*, Wiley, New York, 1967.

(70) G. C. Lepschy, *A Survey of Structural Linguistics*, Faber, London, 1972.

(71) E. Ortigues, *Le Discours et le Symbole*, Aubier.

Miscellaneous

(72) E. Amado Levy-Valensi, 'Vérité et langage du dialogue platonicien au dialogue psychanalytique', *La Psychanalyse*, no. 1, 1956.

(73) D. Anzieu, 'Débat: contre Lacan', *La Quinzaine littéraire*, no. 20, January 1967.

(74) P. Aulanier-Spairani, 'Du désir de savoir dans ses rapports à la trangression', *L'Inconscient, Revue de Psychanalyse*, no. 1, 1967.

(75) É. Benveniste, 'Remarque sur la fonction du langage dans la découverte freudienne', *La Psychanalyse*, no. 1, 1956.

(76) M. Blanchot, 'Freud', *La Nouvelle Revue française*, no. 45, 1956.

(77) A. de Waelhens, 'La force du langage et le langage de la force', *Revue philosophique de Louvain*, 1965.

(78) A. de Waelhens, Preface to Demoulin, *Notions de psychiatrie phénoménologique*.

(79) A. de Waelhens, 'Sur l'inconscient et la pensée philosophique', *L'Inconscient* (VI Colloque de Bonneval) Desclée De Brouwer, 1966.

(80) E. Fink, 'Appendice à l'oeuvre de Ed. Husserl', *Crise des sciences européennes et la phénoménologie transcendentale*, Coll. Husserliana, vol. VI, The Hague, 1962.

(81) A. Green, 'L'objet (a) de J. Lacan, sa logique et la théorie freudienne', *Cahiers pour l'Analyse*, no. 3.

(82) A. Green, 'Les portes de l'inconscient', *L'Inconscient* (VIth Colloque de Bonneval), Desclée De Brouwer, 1966.

(83) A. Green, 'Discussion de l'article de Laplanche et Leclaire, *L'inconscient, une étude psychanalytique*', *L'Inconscient*, Desclée De Brouwer.

(84) A. Hesnard, 'Refléxions sur le "Wo Es war, soll Ich werden"', *La Psychanalyse*, no. 3.

(85) J. Hyppolite, 'Commentaire parlé sur la *Verneinung* de Freud', in J. Lacan, *Écrits* (see 17 above).

(86) L. Irigaray, 'Communications linguistique et spéculaire', *Cahiers pour l'Analyse*, no. 3.

(87) S. Isaacs, 'Nature et fonction du fantasme', *La Psychanalyse*, no. 5.

(88) J. F. Kahn, 'La minutieuse conquête du structuralisme', *L'Express*, no. 884, August 1967.

(89) Kaiser, 'Le problème de la responsabilitè en psychothérapie', *La Psychanalyse*, no. 2.

(90) G. Lapouge, 'J. Lacan veut que la psychanalyse redevienne la peste', *Le Figaro littéraire*, 1 December 1966.

(91) D. Leroy, *Mythologie de l'anxiété*, José Corti, Paris.

(92) Cl. Lévi-Strauss, *Anthropologie structurale*, Plon, Paris, 1968. *Structural Anthropology*, Penguin, Harmondsworth, University texts, 1972.

(93) R. Mack Brunswick, 'A supplement to Freud's *From the History of an Infantile Neurosis*', *International Journal of Psychoanalysis*, 1928.

(94) Maldinev, 'Comprendre', *Revue de métaphysique et de morale*, January–June 1961.

(95) J. A. Miller, 'La suture', *Cahiers pour l'Analyse*, no. 1.

(96) J. A. Miller, 'Action de la Structure', *Cahiers pour l'Analyse*, no. 9.

(97) J. C. Milner, 'Le point du significant', *Cahiers pour l'Analyse*, no. 3.

(98) O. Mannoni, 'Poésie et psychanalyse', *La Psychanalyse*, no. 3.

(99) J. Nassif, 'Le fantasme "on bat un enfant"', *Cahiers pour l'Analyse*, no. 7.

(100) J. Nuttin, *Psychanalyse et conception spiritualiste de l'homme*, Nauwelaerts, 1961.

(101) E. Ortigues, 'Sur la théorie psychologique et la réflexion morale', *Recherches et débats*, CCIF, January 1953.

(102) E. Ortigues, *L'Oedipe africain*, Plon, Paris, 1966.

(103) J. Piaget, *La Formation du Symbole chez l'enfant*, Delachaux et Niestlé, Paris, 1945.

(104) G. Politzer, *Critique des fondements de la psychologie*, Coll. de l'Esprit, Paris.

(105) G. Rosolato, 'Le symbolique', *La Psychanalyse*, no. 5.

(106) G. Rosolato, 'Trois genérations d'hommes dans le mythe religieux et la généalogie', *L'Inconscient, Revue de psychanalyse*, no. 1, 1957.

(107) G. Rosolato, 'Séminaire du 8 mars 1967 sur la métaphore et la métonymie à l'UCL'.

(108) G. Rosolato, 'L'Hystérie', *Évolution psychiatrique*, 1962.

(109) G. Rosolato, 'Sémantique et altérations du langage', *Évolution psychiatrique*, 1956.

(110) M. Robert, *La Révolution psychanalytique*, Payot, Paris, 1964. *The Psychoanalytic Revolution*, Allen & Unwin, London, 1966.

(111) J. Schotte, 'Le transfert (essai d'un dialogue avec Freud sur la question fondamentale de la psychanalyse)', *Revue de psychologie et des sciences de l'éducation*, no. 4, 1965.

(112) C. Stein, 'Fragment d'un commentaire de l'interprétation des rêves de Freud', *L'Inconscient, Revue de Psychanalyse*, no. 1, 1967.

(113) C. Stein, 'Langage et inconscient', *L'Inconscient*, Desclée De Brouwer, 1966.

(114) M. Tort, 'Le concept Freudien de représentant', *Cahiers pour l'Analyse*, no. 5.

(115) A. Vergote, *Psychologie religieuse*, Coll. Psychologie et Sciences Humaines, Dessart, 1966.
(116) H.-T. Piron, *et al.*, *La Psychanalyse, science d'homme*, Coll. Psychologie et Sciences Humaines, Dessart, 1964.
(117) H. Wald, 'Métaphore et concept', *Revue de métaphysique et de morale*, no. 2, April 1966.

Index

Index

Martin, P., 70–1
Martinet, A., 19–20, 22, *62–3*
meaning and concept, 17–19,
    22–3, 40–2, 102
metaphor, 32–3, 42, 52;
    condensation and, 43, 142,
    169, 187–8, 191–2, 199–202;
    definition, 192–3; formula
    for, 96–7, 122; in psycho-
    analysis, 197–9; as schema
    for establishment of
    unconscious, 119, 188, 197–8,
    206–7, Laplanche, 98, 104,
    125, Stein, 142–3
metonymy, 32–3, 42; definition,
    193; displacement and, 43,
    47–8, 142, 169, 187–8, 191–2,
    199–200, 203–4; in
    psychoanalysis, 194–7
Miller, J. A., 67–9, *95–6*
Milner, J. C., *97*
mirror stage (of child), 79–81,
    176–8
misrecognition, 58
mother–child relationship, 82–4,
    87–9, 164–7, 228–9, 234–5;
    see also father
motivation, 48–9
myth, 91; of human genesis, 127

narcissism, 181
Nassif, J., *99*
need, *see* lack
negation (denegation), 74–6
neurosis, 227–8, 230–1;
    hysterical, 228–9; obsessional,
    229
Nuttin, J., *100*

object: of instinct, desire,
    demand, 128–9, 169, 173–5;
    sexual, 147–8
Oedipus, the, 7–8, 58, 100, 166,
    235, 238; role in accession to
    symbolic, 78–92, 179–80;
    see also castration; Phallus
Ortigues, E., 52, 59, 81, *71,
    101–2*; on Oedipus, 90;
    on symbolization, 55–6, 61–2,
    84

other, 62, 169–70, 174, 180–1;
    definitions, 157; psycho-
    analyst as, 217

paranoia, *see* delirium
Pascal, B., xix
Peirce, C. S. S., 14–15, 24, 46–7
Perelman, xiii
Phallus, 59, 129, 175, 229;
    definition, 86, 145;
    transition from being to
    having, 82–3, 87–8, 245; *see
    also* castration; Oedipus
phantasy, 142–4, 165, 189,
    245–6; primal, 189–90
Philippe, case history, 139–41,
    143–5
Piaget, J., *103*
Piron, H.-T., 150, 156, 171,
    189, 198, 228, *116*;
    definition of psychoanalyst's
    role, 217
pleasure, 145–6, 149–50
Politzer, G., ix–x, 135–6, *104*
Pontalis, J.-B., 82, 165, 189,
    42–55
psychoanalysis: anthropology
    and, 63; cure, xxi–xxii, 169,
    220–1, 223–4; discourse of
    patient, 39–40, 69, 73, 136,
    215–16, 223; function of
    language, xx, 215–16, 217;
    function of psychoanalyst,
    217–18, 220–2, 223–4;
    history, xvii; linguistics and,
    3–5, 43–4, Saussure's
    algorithm, 44, 156, 215;
    metaphor and metonymy in,
    194–9; political/academic
    position, viii–ix; processes, 45,
    110, 211; symbolism, 46–9;
    theory and practice, xxi–xxii,
    115, 136; transference, 220–2
psychology of adaptation, xxi
psychosis, 227, 230–8, 248;
    see also wolf man

Real, the, 40–1, 51–2, 115–16,
    120, 233–4; symbolic and, 67,
    and imaginary, 227

264